Perpetuating Trouble

# *Perpetuating Trouble*

A MEMOIR

CHRIS ORCUTT

Perpetuating Trouble
A Memoir
by
Chris Orcutt

Copyright © 2017 by Chris Orcutt

All rights reserved. No part of this publication may be used, reproduced, distributed or transmitted in any form or by any electronic or mechanical means, including information storage or retrieval systems, without the written permission of the author, except where permitted by law, or in the case of brief quotations embodied in critical reviews. This work is registered with the U.S. Copyright Office.

First Print Edition: 2017

This is a nonfiction memoir. While all of the events in this book actually occurred, select details, and most names, have been changed to protect the privacy of the people involved.

ISBN 13: 978-0996278379 (Have Pen, Will Travel Publishing)

The cover artist and book formatter for this book is Have Pen, Will Travel Publishing. Book cover image, "Writer novelist drinking whiskey working on a book using typewriter" (stock photo ID: 530717434) by Peter Bernik, used under license from Shutterstock, Inc.

Also by Chris Orcutt:
Nick Chase's Great Escape (A Comic Novel)
I Hope You Boys Know What You're Doing! (Short Stories & Poems)
A Real Piece of Work (Dakota Stevens Mystery #1)
The Rich Are Different (Dakota Stevens Mystery #2)
A Truth Stranger Than Fiction (Dakota Stevens Mystery #3)
The Perfect Triple Threat (Dakota Stevens Mystery #4)
The Man, The Myth, The Legend (Short Stories)
One Hundred Miles from Manhattan (A Novel)
The Ronald And Other Plays (Plays)

www.orcutt.net

For Alexas:
My Véra, My Hadley, My Muse

Je t'aime, mon petit pamplemousse.

> 'I'll love you, dear, I'll love you
> Till China and Africa meet,
> And the river jumps over the mountain
> And the salmon sing in the street,
> . . . .
>
> — W.H. Auden

Contents

1. Alien Girls 9
2. The Thomas Kinkade Affair 43
3. You Know What's Coming Next 119
4. Absentminded 131
5. The Redhead in the Emerald Slicker 157
6. A Sorry Mendicant 167
7. Accidental Invaders 193
8. Nobody Says Anything 211
9. Love Story to Sweetie 225
10. The Prodigal Student Returns 243

About the Author 325

Excerpt from *One Hundred Miles from Manhattan* 327

"I avoided writers very carefully because they can perpetuate trouble as no one else can…"

— from *The Crack-up* by F. Scott Fitzgerald

1

Alien Girls

I was told to write this book by a pair of alien girls.

Now before you decide I'm a sexist, anachronistic schmuck out of a 1940s noir film, let me say in my defense that at least I didn't call them a couple of "alien *broads*," and that I initially considered "alien women" but it sounded forced.[1] Besides, the two were at that cusp age—in their late teens to early 20s—so "women" didn't fit. In my view girls don't become women until they've had their hearts broken twice and been called "ma'am" at least once. This pair didn't meet my private criteria, so from the moment I picked them up hitchhiking (before I figured out they were aliens), I thought of them as girls.

The other thing I should get out of the way is that I believed in aliens long before the girls told me to write this book.

October 1987. I was 17 years old and had just gotten home from school. I was sitting at the window of our house in Millbrook, New York with a view of Clove Mountain when I spied a UFO hovering above the ridge

---

[1] Also forced were "extraterrestrial girls" and "extraterrestrial women." Anyway, to my ear "extraterrestrial" sounds like a variety of mushroom.

top. This was no trick of light or shadow because it was a crystal clear day and the silvery oblong disc stood in sharp contrast against the deep blue sky. Even though it was early afternoon, there were lights—yes, lights—running along the side like little windows, and I was able to gauge the disc's size from the fire tower it hovered beside. I'd hiked up to that tower several times, so I knew it stood about 50 feet high. The saucer (elegant variation[2]) was about two fire towers tall by six wide (if the tower were turned on its side), or about 100' x 300'. I was on the phone with my friend Tony Scotto and told him what I was seeing.

"It's a UFO. Seriously."

"Yeah, okay." He said this with a jadedness that only a guy originally from Brooklyn could muster.

"I'm not kidding," I said. "I'm looking at it right now."

"What's it doing, beaming up little green men?"

"No, it's just sitting there. Hold on, I'm getting a camera."

I ran into the kitchen and fumbled through the drawers for the stupid "Brownie" camera my mother kept around for moments like this, but of course I couldn't find it. When I ran back to the window, where I'd left the phone, the UFO was gone.

"Shoot, it's gone."

---

2 Elegant variation, or "the stylistic fault of studiedly finding different ways to denote the same thing in a piece of writing, merely to avoid repetition" (e.g., saucer, disc, UFO, etc.), is considered by *Fowler's English Usage*—the premier reference book on word usage—to be a rhetorical gaffe on par with genocide. Then again, I doubt that the Fowler brothers, the authors of *Fowler's*, ever saw a UFO. So there.

Tony scoffed. "Probably heard you were going to take a picture, so they jumped to warp speed."

"I'm telling you, I saw it," I said.

Whether or not Tony or anyone else believed me, from that moment on I had my very own UFO story. Sure it wasn't as dramatic as an alien *abduction*, but if I went to a party and the conversation drifted toward the occult, I had my very own UFO story, which never failed to garner the wide-eyed fascination of nubile young women or the seething envy of competing men.

In a Boston bar once, I brought up the story to a girl I was pursuing, and two others at adjoining stools whipped their heads around.

"Really?" they gushed. "You saw a UFO?!"

"Yes, really," I said. "And it was very scary. Come closer, all three of you, and I'll tell you *all about it.*"

And thus was many a door of possibility opened.

But I digress. Back to the alien girls, the pair that told me to write this book.

It was a glittering October morning in 2008, and the world, as far as I was concerned, was going to hell. The world economy was tanking, my younger sister had been diagnosed with a rare disease, and my fiction career was at a standstill. A dozen editors at major publishers had read my two PI/mystery novels, but all of them, while praising the dialogue, the characters, the plots and the quality of the writing, had decided that somehow, the books "weren't *quite* right for them" or that they "lacked the ability to break out of a crowded market."

This last rejection made me imagine my books, now sprouting arms and legs, trapped in the Grand Bazaar in Istanbul, being crushed by shoppers and rug merchants, and unable to break out. I'd poured the last five years of my life into those two books, and as the rejections for the second one mounted daily, and the future I saw for myself didn't include them, I began to wonder what the hell I should do with my life.

Should I stop writing fiction?
Should I quit writing altogether?

Trouble is, ten years earlier I had tried to quit writing and couldn't. Writing was a compulsion. No, more than a compulsion: an obsession. During the six months that I wasn't writing I developed a mysterious rash all over my torso. My need to write was more than psychological; it was physiological. Like it or not, writing and I were stuck with each other.

All of these concerns were weighing on me that October morning in the Hudson Valley when something (intuition, I suppose) told me to drive my wife Alexas to work and head north. My plan was to meander up Route 9 listening to jazz, find a park along the Hudson River, and sit with my notebook and a pencil and see what came to me.

And that's when I saw them: a blonde girl and a brunette hitchhiking beside an exit ramp. Their clothing was rumpled, and despite approaching them at 60 mph, I noticed that the blonde was in bare feet. The brunette wore a ski cap and held a paper plate with "*NORTH*" scrawled on it in a horror film font.

The second I passed them, a small, still voice inside myself told me to turn around and pick them up. At the first traffic light I encountered, I hooked an illegal U-turn and sped southbound. They were still out there, thumbs angling into the road, as I took my Honda Accord up to 80 mph and peeled off at the next exit. I turned around again and merged back onto Route 9 an exit south of them.

When I reached them I pulled onto the narrow shoulder and rolled down the passenger window. To say they were dirty and bedraggled would be an understatement. They looked like they'd been sleeping on beaches all their lives. The blonde, who was most definitely barefoot, was already reaching for the back seat door. However the brunette with the paper plate sign eyed me suspiciously. I needed to establish my bona fides.

"I passed you a minute ago and saw you two waiting here and didn't want anything bad to happen to you, so I turned around and here I am."

The blonde got in the back, but her brunette friend hesitated. I held up my notebook.

"I'm a writer," I said, as though this somehow enhanced my credibility. "I was driving around looking for inspiration. Where're you two headed?"

I thought she might say Bard College, the bastion of hippie college girls in the area. The brunette wore a pair of crazy drawstring pants, and the barefoot blonde wore a peasant skirt. The idea that they went to Bard wasn't an unreasonable deduction.

"We're heading to the Alpha Holistic Sciences Center," the brunette said. "You know where that is?"

"No, but I've heard of it. It's north of here, right?"
"Yeah."
"Well, get in," I said. "I'll take you."
"Perfect," the blonde said.

I was glad I'd shaved the night before; I don't look good with a beard. Over the years I'd observed that my credibility was inversely proportional to the length and scragginess of my beard. If I didn't shave for a week, I looked borderline psychotic—like the survivor of a shipwreck still in denial about his ordeal.

Today I was clean-shaven and highly credible, and my car was immaculate from a recent wash and vacuuming. As the grubby blonde curled up on the back seat, I winced for the upholstery and wished I had a sheet or a cardboard box for her to sit on. I hoped she wasn't carrying fleas or, worse, bedbugs. Even in the rearview mirror I could see that her nose pores were blocked up with crud. *Damn, spring for a box of nose strips, girl!* When they both clicked their seatbelts, I pulled back onto the highway.

"Yeah," I said. "I was taking the day off anyway, so it's no problem for me to give you a ride. But when we get close, you'll have to give me directions."

The brunette in the front seat was rolling a cigarette. She glanced over her shoulder.

"Hear that, Astrid?"
"Yeah, that's so cool."
"Excuse me," I said to the one with the rolling papers, "did you call her *Astrid*?"
"Sure. That's the name she gave herself. Mine's Hoku Lani."
"I'm Chris. So what are your real names?"

"You mean the ones somebody else gave us?" Hoku said. "The ones we had no say in?"

"We don't use those anymore," Astrid said.

Hoku finished rolling her cigarette and pulled out a lighter.

"Not in the car, please," I said. "I'm allergic."

"Oh, okay."

I'm not allergic. I'm simply a fastidious guy with a profoundly sensitive sense of smell, and I knew if anyone ever smoked in this car, I was going to smell it for the entire life of the car. Hoku tucked the cigarette behind her ear.

"So, Chris," she said, "do you like your name?"

"It's all right. Why?"

"If you could give yourself a new name, one that matches your personality, what would it be?"

Apparently Hoku was used to asking this question of people who had never considered it before. I, on the other hand, *had* contemplated alternative names and how their nuances might have influenced my development. My alternatives were usually thinly guised homages to, or outright rip-offs of, fictional characters and classic movie stars I admired, like Rhett, Clint, and Cary. But I did have my standard backup name for just such a situation.

"Wyatt," I said. "As in Wyatt Earp. I've always thought that if I'd lived during the Old West, I would have been a gun for hire."

"Maybe you were!" Astrid poked her head between the seats.

"Well, Wyatt," Hoku said, "thanks for the ride. We mighty appreciate it."

"No problem. Minute I woke up this mornin', something told me I was supposed to come up this way, like I knew I was gonna pick you up or something. Does that make sense?"

"Yes," Astrid said. "Hoku, remember last night, when we were at that performance art thing in Manhattan and I said, 'We have to get back upstate. Somebody needs our help.' Remember? And Chris—sorry, Wyatt—these people we were with kept going, 'You two are so weird. What are you, a couple of *aliens?*' We laughed and were like, 'Yeah, ha, ha, we're aliens from another planet, and we just beamed down from our spaceship to go to this stupid art show, for sure.'"

"So, Wyatt," Hoku said, turning to me. "What's troubling you?"

"What do you mean?" I said. "I'm fine."

Astrid touched my shoulder from the back seat. Her hand was very warm, like she had a fever of 200°F.

"It's okay," she said. "You're safe. We're here to help you."

Her touch had an immediate calming effect on me. My fingers loosened on the steering wheel to the point that I felt like the car was driving itself. Outside, peak foliage whisked by. We passed the Culinary Institute of America, the FDR Mansion, and the Vanderbilt Mansion. After a few minutes of quiet, I decided to share how I was feeling. I didn't have any answers, but maybe these two precocious 20-year-olds did.

"Well, as a matter of fact, there *is* something troubling me."

I told them the saga of trying to get my mystery novels published. Because if there's one thing people universally want to hear about, it's a writer's struggles for publication and recognition.

"I don't get it," I said, finishing up. "I thought these books were *it*. I thought they were what I was supposed to be writing. I'd just like to know when it's going to break for me."

Hoku leaned her seat back and covered her eyes with the ski cap.

"Look, Wyatt," she said, "you need to understand something. The universe is like a giant catalog. There are all of these great things you can order…like experiences, people, places, accomplishments and material possessions, right?"

"Okay," I said.

"Think about it this way," she continued. "If you ordered something from a catalog or online or whatever, you wouldn't worry about whether it was going to get to you. You'd simply *trust* that it would get there, correct?"

I thought back to my most recent online order for a new computer, and how I had refreshed the tracking info page on my web browser every hour until it arrived, three days later. I wasn't one to trust that *anything* was going to reach me.

"Sure," I said.

"Well," Hoku said, "the same thing is true of your books. You've submitted your order from the catalog of Life, and your only job now is to trust that it will get to you exactly on time."

"Listen," I said, "it's not that I don't trust it'll get to me…eventually. It's just that I wouldn't mind paying extra for overnight shipping once in a while, you know what I mean?"

At the stoplight in Rhinebeck, Hoku told me to turn right. She then sent me down a road I'd never driven before, which was unusual. In my early 20s I'd been a local newspaper reporter and knew almost every road in the county.

"I think this is the road," Hoku said.

"You *think*?" I said. "You're telling me you girls don't know where this place is? Boy, am I glad *I* picked you up, and not some psycho."

"Oh, Wyatt," Astrid said sweetly from the back seat, "nothing can happen to us."

"That's what you think," I said.

Hoku glanced over her shoulder at her friend. "We can't go back yet. We're not finished here. He doesn't get it."

"Get what?" I said. "And what's with the third-person *he* stuff? I'm right here."

"Wyatt," Hoku said, "there's a nice park up ahead. Are you up for a little hike?"

"Sure."

"It's right up there. Slow down or you'll miss it. Yeah, turn in here."

The sign at the entrance read "Burger Hill Park," and it promised panoramic vistas of the entire Hudson River Valley, including the river, the Catskill and Taconic Mountains, and the Berkshires. The second I parked the car, Hoku and Astrid hopped out and lit their hand-rolled cigarettes. Clouds now obscured the sun. It was cool out. I shook my head at the girls' smoking.

"You know," I said, "they have filtered ones now. You ought to save your lungs."

Hoku chuckled. "These things can't hurt us."

"Apparently you two haven't heard of a little thing called the Surgeon General's Warning."

They ignored me and hiked at a breakneck pace up a long, steady hill, inhaling their homemade cigarettes with every step. In no time they were 50…100 yards…a football field ahead of me, and when I finally reached the top, panting, they were sitting casually: Hoku, on a granite slab with her legs crossed, twirling a Mukluk boot; Astrid, Indian-style on the grass in her bare feet. There was something inhuman about how fast they'd climbed this hill. I was a pretty good walker (a couple miles a day usually), yet these two smokestacks had dusted me, like they'd floated up here. Come to think of it, I wasn't certain I'd seen their feet touching the ground.

"So, Wyatt," Astrid said, flicking away her spent cigarette. "I've been thinking more about your situation. Would you like to hear my conclusions?"

"Absolutely," I said.

"Well, clearly the reason your mystery novels haven't been published is because you don't want them to be."

"And why is that?"

She shrugged. "Because they're not what you really want to say. Deep down, you want to be writing about your own life, your own adventures, the things *you've* learned. Not the stuff some *character* has learned."

I sat up and gazed at the colorful view. In every direction the hills were giant, vibrant scoops of rainbow sherbet. I thought back to when I'd finished the second novel in my mystery series: I was worried the first novel would be published, then the second one, and before I knew it I'd be typecast as a Mystery Writer. At book signings, the *real* writers, the literary writers, would snidely whisper, "He's a hack. He sold out and wrote work the market wanted, not what *he* wanted."

"You might have a point," I said to Astrid. "I've thought about it, that's for sure. But how did you know?"

"It's what you've been putting out into the universe," she said.

"Ha, ha," I said. "But really."

"No, that's what you've been putting out there."

"But how could you know?" I said. "It's impossible."

"There's nothing impossible about it, Wyatt," Hoku said. "Astrid and I were meant to meet you today. It's why we're here."

I wanted to say, "No…you're *here* because I stopped and gave your grubby hitchhiking asses a ride." But I didn't.

"I guess so," I said.

"Go within," Astrid said, "and you'll know we're right. You need to be writing about your own experiences. It's how you can make a difference. It's your *destiny*."

When she said the word "destiny," I shivered. I thought of the scene in *The Empire Strikes Back*, when Darth Vader corners Luke Skywalker (to whom he's just revealed he's his father) and tells Luke that his ruling the galaxy with him is his *destiny*. Astrid's pronouncement felt similarly ominous.

"Maybe," I said. "We should probably go now. It's getting cold."

On our way down the hill, Astrid laid her hand on my shoulder again. Even through my leather jacket, it was as warm as a radiator.

"Don't worry, Wyatt," she said. "The answers will come. The most important thing is to not fight this. You're supposed to write about yourself. Just make sure you go deep within before you start."

Honestly, at this point I was a little annoyed by these two 20-year-old New Age chicks predicting my future.

"Okay," I said. "Let's drop it now."

When we got back in the car, the smell of their cigarettes and body odor was overwhelming. I drove the next few miles with the windows rolled down. This flushed out the unpleasant smells of two dirty hitchhikers and replaced it with two of my favorites: the sour scent of leaf tannin from the fallen leaves, and the faint tinge of manure. When I came out of my reverie the road had narrowed from a two-way blacktop road to a one-way dirt lane, pockmarked with potholes and flanked by crumbling rock walls. This, Hoku explained, was the service entrance.

"For us employees," she said. "The nice road's for paying guests."

"It's up here on your left," Astrid said.

I pulled into a scrubby lot in front of a long bunkhouse. Immediately I thought of George and Lenny's quarters in Steinbeck's *Of Mice and Men*. Several of the windows were covered with plastic on the outside, and there was more bare wood than paint on the building.

"Well, it was great meeting you," I said. "So, do you two have business cards?"

The second I said it, I realized it was a stupid question. These two didn't have deodorant or shoes, and I expected them to have business cards?

"No, sorry, Wyatt," Hoku said. "We don't even have a permanent address."

"You're homeless?" I asked.

"No," she said. "We go from place to place helping people, and when our work is done, we move on."

A thought occurred to me. "Hey, have you two ever heard of Peace Pilgrim? You remind me of her."

"Who is she?" Astrid asked.

I told them how Peace Pilgrim was this woman who, back in the early 1950s, decided she didn't want anything to do with her former personal history, so she destroyed all of her identification, gave away her possessions, relinquished her given name and walked all across North America, spreading a message of peace. I mentioned two other tidbits about her: the fact that in 1981 she was hit by a car and killed, and that once in the mid-1960s when she was in Bangor, Maine, my parents, Al and Susan, put her up for the night. When Peace Pilgrim told them what she did with her life, Big Al said (in his inimitable Down East Maine accent), "Yeah, but how the hell d'ya make a livin'? I mean, Jeezis, how d'ya *feed your face*?" Years later, Al told me how, try as he might, he couldn't perturb the woman—something he always respected about her.

"She sounds interesting," Hoku said. "We'll have to look her up."

"I want to give you some money." I took out my wallet. "Twenty bucks?"

"We don't need your money, Wyatt," Astrid said.

"Well...here...take my card."

"That's okay," Hoku said. "We'd lose it anyway. Besides, our work here is done."

"Done," Astrid seconded, laying that hot hand of hers upon my shoulder.

"Hold on a minute," Hoku said. "I've got something for you. Astrid, tell Wyatt about the lunch. I'll be right back."

While Hoku jumped out of the car and ran around the building, Astrid described the gourmet vegan lunch at the dining hall starting at noon.

"Go to the administration office," Astrid said, "tell them you're our guest, and they'll give you a ticket for a free lunch."

The notion of vegan *anything*, even if it was gourmet, didn't appeal to me. However, out of respect to their generous gesture, I said I'd check it out.

"And walk around and stuff," Astrid said. "There's a little cafe, and down by the lake there are hammocks and meditation areas and kayaks."

"Kayaks? I've always wanted to try one of those."

Hoku materialized by the side of the car, opened the passenger door and tossed a lump of olive fabric in my lap.

"What's this?" I asked.

"Special pants," Hoku said. "Super comfortable."[3]

"Yeah," Astrid said, smiling in the rear-view mirror. "You should wear them when you write your new book. The one about yourself."

Hoku leaned across the passenger seat and grabbed my wrist. Her grip was surreally strong, evoking an image from my childhood: Lindsay Wagner in the 1970s TV show *The Bionic Woman*. Then she stared deeply into my eyes; I now understood how it felt to be mesmerized.

"You've had an interesting life," she said.

"But I—"

"You've had an interesting life, and you have things to say. You are going to write this book. Now say it."

"I'm going…to write…this book."

"Good," Astrid said. "I think he's ready."

Hoku let go of my arm. "Farewell, Wyatt."

I was still in a trance while they shut the car doors and disappeared around the corner of the bunkhouse. Shaking my head, as though awakening from a deep sleep in a strange place, I marveled at how two 20-year-old girls could be so wise. I backed out and drove to the visitor's parking lot.

I'd never been to the Alpha Institute before, so I spent the next hour wandering the paths that snaked through the woods between bungalows, and reading flyers for workshops on everything from realigning chakras to becoming a healer. People passed me on the paths wearing

---

3 These pants are crazy. They're 3/4-length, leaving my shins exposed like women's koolats. They have a string to tie them tight and a pouch for my nethers, but no pockets. Alexas calls them my "alien pants," and I've relegated them to pajama status.

signs around their necks that read "SILENT." Later on I learned that rather than rudely ordering me to be quiet (as I originally thought), the signs identified people who had taken a vow of silence for the duration of their stay.

I found a café and enjoyed a mug of "karma mint tea," which the cashier assured me would bring me good karma, especially if I dropped a dollar tip in the "karma pot." I did. For the next 20 minutes as I drank my tea, I admired the slinky, feline movements of a young blonde yoga instructor. I'd seen her headshot on a poster earlier.

Warmed by the tea, I walked down to the lake and lay in one of the hammocks. A glittering gold maple rustled above me in the breeze. Leaves rained down and covered me. There was a word for this kind of day: serendipitous. Serendipity: *the aptitude for making desirable discoveries by accident.* Knowing I had the rest of this gorgeous fall day ahead of me, knowing I had no office to go to and nowhere I had to be, I laced my fingers behind my head and let the breeze rock me to sleep.

I awoke with a start, which was a problem: I'd forgotten I was in a hammock. The momentum of my sudden sitting-up pitched it sideways, dumping me in the leaves. On a dollhouse-sized beach 20 feet away, a man and woman were dragging a kayak into the water. They dropped the kayak, ran over and helped me up.

"Are you okay?" the woman asked.

"Quite a spill you took there," the man said. "Gotta be careful on those things."

"What time is it?" I asked.

"Quarter to two," the man said.

"That late? Really?"

"That's the time."

"Do you know if the dining hall's still open?"

It's not as if during my nap I had suddenly developed a taste for vegan cuisine; it was the idea that I might miss out on something *free*—a "free lunch" no less, in a world that claimed there was no such thing.

"I think they close at two," the woman said. "Maybe if you hurry."

"Thanks."

I jogged down the main path, following the signs for the administration building. When I got there I paused outside for a minute to catch my breath. It wouldn't do to go inside panting uncontrollably and asking for a free lunch. As soon as I composed myself, I walked in with a smile and stepped up to the counter. A woman in her early 30s got up from a desk.

"Can I help you?"

One of my problems, a problem that especially plagued me for the first 40 years of my life, is that in response to innocuous questions I invariably give *way* too much information. I'm not sure why I do this, but I think it has something to do with the fact that I'm perpetually convinced that even the simplest of simpletons can see right through me. So, to assuage the ever-present fear I have of being declared a liar and a fraud, I offer the questioner *the whole story*, allowing him to sort it out himself. This, I imagine, is where the trope of "digging yourself into a hole" came from. Allow me to demonstrate.

"Yeah, hi," I said to the woman. "I live in the area—Millbrook, actually—and I was driving around this morning—I'm a writer, so I work at home, you see, and I gave myself the day off. Anyway, I was driving up Route Nine when I saw these two young girls—uh, young women actually—hitchhiking and I didn't want anything bad to happen to them, so I turned around and gave them a ride. It turns out they work here, and they said if I came in here and told you I'd helped them, you'd give me a ticket for a free lunch at the dining hall."

"That was very kind of you," the woman said. "What are their names?"

"Well, that's the problem. They didn't give me their real names. They gave me the names they gave themselves, if that makes any sense."

"Actually," she said, "a lot of the young people who work here do that. What names did they use?"

"Hoku and Astrid."

She raised an eyebrow. "You're sure?"

"Absolutely," I said. "I spent the entire morning with them."

"Hmm, that's strange. Hold on a moment."

As she disappeared down a dark hallway, a tight-faced man in his late 50s—a man who looked distinctly as if he hadn't taken advantage of the yoga or meditation classes—eyed me from an adjoining office. I felt self-conscious standing there with nothing to do. This would have been an ideal moment to read the spines of books or to peruse a painting, but alas there was nothing in the room worth studying, and if I focused on the electric pencil sharpener, I'd look nuts. So I stood still with my hands in my pockets, trying to affect a casual pose. It didn't work. In my periphery I saw him staring at me until he finally got up from his desk.

Damn it.

One exasperating byproduct of lying for a living (that's what fiction writing is, Dear Reader—making stuff up, stretching credulity, and presenting your story with authority so that it seems like it really happened) is this: You lose the ability to discriminate between real life and the fantasy world you create in your head. Then, when you're actually telling the truth, you often don't believe yourself. This is especially a problem when you have to explain yourself to authority figures, like this administrator at Alpha. You don't trust your own story, and the person to whom you're speaking picks up on this glimmer of doubt and thinks you're lying. Frankly, it's a pain in the ass, which is why I avoid authority figures as assiduously as I do sinkholes.

He walked out to the lobby clutching a piece of paper officiously at his side, but the worst thing about him, the thing that made me dislike him immediately, was that he scrutinized me over a pair of half-glasses. You know—those things people buy off revolving displays at pharmacies? I guess they're really called *reading* glasses, but that name doesn't connote the sinister quality of the glasses or their wearers the way "half-glasses" does.[4] Half-glasses are by definition noncommittal, and they imbue the wearer

---

4 The only person I ever liked who wore half-glasses a lot was my grandfather's niece, Anne Knowlton Decelles. A Smith College graduate and Hartford, Connecticut librarian, she encouraged my interest in books and always chose me for her team in Scrabble.

with an unearned air of discernment that for some reason makes them believe they're qualified to weigh in on any matter in their purview.

"Can I help you, sir?" he said.

The man removed his half-glasses and let them dangle precariously from his fingertips. All of these people *must* go to the same school of holier-than-thou assholery; their gestures are universally the same.

"No, I'm fine," I said. "Actually, the woman who was just here is helping me. I drove a couple of your kitchen workers here, and they said that you fine folks might give me a ticket to the dining hall for lunch."

"Let me see if I have this straight," he said, loud enough that it drew the glance of a man passing between offices. "You were driving up Route Nine and saw two young women hitchhiking, so you brought them here and they promised you a free lunch. And now Julie is saying we don't have *anybody* working here by the two names you mentioned."

"I don't know if you do or not," I said. "That's what Julie went to find out."

Julie returned. I looked hopefully at her face for a sign that I wasn't crazy, that the two girls I'd brought here did indeed work here, and that I would be immediately vindicated: Mr. Half-Glasses turning instantly sycophantic, apologizing profusely, scurrying around the counter to open the door for me, cringing at my slightest movement. But none of that happened. Julie's face pinched up in confusion.

"I checked the master employee list," she said, staring at me, "but there's nobody by those names. Are you sure they didn't give you their, uh, birth names?"

"Positive," I said.

"Well, Richard," Julie said, "he looks like an honest guy. I say we give him a ticket."

At this point, I'd lost interest in the lunch. Vegan? Gross. It was probably loaded with tofu: tofu turkey breast, tofu bread, tofu potatoes. To hell with it. But I couldn't tuck tail and leave, because then *Richard* would think I'd been lying the whole time. I had to stick to my story. It was time to double down. It was time for a little righteous indignation.

"You know," I said, "this is incredibly offensive. You're acting like I made all of this up, like I woke up this morning with the intention of defrauding your institute out of a free lunch. Come on. Have you ever had somebody come in here claiming to have aided two of your workers, and who wanted a free lunch?"

"I never have," Julie said.

"Well *I* have," Richard said.

"All right then. There's a simple way to clear this up," I said. "Let's go over to their barracks and you can ask them yourself."

"Let's do that."

Before I realized what was happening, Richard had thrown on his coat and gone out the door.

"Here," Julie said, handing me a lunch ticket. "Take it."

"Thanks." I went out the door. Richard was already fifty yards down the path, marching like Sherlock Holmes in pursuit of a murderer. I jogged after him and caught up where the path turned into a gravel lane.

"Listen," he said, "I'm not saying I don't believe you. But I wouldn't be doing my job if I let everybody waltz in here and get free lunches. Besides, I have the safety of the employees to consider."

"Come on, Richard," I said, "are you saying I look *unsavory*? Because, seriously, I shaved this morning, so I know I look anything but."

Richard ignored me. Despite the fact that he was a couple inches taller than me and had a longer stride, I marched right alongside him. The foliage was resplendent in the cool air, and I breathed deeply of the smells of tannin and peaty soil and ozone and everything clean and fresh about this, my favorite season.

Soon Richard and I fell into a rhythm: two autumn-loving guys out for a brisk walk. Without thinking, I started whistling the theme from *Bridge Over the River Kwai*. For thirty seconds the two of us were lockstep. Suddenly Richard noticed he was enjoying himself, and accelerated to break out of our hypnotic rhythm. I stopped whistling; we weren't having fun anymore.

Clearly, Richard was determined to get to the bottom of this. At this point he was walking so fast that he was actually on the cusp of a jog, but I could tell he didn't want to appear too eager. Instead he quick-stepped up to the bunkhouse door and knocked three times.

After he had knocked a few more times a girl came to the door wearing nothing but a T-shirt with a giant cannabis leaf on the front, and forest green panties peeking out at the bottom. She was tall, and with her long legs and the musky smell of cannabis and incense that surrounded her, she reminded me of my first college fling, Deirdre. She held a paperback of the *Bhagavad Gita*, with her forefinger in the book to mark her place.

"Hi," Richard said, "we're trying to clear up a bit of confusion. I'd like to speak to…" Richard turned to me. "What are their names again?"

"Hoku and Astrid," I said.

"Hoku?" the girl said. "And what was the other one?"

"Astrid," I said.

She gazed over my shoulder. After a long, awkward moment of silence and utter vacancy on her face (a moment during which Richard stood as imperturbably as a Queen's Guard at Buckingham Palace), she shook her head.

"Well," Richard said to me, "why don't you describe them?"

I was pressed for how to do this. Astrid: a tall blonde with a warm touch and blocked pores? And Hoku: a brunette of average height wearing a ski cap and crazy pants?

"Well?" Richard said to me. "This young lady doesn't have all day."

"Actually, I do," she said. "I'm not working today, so it's fine."

"All I can tell you," I said, "is that the one that went by Astrid was about your height, and she was blonde with widely spaced blue eyes. Hoku was a short brunette and wore a ski cap."

The girl fell into her trance for a moment, then shook her head.

"Sorry," she said, "there's nobody like that here."

I was getting angry. The whole thing felt like a conspiracy.

"This is ridiculous," I said. "I *saw* them go inside here. Hoku went in and brought out a pair of pants for me. If you don't believe me—"

"Thank you very much, miss," Richard said. "We won't trouble you anymore."

As the girl went inside, Richard starting walking back, forcing me to follow.

"So that's it?" I said. "That's your proof?"

He walked clasping his hands behind his back. Richard probably picked up this mannerism at the same School of Assholery where he got the dangling half-glasses bit.

"We spoke to a young lady who lives in the same quarters as the two you met," he said. "The young lady just said she hasn't seen two people who match the descriptions you gave. *Ipso facto*, those two women—if they exist at all—don't live there."

"*Ipso facto*?" I said. "I think you mean *ergo* or *therefore*."

"No…I mean *ipso facto*."

I winced and shook my head. "No, I have a degree in philosophy, Richard, and you're wrong about that. '*Ipso facto*' means 'by the fact itself'—in other words, that a phenomenon is a direct result of the action in question. It'd only be '*ipso* facto' if the girl not recognizing their descriptions actually *caused* them not to live there. You see the difference?" I smiled walking alongside him and craned my neck in his direction. "But I bet you've been waiting a long time to use good old *ipso facto*. Five, ten years at least. Right?"

He mumbled something, then ignored me all the way back to the administration office, where he finally stopped at a fork in the path.

"You seem harmless enough," he said.

"Yeah, I'm pretty harmless."

"Why don't you go have lunch, walk around a bit and then leave?" Richard said. "I have no doubt you gave two young women a ride here, but I don't think they work here. I'd appreciate it if you dropped this, okay?"

"No problem," I said. "I enjoyed our walk."

"Come on inside then, and we'll give you a meal ticket."

"Julie already did."

With a nod, he leaned towards me and stretched out his hand. But when he saw that I wasn't planning to shake his hand, he tried to pretend he'd only been loosening his arm in his sleeve before putting his hand in his pocket. Had I been 20 years younger, I probably would have shaken his hand to alleviate the tension, but the older I got, the more I enjoyed making jerks uncomfortable.

"Well then," he said finally. "Good day."

"Yes, it is, isn't it?" I said.

I followed the signs to the dining hall. There was no way I was letting this go. I wanted to know where the hell Hoku and Astrid were, and I wanted to chew them out for making me look like a schmuck. The second I reached the dining hall and the hostess at the door took my ticket, I asked her about Hoku and Astrid, and whether two women matching their descriptions worked here.

While doing research for my mystery novels, I'd read a lot about facial tics and eye movements that revealed whether somebody was holding something back or outright lying. This girl's face, besides having some of the most radiant skin I'd ever seen (must have been the vegan diet), showed only confusion.

"No, they don't sound familiar," she said. "Sorry."

"No problem."

"Are they in some kind of trouble?" she asked.

"No, why?"

"Because the way you were asking me those questions, for a second I thought you were a cop."

I chuckled. "No, I'm Astrid's cousin. They said they were working here and I'm supposed to meet them."

"Well, enjoy your lunch."

The dining hall was a knotty pine deal with vaulted ceilings. It had the feel of an upscale summer camp, probably because the Alpha Institute basically *was* a camp—for wealthy, New Age adults. Instead of arts and crafts and Capture the Flag, there were chakra realignments and Tai Chi. The dining hall was arranged with the food in a buffet setup down the middle of the space, seating on each end of the hall, and drinks, plates, condiments and napkins along the back wall. I sat down with a plate of vegan lasagna, spinach salad, two glasses of apple juice and a cup of coffee. I laughed to myself. Compared to my previous encounters with all-you-can-eat buffets, this one was tame.

Certainly tamer than the one in Virginia Beach, where, as a teenager, I'd accompanied my friend Carl Kropp's family on vacation. At a restaurant that served all-you-can-eat Maryland blue crab, Mr. Kropp and I mortified Mrs. Kropp, Carl, and his younger siblings by interpreting the "ALL YOU CAN EAT" sign literally. Our primal grunts as Mr. Kropp and I ripped open those soft shells were probably a bit much. Our lips stung from the thick coating of Old Bay seasoning the cooks had applied as a deterrent to further eating, but Mr. Kropp and I were seasoned ourselves. We knew we were better off simply to continue eating, thus dulling our pain receptors to the spiciness, than we would be if we tried to cool our tongues with water, which would only fill our stomachs and prevent us from consuming more crab. As an insurance policy, Mr. Kropp wrapped half a pound of shelled crabmeat in a napkin and dropped the bulge down his wife-beater. Around the fifth platter, the cook and the manager stood at the kitchen doors, both of them with their arms bizarrely akimbo, and frowned at us.

Now I was sitting at a window table alone, watching the Alpha instructors dine with guests. I sipped my coffee.

Hoku and Astrid had said they worked in the kitchen.

Well…what was stopping me from going in there and seeing if they worked here?

Nothing, that's what.

I bussed my tray, going through the convoluted process of composting and recycling. The complicated litany made me long for my 1970s childhood, when we simply threw everything *the hell out.*

For a minute I stood in the corner wondering how I could get to the bottom of the Hoku–Astrid mystery.

What would my detective, Dakota Stevens, do?

He'd ask himself what his hero, PI Jim Rockford, would do.

And what would Jim Rockford do?

He'd give himself a cover story and pose as somebody else.

I noticed a side door into the kitchen. If anyone asked, I was a temp in Administration and had been sent up here by good 'ole Richard to find Hoku and Astrid. Those two had some *splainin'* to do.

Steeling myself by standing up straight and raking my hands through my tousled wavy hair, I took a deep breath and plowed through the double doors.

A pair of dishwashers, a guy and a girl, hosed down plates and loaded a machine. I kept walking. Rather than meekly asking each employee one by one, I decided I'd be better off making a show of strength by accosting a group of them.

In the main kitchen area, a group of cooks and sous chefs, and a woman in a navy pantsuit who looked like a manager, were cleaning up. They saw me coming and weren't at all fazed by having an outsider in a leather jacket wander into their place of work. I sensed that with a soupçon of bluster, I could get the information I wanted.

"What's up?" said the woman in the pantsuit.

"*What's up?*" I parroted back at her. I jerked a thumb over my shoulder. "Richard's pissed, that's what's up. You know…Richard down in Administration? He sent me up here to find out if you have a couple of girls working in the kitchen. I guess some guy claims he picked them up hitchhiking. They said they worked in the kitchen and promised him a free meal, and Richard wants to get to the bottom of it."

"Crazy," the manager said.

"Yeah. Anyway, they go by Hoku and Astrid. One's a tall blonde and the other's a short brunette. We thought they lived in the dorm down by the—"

"Dorm?" she said. "You're kidding, right?"

The chefs laughed.

"Ha, I get it," I said. "So, it seems they don't live there, and Richard wants to know if you have anybody like that working here in the kitchen."

"Tell him we don't," she said. "Right, guys? Hoku? Astrid?"

They shook their heads.

"You know," one of the others said, "they might live in a tent. There are a few workers who do that. Did you look around for a tent? Down by the lake?"

"No, I didn't. Thanks."

"Good luck."

I went out the back door and picked up a path that ran behind the dining hall. I was seriously beginning to doubt that Hoku and Astrid were real. *But I had those pants.* Then something occurred to me: the dining hall wasn't the only place on the Institute campus with a kitchen. There was also the café where I'd had the Karma Mint Tea. I went in the rear entrance, made sure Richard wasn't around, and asked the young woman at the counter if Hoku and Astrid worked there.

"No, there's nobody like that here," she said.

I left via the back again and followed a path to the barracks. There was no tent nearby. There were no signs of flattened brush or a clearing that might have contained a tent either. Unless those two were sleeping under the stars, they weren't out here.

I continued through the woods to the edge of the lake. There was a big green cabin tent. I went over, knocked on the tent pole.

"Hello? Anybody home?"

No answer. The beach and the hammocks were empty. I thought about going in the tent to see if there was anything (like a pair of those crazy pants) that would prove their existence, but I decided just to peek through the mosquito netting instead. The front flap was zipped shut, so I walked around to the back and peered in. Everything was bathed in a green glow, so it was impossible to make anything out.

"Hey, can we help you?" a man's voice said.

A guy and a girl, holding hands, emerged from the path behind me. Startled, I tripped on the guy line and stumbled over to them.

"I know this looks bad," I said, "but I'm trying to find two girls."

I couldn't take it anymore. I wanted to know who those two girls were, and more importantly, *where* they were, so I dumped the entire story on these two 20-somethings, throwing myself on their mercy. I told them about picking up the girls when they were hitchhiking, going to the park with them, the crazy pants they gave me, and how I'd spent the last couple of hours searching for them around the Institute.

"I don't get it," I said. "It's like they just vanished."

"Weird," the guy said.

"Yeah, weird," the girl said.

"Have you seen anyone like them camping out around here?"

They shook their heads.

"Hey, listen," the guy said, "we're late for a class. Good luck, okay?"

"Thanks," I said. "And thanks for not thinking I'm nuts."

I walked down to the tiny beach by the lake, and when I glanced over my shoulder, the couple was hustling up the path towards the administration building. The girl looked back, saw that I was looking at her, and the two of them jogged around a bend in the path and out of sight.

Great, a couple of hipster narcs.

I couldn't go directly back to the parking lot because it was on the path leading to the administration office. But what if I approached it from the lake? They wouldn't expect that. I glanced at the shiny kayaks lined up like new cars on an auto lot. I went to a small shed, grabbed a double-paddle oar and dragged a kayak to the water.

The water was only a few inches deep next to the shore, so I had to take off my shoes and socks and drag the kayak in until the water was up to my calves before I could get in it. Once I balanced myself on the seat, I shoved off with the oar and started paddling. Although I'd been pretty good in a canoe in my Boy Scout days, I'd never used a kayak before, and my first strokes sent me curving in one direction, then the other. Soon, though, I found a good rhythm and was gliding across the flat water, into a tiny cove at the woods' edge. I plowed through a mass of cattails, turned the kayak parallel to the bank and hauled myself out. I also pulled the kayak up on shore; if nothing else, I didn't want Richard thinking I was irresponsible with the Institute's equipment.

Now on dry land, I put on my socks and shoes and jogged through the woods until I reached the parking lot. My Honda was 100 feet away, between an SUV and a van. I broke out of the woods and ran full-tilt, or as full-tilt as a reasonably fit middle-aged man bent double can run. I unlocked the car door with the remote key before I got there and jumped in. In the rear-view mirror, I saw Richard and the hipster couple walking towards the lake. I started the car and crept out of the lot.

As I passed the bunkhouse, I began to seriously question whether Hoku and Astrid were real, and whether I'd imagined the whole thing. But that couldn't be because I had the strange olive drab drawstring pants right beside me on the passenger seat. I thought about spending the morning with the two of them, how they had insisted I write about myself, and then how they simply vanished. And then I remembered something else: how people in Manhattan last night had called them aliens.

Suddenly I knew what the answer was. They were alien girls—alien energy spirit creatures in human corporeal form—sent here to encourage me to write this book. The book you are now reading.

Hoku, Astrid: Wherever you are, whatever planet you hail from, thank you.

2

The Thomas Kinkade Affair

Before Alexas' great-Uncle Walt started sending us Thomas Kinkade paintings, I had never heard of the "Painter of Light."

I enjoyed art very much and had some framed prints of painters I admired: Andrew Wyeth, Maxfield Parrish, and Edward Hopper. But I knew nothing about this guy Kinkade. So when Uncle Walt sent us our first one as a Christmas gift—an innocuous scene of the Golden Gate Bridge—I said to Alexas, "Hey, nice."

Since Alexas was born in San Francisco, the Kinkade picture was an unobtrusive reminder of her home. We only got back to the Bay Area about every five years, so the least I could do was hang the 18"x12" picture in what I'd dubbed the Library of our pre-war apartment.

And there it sat, unobtrusive and unnoticed, for a year.

The following year, for our wedding anniversary, Uncle Walt sent us another Kinkade. This one was of a cottage on a nameless cliff by the sea. "Okay," I said to Alexas when we got it unwrapped, "but I get it. Is this another place on the California coast?"

"Not that I know of," she said.

I shrugged. "Well, it was nice of him to think of us. We'll put it in the living room near the Wyeth sketches."

The fact is, I hated the damn things, but I couldn't put my finger precisely on what I loathed about them. Was it the saccharine color scheme? The maudlin use of light? Or was it the fact that every one of his "paintings" came with a Certificate of Authenticity? I wasn't sure.

That Christmas, barely two months after our anniversary, Walt sent us two more Thomas Kinkades.[5] I voiced my consternation to my wife.

"What the hell, Alexas?!"

"I know, I know," she said.

Alexas retreated to the bedroom and called her younger sister for advice. When she reemerged, I was watching *Butch Cassidy and the Sundance Kid*. Actually I was watching a playback loop of my favorite scene: Butch delivering, to a mutinous Hole-in-the-Wall gang member, "the most aesthetically exquisite kick in the balls in the history of the modern American cinema."[6] After the loop had played 6 or 7 times, and I'd laughed so hard my stomach hurt, Alexas rolled her eyes and shut off the DVD player.

"Do you want to hear about the Kinkades?" she asked.

"Yes."

According to Alexas' younger sister, we were getting off easy. She and her husband had received eleven Kinkades already.

---

5 This entire affair happened between the years of 2003 and 2009. Thomas Kinkade died in 2012.

6 This is how the screenwriter, the great William Goldman, described the scene in the script.

"*Eleven!?*" I said.

"Yes, eleven. And it's *not* Uncle Walt who's buying them. It's his new girlfriend, Darla. She's like thirty years younger and apparently a shopaholic. She likes spending Uncle Walt's money on crap."

"So what are we going to do?" I asked.

"My sister is going to talk to Walt about it. He likes her, says she's got spunk. It'll be better if it comes from her."

"I doubt it'll work," I said, "but okay."

The two Kinkades went into a closet, and for ten months I didn't think about them at all.

Then October came, the month of our anniversary again. I had ordered a new computer, and the morning I expected it to arrive, our UPS guy, Neville, met me at my apartment door. I flung it open and rubbed my hands together.

"A new Mac, Neville! I can't wait."

"I don't think it's a computer, Chris. Did you guys order a flat-screen TV?"

"No, why?"

Neville went around the corner and wheeled the package up on a hand truck. It was a plain cardboard box of the same dimensions of a flat screen TV, and it was a big one—at least 60 inches! Alexas and I were legendary cinephiles, and a big flat-screen TV was the perfect gift for us.

"Thanks, Neville," I said. "Have a great day!"

I dragged the box into the living room, freshened my coffee and got a knife to open it with. Our cat, Sweetie, came out of hiding to see what the fuss was about. She sat on the armrest watching me with her front paws folded demurely in front of her.

We had recently bought a new TV, a 32" Sony Trinitron. Since it used the old CRT technology, the thing barely fit into elevators and required two Samoans to carry it. But if this box contained an HDTV, the Trinitron would be out on the street in an hour.

After I had a long sip of coffee and surveyed our free wall space for the TV, I opened the box. Heavy styrofoam protected the corners, and the entire unit was bagged in thick plastic. I'd never gotten a flat-screen TV before, so I didn't know if the protective plastic was standard, but I knew that the gold color I saw underneath was *not* standard. I looked up at our apartment's freakishly high ceilings.

"*Please* no," I said.

I said a quick, silent prayer that the contents of the box wouldn't be another Kinkade, that somehow Walt, a reputed lifelong practical joker, had bought us the only flat-screen TV available in a gold leaf frame. I closed my eyes, took a breath and cut the plastic away. I leaned the box toward the light from the window, pushed the cardboard to the side, and peered in. A kaleidoscope of garish colors and glowing windows sneered back at me.

I couldn't believe it. Another Thomas Kinkade.

What bothered me most was that I had gotten my hopes up for a flat-screen TV, and within seconds those hopes had been dashed. We were going to host epic parties with the 60" flat-screen TV as the draw. The neighborhood barber Lazar, the butcher Frank, the newsstand guy Elio, the typewriter repairman Sol, the guys I knew from the diner—they'd all come to our place to watch the World Series and the Super Bowl. Alexas would prepare endless trays of her delicious canapés, and she and the women would sip wine and play cards and gossip in the kitchen while we men shouted at the TV in the living room. The men would give me a nickname (a better one than my usual "Orcutt"), something like "Mirado Warrior" (as a tribute to my love of pencils) or my freshman dorm nickname of "Elway" (like NFL quarterback John Elway, I threw the football really hard when we played).

Now, alas, now all of that was gone. There would be no parties, no Super Bowl, no nickname.

I moped into the kitchen and called Alexas at work.

"Well," I said, "we got another one."

"Another what?" she said.

"What do you think? Another Kinkade."

"You're *kidding*."

"Nope," I said.

"What's it look like?"

"No idea. I didn't take it out of the box."

She sighed—a throaty one that rattled the line. "All right…we'll put it in the closet with the others."

"It won't fit."

"What do you mean? How big is it?"

"Let's put it this way," I said. "I thought it was a flat-screen TV."

"Jesus," she breathed into the phone

I waited until she got home before taking it out of the box. It was a Kinkade all right, a 48x36-incher entitled "Boston Celebration." Both Alexas and I had gone to college in Boston, met in the city years later and fallen in love there. Clearly Darla had done more research this time to find a Kinkade relevant to us as a couple. But again, I *hated* it: the composition was hideous, and also, "Boston Celebration" my ass; neither of us could tell *where* in Boston the scene was located.

"I say we get rid of it," I said. "Sell it and buy something from a *real* artist. You know…one that actually puts *paint on canvas*."

"We can't do that," Alexas said. "My mom knows about Uncle Walt's gifts. When she comes out, she'll want to see them."

"Well we're not hanging this one, that's for damn sure," I said. "We'll keep it in the box, and if she comes for a visit we'll hang it then. In the meantime, tell your sister to tell Darla that there's no more room at the inn. Tacky artwork? Sorry, all full up here."

"Understood."

This worked…for a while. Then, right around the time that Walt was breaking up with Darla, we received several more, smaller Kinkades (all lighthouses), and when Alexas asked her sister about them, she learned that Darla, in a spiteful final shopping spree, had taken Walt's credit card to the local Thomas Kinkade gallery and bought over a dozen for Alexas and her sister. These were kept in their boxes and shoved under the bed.

In December of 2006, Alexas was burned-out from working in the fashion industry, and we were both tired of having to maintain a large income for basic things like rent. Our needs were few—movies and books for both of us, pencils for me, popcorn for her—so we decided to move to the country, to the small town 100 miles north of New York City where I had graduated from high school: Millbrook. For a guy who had moved 20-plus times as a kid, Millbrook was the closest thing I had to a hometown.

We had moved on savings and faith, neither of us having a steady job before we took the leap. We found a small second-floor apartment (an actual *garret*) right in the village. While I took a web design assignment for a few weeks, Alexas painted the apartment, and it was then that we discovered how little wall space the place had. Once our favorite prints were hung, there was zero space for the Kinkades—*if* we had wanted to hang them, which we absolutely didn't. Alexas and I now had enough Kinkades in my parents' garage across the street to start a Thomas Kinkade "gallery" of our own.

One spring weekend morning after we had settled into the apartment, the two of us were retrieving some items from storage when I pointed at the paintings. A beautiful network of spider webs connected the boxes. There were a dozen Kinkades.

"We have to get rid of them," I said.

"I know," Alexas said.

"See if you can sell them. Put them on Craigslist."

"I will."

"All of them," I said. "I hate looking at the things."

Alexas shook her head. "Darla. What a twit."

For the next six months, Alexas tried every tactic and scheme she could come up with to rid us of the Kinkades. After considerable research, she listed them on

Craigslist for well under their purchase prices; but the only responses she got were from cheapskates offering her $50 for the lot. She created an Ebay account and tried to auction them; but none of the bids ever cleared the minimums we set. She even called the nearest Kinkade "gallery" to get *them* to buy the things back. As I listened in on the extension, the woman explained that a lot of people tried to do this; unfortunately, her "hands were tied" because the dealers were required to buy directly from the Thomas Kinkade corporation.

"So, basically you're an Amway," Alexas said. "A cult."

I stifled a laugh. I loved it when Alexas went on the offensive; she so rarely did it, and, as a trial lawyer's daughter, she did it so well.

"Absolutely not," the woman protested.

"No," Alexas said, "because if you were an actual *gallery*, you'd buy and sell from anyone to anyone."

I said, "Alexas, ask her about the Certificates of Authenticity?"

"Yes, what about *them*?" Alexas said. "All of ours still have their certificates."

"This is very unfair," the woman said. "I can't talk to two of you on the phone. If you'd like to come in, perhaps—"

There was blood in the water. God forgive me, but I loved it.

"That's not going to happen," I said. "Now what about the certificates?"

"I'm afraid they don't matter," she said.

"So you're saying they're all bullshit," I said.

"I'm sorry," the woman said, "but I have another customer on the line."

"Did you hear that, Alexas? A *customer*."

"Go ahead," Alexas said. "Go recruit a new sucker for your little *cult*."

"Goodbye," the woman said.

When we hung up, I went out to the kitchen. Alexas was angry-scrubbing the sink.

"Alexas, where is this place?" I asked.

"The Westchester mall, why?"

"What if I took the paintings up there right now and threw them through the window?"

She drummed her fingers on the counter. "Hmm…well…one, you'd go to jail. And two, I still think we can sell them."

"All right," I said, "you've got one more chance. Then we're going with my through-the-window plan."

Alexas arranged to sell them at my younger sister Mandy's yard sale. Mandy was an apprentice-level hoarder, so lumping the Kinkades in with all of her stuff made sense. The day of the sale, instead of putting prices on the pictures, Mandy simply called us with the customers' offers.

"Mandy says a guy will give us a hundred bucks for all of them," Alexas said. "I guess he does the flea-market circuit and can resell them easily."

"Tell Mandy to tell him to blow it out his ass," I said. "That won't even cover the *gas* we've used hauling them around."

"So, no," Alexas said.

"Hell no."

"Sorry, Mandy," Alexas said into the phone. "That's not enough."

Make no mistake, I hated the things, but I wasn't going to be ripped off either. I could see this greasy-haired, saggy-jeaned, no-assed leech snagging the paintings for $100, then turning around and getting thousands for them at his next flea market. Screw him. I'd burn the things in front of him before I let that happen.

The yard sale was a bust, of course. The only picture that sold was the one I hated the least—*Golden Gate Bridge*—and only for a measly $40. I tried giving the paintings to Mandy, but even my pack-rat sister had enough aesthetic sense not to want them hanging in her house.

II

In June, Alexas was invited to a work-related conference at Middlebury College in Vermont. Spouses were welcome. Born in Maine, I felt a kinship with all of New England, but I especially loved Vermont. And after the extremely wet spring we'd had in the Northeast, the Green Mountains in July would be profoundly verdurous.

In the weeks before our trip, every time I turned around, there he was—Thomas Kinkade. I'd been reading a number of books on mental attraction, books full of phrases like "what you focus on expands," so I'd worked hard at *not* thinking about him and his work. Despite my best efforts, though, I couldn't avoid the bastard.

While I was flipping through TV channels one afternoon, the remote got stuck at QVC, where a Thomas Kinkade sales blitz was underway. I shut off the TV. A flyer for a Thomas Kinkade event at a local Holiday Inn came in the mail. I balled it up and threw it out. The next day another one appeared in my mailbox. I burned it and flushed the cinders. Never mind the Thomas Kinkade catalogs we'd been getting for two years because Darla had put us on their damn mailing list.

But the last straw was when I saw a *60 Minutes* piece in which Thomas Kinkade said of Pablo Picasso, "I don't believe, in time, that he will be regarded as the titan that he is now."

My jaw dropped. There was no way Kinkade could be so self-deceived; I *must* have been hallucinating. There was no way he could think that his work and his influence on Art would stand the test of time against a guy who shattered the idea of what Art *is*. But no. Kinkade actually believed that because his flea-market pictures had sold more than Monet, Manet, Rembrandt, Renoir, Van Gogh, Gaugin and Picasso combined; because his company had sold over $1.7 billion of artwork at retail; because an estimated 1 in 10 U.S. homes featured some form of his art or licensed products; and because his customer base was approximately 25 million people, that these facts meant his work was objectively better.[7] The

---

7 Source: "The Thomas Kinkade Brand: Discover How You Can Be a Thomas Kinkade Dealer," Adobe PDF document: http://www.sellkinkade.com. The entire footnoted sentence is one long logical fallacy—*argumentum ad populum*, to be precise—and the only thing these numbers prove is that there are a *lot* of people in the world with abysmally bad taste.

idea that Picasso, an artist who had changed the way people *see* the world, would in time be less highly regarded than Thomas Kinkade was absurd. In my own small way, I had to put a stop to this, and I had to get his damn pictures out of my life—forever. Then, in one of those serendipitous moments of such sublime synchronicity, one of those moments so rare and perfectly timed that you know it's been divinely orchestrated, I got my chance.

In anticipation of the Vermont trip, I had begun to research recreational opportunities in the Middlebury area, and I discovered that the college had an art museum. During the week of our trip, the museum was featuring an exhibition on the work of—I couldn't believe my eyes—Thomas Kinkade. As I read the exhibition description, my lips curled into a Grinch smile. I started to conceive a masterful plan to rid myself of the Kinkades once and for all. Here is the exhibition description:

> **Making Sense of Thomas Kinkade**
> May 21–August 9, 2009
>
> It is easy to dismiss the work of contemporary landscape painter Thomas Kinkade and brush aside his popularity as only a successful marketing phenomenon. But to do so ignores his sincere zeal and the deep resonance his work holds for people. This exhibition, guest-curated by Michael Clapper, associate professor of art history at Franklin and Marshall College, considers Kinkade in the context of work that ranges from Norman Rockwell to Komar and Melamid.[8]

Coincidentally around this time, I rented the original and the remake of the movie *The Thomas Crown Affair*.

---

8 Source: Middlebury College Museum of Art exhibition brochure.

I preferred the original for ultra-cool Steve McQueen,[9] and for the sexy opening shot of Faye Dunaway: a multiple-shot extreme close-up of her flawless skin and fine profile, her giant hat and big sunglasses, and her iron dominatrix expression. But the remake, in which Thomas Crown is an art thief instead of a bank robber, was more relevant to my current situation. I watched it several times in a row, and not solely for redhead Rene Russo's topless scene. I was looking for ideas; ideas not on how to steal paintings, but on how to rid oneself of paintings one doesn't want.

The most important idea I gleaned from watching both versions of *The Thomas Crown Affair* (besides the virtues of a sexy antagonist and a well-tailored suit) was that one needed to do one's research. I would have to assume a false identity, and to do that I would have to do something that made me cringe: I had to become a lay expert on everything Thomas Kinkade.

Reluctantly I perused the Thomas Kinkade website, as well as the blogs of collectors and admirers, and I learned several things. First, the passion and vehemence most of them expressed scared me. Their arguments reminded me of discussions of religion I'd had over the years with people who a) didn't know what the hell they were talking about, and b) tacitly considered it their mission to proselytize every person every chance they got. I learned there was a Thomas Kinkade Collector's Society,

---

9 Steve McQueen is one of several personal idols whose birth number is the same as mine—the master number, 22/4. They are all renegades, men known for doing things "their way": Frank Sinatra, Clint Eastwood, Woody Allen, Mark Twain, Immanuel Kant, J.D. Salinger, P.T. Barnum, and J.D. Rockefeller III.

and while I was damned if I was joining, for $50 one would get a brushwork of *Lakeside Manor* in an elegant gold frame (an $89 value!), a quarterly magazine, access to the Collector's Society exclusive store, a membership card, and a red heart-shaped membership pin with "The Love of Home" and a gas street lamp in embossed gold on the front. I studied the pin closely. Based on what I'd read about these people, it was exactly the sort of thing they'd wear to broadcast their allegiance, like the Nazis did with their little pins. If I saw the pin on somebody while up at Middlebury, I'd know I had a sucker.

For my secret identity, I decided to pose as an entrepreneur who was considering opening a Thomas Kinkade gallery. For this, I studied the PDF on becoming a Thomas Kinkade dealer, absorbing illuminating tidbits like, "known to Presidents, Popes, Kings and Queens, Thom's fame reached around the world" and, "during 2005 and 2006, Thomas Kinkade was the spokesman for the Points of Light Foundation, founded by former President George H.W. Bush."[10] I was shocked to learn that if I wanted to own a "Signature Gold Gallery," I would need between $80,000 and $300,000 in startup capital.

The night before we left for Middlebury, I put all of my Kinkade research into my carpetbag, along with 100 copies of a color trifold brochure of our paintings that I'd had printed, and told Alexas to pack my khaki summer suit. I hadn't worn it since a corporate speechwriting gig

---

10 And there was this important fact, which I planned on shoehorning into conversation at the next dinner party I attended: "Thomas Kinkade has become such a pervasive force in the culture that the term 'Kinkadian' has entered the popular Lexicon." I couldn't *wait* to use this.

in 2007—during a junket at a posh resort in Scottsdale, Arizona—so naturally Alexas was curious.

"Why the suit?" she asked.

"Because if we're going to find anybody who likes Kinkades enough to buy ours," I said, "it's going to be at this exhibit, and I don't want to look like I *need* the money."

Alexas grinned conspiratorially at me.

"Besides," I continued. "I think this Middlebury exhibit is going to bring scads of these freaks out of the woodwork."

" 'You keep thinkin', Butch,' " she said. " 'That's what you're good at.' "

" 'I got vision and the rest of the world wears bifocals,' " I said.

The next afternoon we drove north up pastoral Route 7, through Stockbridge, MA (hometown of one of Kinkade's influences, Norman Rockwell), through the verdant Green Mountains, to quaint Middlebury, Vermont. We checked into our hotel and went in search of food. For an hour we searched for a place to eat and only found two prospects: a restaurant with a neon "EAT" sign on the side (which read as "E T" because the "A" was burned out) and a place called "Mister Up's"—where they spelled out "Mister" instead of simply using "Mr." The use of "Mister" annoyed me; not only was it an obviously calculated attempt by the establishment owner to gain instant credibility, but "Mister" made the restaurant sound sinister.

"Who the hell is this 'Up' guy anyway?" I said to Alexas. "Oh, but I guess I'm supposed to trust him because he's *Mister* Up. Screw him."

Alexas sighed. "What if we get a bunch of fruit and cheese and have a carpet picnic back at the hotel?"

I raised an eyebrow. "The Home Run Derby's on tonight."

"Well," she said, "that settles it."

The next morning after breakfast, I dropped off Alexas at her conference, put on my suit, and drove to the museum. As I walked inside, I made up my mind that no matter what happened, I would stay in character. I was a Kinkade collector with 26 of the Master's paintings, and I was considering starting a gallery. I had doubles of a dozen paintings, and to raise money for my new business venture, I was looking to sell them to another collector.

Adjusting my Armani glasses, admiring the drape of my trousers and the buff of my chestnut loafers, I whipped open the museum door and jogged toward the check-in desk with feigned breathlessness. An elderly woman peered over the desk at me.

"Excuse me," I said, "where is the…Kinkade exhibit? I've come…all the way…from New York to see it."

"Yes, it's just inside." She produced a map and pointed at it with a pen. "The Kinkades are here, on the first floor. And on the second floor there's a terrific exhibit of Luigi Lucioni's work. He did a lot of Vermont landscapes, among other things."

Lucioni was the guy whose work I really wanted to see, but I had to maintain my cover: I was here for the Kinkades, plain and simple.

"I'll check out Lucioni's stuff if I have a chance." I took out my wallet. "How much do I owe you?"

"Nothing. It's free."

"Really?!" I said. "That's so generous of you folks. Boy, I've been a collector of Kinkades for years and this is the first time any museum has given his work the respect it deserves."

The old woman smiled crookedly. "How nice."

"I'm Chris by the way."

"Helen."

"I love that name." I leaned on the counter. "Do me a favor, would you, Helen?"

"If I can."

"I'm selling a few of my Kinkades, so if you meet any avid collectors, could you send them my way?"

"I can do that."

"Great." I gave her one of the printed brochures and wrote my name and the hotel phone number on it.

"Oh, lovely," she said.

"I'm in town until Thursday. Tell people they can call me anytime, day or night."

"Okay, Chris."

"Thank you, Helen. I love your hair by the way." It was a shimmering silver and terrifically full. "Take care."

I strolled into the Thomas Kinkade exhibit. On the walls were a dozen of his paintings, along with a few of his "influences." I decided that if I was going to pretend to be a Kinkade lover, I needed to find something to appreciate in the things. So, starting with the first painting, I studied each work and its description card closely before moving to the next one.

By the time I took in my third well-lighted cottage, and saw yet *another* San Francisco street jammed to the curbsides with cable cars, tourists, taxis, rickshaws, delivery trucks, shop owners, cats and dogs, I figured out why I loathed Thomas Kinkade's work: It was all too much. The guy knew nothing about restraint, nothing about the principle of "less is more."

"Why have one lighted window when they can *all* be lit?" he probably thought.

Instead of having a single, striking bed of flowers, he'd put ten flowerbeds in the picture, all in jolting hues, creating a battle royal of color for the viewer's attention. And worst of all, he never allowed one iconic image to own the scene; instead he turned every painting into a game of *Where's Waldo?* "Look, honey! The Chinese food delivery guy! I found him!"

Almost as bad as his over-stuffing every painting was Kinkade's blatantly repeating himself. As Kenneth Baker, critic for the *San Francisco Chronicle*, expressed it, "He has a vocabulary, as most people do. And it's a vocabulary of formulas, unfortunately. And he shuffles the deck every so often. Lighthouse, cottage, sea, ships, sky, so on, so on. Little bit of waves, so on, rocks. And you end up with this."[11]

To show Kinkade's influences, the exhibit featured a small village scene by Norman Rockwell and a Yosemite landscape by Albert Bierstadt. But the second I saw those exquisitely crafted, idyllic visions next to Kinkade's

---

11 Source: "Thomas Kinkade: A Success," *60 Minutes*, CBS News, November 21, 2001.

"paintings," the hideousness and inferiority of Kinkade's work became instantly obvious.

A night scene showed a busy small town street, glaringly lit. The descriptive plate beside the picture explained why Kinkade was so enamored of windows with a warm yellow glow: to him, the lighted windows conveyed comfort, home, openness, and safety, and they're also intriguing, prompting the viewer to imagine what's going on inside. However, the effect is lost when *every single window on every single structure* glares like there's a porn set inside.

My favorite painting of a lighted house is one by Maxfield Parrish: *Hilltop Farm Winter*. In it, a simple Colonial country farmhouse sits atop a knoll. There is snow on the ground, a trickle of smoke coming from the chimney and *one* lighted window, forcing the viewer to imagine the scene inside. It's a paragon of composition and restraint, and the delicious ambiguity of the light on the distant horizon leaves you perpetually wondering what time of day it is—dawn or dusk?

So far, all this visit had done was entrench my views about Thomas Kinkade and the low worth of his art. I had studied every painting and read every description plate. My hatred for his work and his gauche marketing practices was now fully justified. It was time to get back into character as a Kinkade collector and aspiring gallery owner.

Across the room, a skinny college girl snorted at a painting of a lighthouse. She wore a Middlebury College T-shirt, shorts and track shoes, and she was mildly perspiring, like she had sprinted over here straight from practicing the high jump. Here was a chance to put my devil's advocate skills into practice. Sidling up to her, I stood with my chin poised thoughtfully in my palm.

"I take it you don't care for his work," I said.

She closed her eyes and shook her head vigorously. Her ponytail wagged.

"So, that's a no," I said.

"It's *so* bad," she said. "I mean everything…the colors, the textures, the themes. Can you *have* any more cottages? Awful doesn't even begin to describe it."

"Are you an art student?"

"Art history, actually." She appraised my suit. "What are you, a docent or something?"

"No, just a collector."

She gulped. If she'd been eating something, she would have choked.

"A collector?" she said stridently. "Of *this* stuff?"

"Sure," I said. "There's a lot to like about it. It's cheery and optimistic, and it's simple. There's nothing to *get*."

"But one of art's purposes is to make us *think*," she said. "To expand us as human beings. This stuff doesn't *expand* us, it contracts us. It dumbs us down. This is the Burger King of art. 'I'll take the number three Whopper cottage with onion rings and a Diet Coke.'"

"Clever," I said. "You'd be an excellent critic."

"Seriously," she said, "how can you collect this guy's junk? He's lowest common denominator."

"Humor me for a moment, okay?"

She crossed her arms. "All right."

"What if Kinkade *knew* his stuff was mediocre, but the piece of art he was really trying to create was the mass controversy? *This*—people like you and me arguing over what art is and what makes it good or not? What if *that's* what he was aiming for all along?"

"I think you're giving him *way* too much credit," she said. "I've seen the dude in interviews. He's not that deep. All he cares about is the money."

"Maybe," I said. "All I know is, after a long day at the office, I like seeing his stuff on my walls."

"Ah, anesthetize yourself. Some squishy paintings and a tall gin and tonic to shut out the big bad world."

"Interesting. What year are you in?"

With her arms still crossed, she looked at me defiantly. "Junior. Why?"

"Well, about a year from now, you're going to find out what a big bad world it is out there. Bet on it."

"What-*ever*. Have fun with your classy Kinkades, jerk."

"And *you* have fun trying to get a job after graduation, little girl," I said.

She gaped at me in shock for a moment, then stomped out of the room.

The exhibit was empty for a while, so I used the time to stroll around and practice my expression of feigned reverence. Other scoffers came in, but I didn't waste my energy with them; I was now confident that I could play a Thomas Kinkade lover and collector as well as Daniel Day Lewis.[12] All I needed were some suckers.

I thought I'd hit the jackpot when a tour group of Florida retirees shuffled in and fawned over each

---

12 Readers of 2050 and beyond: Daniel Day Lewis was one of the greatest actors of the late 20th and early 21st centuries.

painting. Two couples wore the Collector's Society heart pins. Bingo. I didn't have a Collector's Society pin, but I was wearing my WWII and D-Day pins on my lapel. As casually as Cary Grant, I walked over.

"Fellow Society members I see." I put a hand on my chest. "Chris Orcutt, New York."

"Where in New York?" asked one of the men. "Lot of us are from Queens originally."

"Upstate. Dutchess County."

"Oh." They nodded perfunctorily.

"Let me ask you," I said. "Would any of you be in the market for some of these?"

I pulled a sheaf of my convenient trifold brochures out of my jacket pocket. The men each took one and passed the rest along.

"Why're you getting rid of them?" one of the men asked.

"I have doubles of them," I said.

A man in a straw fedora let out a long whistle. "Doubles?!"

"Yes, so I was in town—"

"Vermont?" a lady said. "What are you doing here?"

"Visiting my great-aunt," I lied. "She turned one hundred yesterday."

"*Awwww*," two of the ladies said simultaneously. "How sweet!"

"Yes, I love her immensely. Anyway, I heard about this exhibition and thought—"

The lead man handed back the brochures. "We've got all these. What else you got?"

"Nothing, I'm afraid. Those are my only doubles."

One of the old-timers in the back stepped forward. He wore a navy blue and gold baseball cap that read "WWII VETERAN." He pointed at my lapel with his cane.

"I like your pins, young man."

"Thank you, sir. My wife and I were founding contributors to the WWII Memorial in D.C. and the D-Day Museum in New Orleans."

"Seen 'em both," he said. "Not bad."

"Were you in the war, sir?" I asked.

He set his jaw and nodded. "Jack Gregor. Omaha. First Infantry. My unit landed in the second hour."

"That's amazing, Mr. Gregor. May I shake your hand?"

He gave me the nod, and I shook it.

"Your generation saved the world," I said.

"We were just doing our jobs. The real heroes are the guys who didn't make it…our buddies."

"I'm very sorry, sir. Well, from my generation to yours…thank you."

He gave me another somber nod, and the entire group shuffled out of the exhibit. I thought I was alone until a kid in a beret and flip-flops (yes, flip-flops) walked in front of me. He was followed slackly by his buddy, who sported a blonde goatee with a pointy chin-beard. He looked like Lenin's retarded cousin.

"Could you believe those old coots?" Goatee said. "They *collect* this shit."

"Unbelievable," said Beret.

There was absolutely *nothing* that I liked about these two. Not their supercilious attitudes, not their slouching posture, not their perfect tans, not their wrinkled polo shirts. Most of all, I resented that they apparently had such a surplus of leisure time that they could attend an art exhibit they didn't like and make fun of it. Bored, I decided to pick a fight with them. I walked over to them slapping my brochures menacingly against my knee.

"You know," I said loudly, "I collect Kinkades."

"So?" Goatee said. "Good for you."

"I heard you call those old gentlemen *coots*," I said. "One of those 'coots' was at Omaha Beach on D-Day."

They ignored me and stepped to the next painting. I followed them and stood a foot away from Goatee.

"It's because of so-called coots like him," I continued, "that you two can prance around the countryside acting superior to everyone and everything. If it weren't for men like James Gregor, *you two* would be mopping floors in a Vermont Gestapo office."

"You're assuming the Germans even had a chance of winning," Beret said. "Everybody knows the Germans were finished after Stalingrad."

"*Finished?!* Are you kidding? Tell that to the guys surrounded by SS Panzer divisions at Bastogne. See what they think of your theory."

"The Battle of the Bulge has been mythologized by Hollywood," Beret said. "Patton made sure of it. That way, when he rescued them, he got to be a big hero. I saw it all on the History Channel."

"And I suppose the Holocaust never happened either," I said. "Sounds like *somebody's* been smoking a bit too much of that revisionist stuff. Read the first-hand accounts, from soldiers. Then we can talk."

"I saw *Saving Private Ryan*," Beret said, "I get it."

"You're an idiot, kid, you know that?"

"Come on, Doug," Goatee said. "It's not worth it."

I made a mental note: beret equals Doug.

"You're lucky he's making me go," Doug said over his shoulder.

"Sure I am," I said. "Now get lost before I shove *Lighthouse Number Eleven* up your ass."

They shambled away. A couple minutes later, Helen from the reception desk came in with a security guard. I sighed. This kind of thing happened to me a lot.

"Chris," Helen said, "two young men just complained that you threatened them."

"I did no such thing," I said. "They insulted Kinkade collectors, and when I said I was one, they insulted a WWII vet in that group, and I won't stand by when veterans are attacked."

The security guard pursed his lips and nodded. He looked old enough to have been in Vietnam, so I poured it on like Vermont maple syrup on blueberry pancakes.

"Somebody has to say something to these kids," I continued. "That's the trouble with this country. Everybody looks the other way when they're disrespectful, and it only gets worse. Ask guys who were in Nam, they'll tell you."

"Right on, brother," the security guard said.

"Yes…well, actually," Helen said, "this isn't a forum for political discussion. It's an art museum. You need to keep your political views to yourself."

I was too tired to argue anymore. "You're right. Think I'll go check out Lucioni for a while, if that's okay."

"That's fine," she said, "but no more arguments, please."

When Helen had turned the other way, the security guard gave me a thumbs-up and followed her out.

After spending two hours skulking around the Kinkades, I needed to cleanse my aesthetic palate, and Luigi Lucioni's work did the job nicely. The museum curator had wisely chosen the crisp landscapes of Lucioni to contrast with the muddled Kinkades, as if to say, "You think those are paintings? No...*these* are paintings." Included among Lucioni's landscapes was a Mona Lisa-ish self-portrait in which one of his own paintings hung on the wall behind him. It was refreshing to see such clean, masterful paintings after Kinkade's flea-market crap.

The Kinkade exhibit was empty when I returned, so I left the museum and walked across the parking lot in the hot noontime sun. A deer fly buzzed around me and landed on my suit jacket. I swatted it. A couple cars down from mine, Goatee and Doug sat in an aging SUV passing a joint back and forth. They spotted me and snickered.

I got in my rental car, turned on the A/C and took a few slow, deep breaths.

Picking a fight with two spoiled pricks. What the hell is wrong with you, Chris?

You forgot to take your medication three days in a row and you're manic and irritable. That's what's wrong with you.

As I was backing out, Goatee and Doug looked at me, said something and laughed. They started out of the parking lot. Recalling a scene from one of my favorite novels, *Lolita* by Vladimir Nabokov, in which a mysterious vehicle follows Humbert Humbert and his prepubescent companion, I slapped the gearshift into drive and tailed the two stoners.

They cruised down Route 30 towards the Middlebury town square. At one point Doug glanced in the side mirror and saw me. They made a sharp left down an alley. I followed them and cut through a parking lot that belched us onto another road. We passed the gleaming white marble buildings of Middlebury College and were soon whizzing down an empty rural road, past cows in scrubby pastures.

On a mile-long straightaway, I saw them slowing down, so I slowed as well, leaving a 100-yard gap between their vehicle and mine. In Stanley Kubrick's film of *Lolita*, this is what the car pursuing Humbert Humbert does, making it memorably sinister.

Doug, now sans beret but still wearing the flip-flops, got out of the SUV and loped along the sandy shoulder toward me. I rolled down my windows. Then Goatee jumped out.

"Doug, stop! The guy might have a gun or something! He's not worth it!"

Doug halted and cupped his hands around his mouth.

"What the hell do you want, psycho?! Leave us alone or we're calling the police!"

I didn't say anything. He took a few steps towards my car. To maintain the sinister distance between us, I put the car in reverse, backed another 50 yards down the long straightaway, and stopped. Doug ran after me. I reversed some more. A tanker truck barreled towards me in the rear window and passed me blaring its horn. When I stopped again, Doug was still jogging after me. He'd lost a flip-flop. Doubled-over, out of breath, he put his hands on his knees.

"What's your *problem*, man?!" he yelled.

I was now a good 300 yards away from Goatee's SUV. Doug was stranded between the two vehicles. The stifling, ammoniacal smell of fertilizer hung in the air, and the heat shimmered off the blacktop around him as fiercely as though this were the Mojave Desert. Somewhere in the trees beyond the roadside pasture, a cicada chittered to a high-pitched crescendo. Then, as it tapered off to a soft rattle, a horn honked. Way up the road, Goatee had an arm inside the open car door. He honked two more times, then walked to the back bumper.

"Damn it, Doug! Come on! Forget that jerk!"

As if receiving a relay baton, Doug glanced back at Goatee, then turned around and shouted in my direction, "Asshole!"

I craned my neck out the window. "Dug-eeeee!"

Slump-shouldered, Doug began the long hike back to the SUV. When he was a distant speck, I did a 3-point turn and roared back to Middlebury. I was supposed to pick up Alexas at the Middlebury Inn, where her conference was, at noon, but I was late. She had the afternoon off. We were going to take a small ferry across Lake Champlain to Fort Ticonderoga. I wondered if there was any connection between the fort and Dixon–Ticonderoga pencils. Doubtful.

When I pulled up to the inn porch, Alexas smiled at me from a rocking chair. She skipped down the steps and got in the car. Today for some reason—probably because it was lunchtime—the traffic was a snarled nightmare.

Like Bastogne, about ten roads converged at the Middlebury town square, and no matter where you entered the square, you had to go all the way around it to get out of town. I dreaded having to do this again. The first time, it was quaint because Middlebury was vaguely reminiscent of some of the Maine towns I lived in as a boy: Machias, Guilford, Dexter. Now the thing just made me angry.

"Yeah, yeah, you drive *around* it," I said to Alexas. "Oh, how adorable…they have concerts at the band shell and people picnic on the grass. Ever heard of a traffic light? Douchebags."

I forced my way into traffic—New York style. The way I figured, no matter how courteously I drove, Vermonters were going to see my New York license plate and decide I was a prick anyway, so I might as well drive assertively. Behind me, a woman blared her horn. I waved at her in the rear-view. Interestingly, I've discovered that this annoys people more than giving them the finger.

Alexas straightened my hair. "How was the Kinkade exhibit?"

"Awful. I ended up arguing with some people."

"Shocking," she said. "Let me guess. They were Kinkade lovers and you couldn't bite your tongue."

"The opposite actually," I said. "A college girl and a couple of stoners. They were insulting Kinkade collectors, so I had to say something."

"But you *hate* Kinkade."

"Yeah," I said, "but I'm pretending to be a collector. They insulted collectors, so they insulted *me*."

"God you're weird."

"I'm acting. Isn't that what actors do?"

I asked Alexas this because she was a trained actress who had performed in many plays and done TV commercials.

"Make their lives a living hell for a part?" She opened a map and spread it out on the dashboard. "The weird ones do. When we get around the square, drive out past the college. That's how we get to the ferry."

"Have you eaten?" I asked.

"Yes, they gave us a very nice lunch at the hotel. But I wouldn't object to some ice cream."

"Okay. With all these cows around, I bet we can find some really good homemade stuff someplace."

I drove out of town on Route 30, the same road on which I'd been following Doug and Goatee half an hour ago. We cruised down the long "Lolita" straightaway, passed a couple dairies and lots of corn. On a grassy hillside, a tractor cut hay, followed by another one that spit out square hay bales. Fifteen minutes later, there were still no signs of ice cream.

"Maybe we should turn around," Alexas said.

"No, there's ice cream out here. I can smell it."

At a T-intersection ahead was a general store. There was an old-fashioned gas pump in front and a sandwich board by the side of the road that read

> Maple Syrup, Fudge,
> Cheddar Cheese, Moccasins,
> & Hand-Packed Ice Cream!
> Come on in!

"Good job." Alexas glanced at the map and pointed at the turn in the road. "The ferry is down that way."

I parked in front of the general store and cut the engine. "What kind of place sells cheddar cheese *and* moccasins?"

Alexas chuckled.

"And what the hell does hand-packed mean?" I said. "Is that like homemade?"

She shrugged. "Who cares? It's ice cream. Get me chocolate chip if they have it. If not, plain chocolate."

"Okay."

I got out and climbed some sagging stairs to a weathered wood porch. The store had a screen door, and when I opened it, it creaked exactly like the one on the TV show *The Waltons*. I noticed I was still wearing my suit and felt conspicuously overdressed. I removed my tie, stuffed it in my pocket, and unbuttoned my collar.

The store interior was similar to other general stores I'd seen: cool and dimly lit; tin ceilings with slowly turning ceiling fans; souvenirs, T-shirts and jars of loose candy up front, and an old-fashioned cash register on the side. A man in glasses looked at me over his newspaper as I marched to the rear of the store, where the ice cream was. The area behind the counter was empty. I checked out the flavors in the case. They had Alexas' requested flavor, chocolate chip.

"Hello?" I said.

A chirrupy woman's voice rang out from the back room: "Just a sec!"

A moment later, a flimsy black curtain parted, and in walked a vision, wiping her hands on an apron. Her hair, thick and tawny, was in a ponytail. A couple stray strands dangled on her cheeks. She wore a tight white tank top with a mysterious cherry-red proclamation bulging across her chest: "DOUBLE CHERRY." Perhaps 25 years old and gorgeous on a primal level. A young woman so desirable that, the shock of seeing her when I least expected it, in a Vermont general store, staggered me. The last place I'd encountered a young woman this desirable was in the pages of *War and Peace*, in the form of the man-eating Princess Hélène Kuragina. I actually swayed on my feet and had to take a step backwards to steady myself.

"So, what can I get you?" she asked.

Eternally sensitive to language and meaning, I mused briefly on what DOUBLE CHERRY might be referring to—a fashion brand name, the size of her breasts, the state of her virginity, the grade of her sexual prowess (like Grade AA maple syrup)—before managing to cough out a reply.

"Ice…cream," I said.

"*Okay*. Flavor?"

I swallowed hard and mustered up all my self-control. Yes, this was a gorgeous young woman, but I was a relatively accomplished middle-aged writer, and handsome in a well-tailored suit—all of which, in my own mind at least, made us equals. I stood up tall and smiled.

"The raspberry…is that sherbet or ice cream?"

"I'm not sure," she said. "Want me to check?"

"That's okay, I'll take it. That and the chocolate chip."

"Cones or cups?" she asked.

"Cups."

"Small or large?"

She put a small cup in one hand, a large one in the other, and playfully raised and lowered them front of her protuberant DOUBLE CHERRY backdrop. When she punctuated her demonstration with an ingénue's smile, I was crushed by a sense of longing for my vanished youth. Dear God, if only I were ten years younger and single.

"Large," I sighed.

"Both large?"

"Yeah, thanks."

She grabbed an ice cream scoop, flipped it in her hand with panache, and leaned into the ice cream case. The open neck of her tank top afforded me a view as wondrous and as rare as Halley's comet, and as such it would have been criminal for me not to savor this moment. Her cleavage was epic. Cold steam swirled out of the case, around her neck and hair, making the view hauntingly memorable. But as she scooped the ice cream and her exertions showed in her face, my attention shifted to her arm. She had the lithe, muscular arms of action movie heroine Sarah Connor in the second *Terminator* movie. Each time she dug into the vat of rock-hard ice cream, her entire arm tensed up, revealing a shoulder and bicep that outclassed those of most men.

"Damn, that arm of yours looks strong," I said. "Ever tried arm-wrestling? I bet you could take any of the old geezers that come in this place."

She smiled. "And most of the young ones. Thanks for noticing."

Finished with the cup of chocolate chip, she placed it atop the case and she moved on to the raspberry.

"So," I said, "are you in school, uh…?"

"Dani. No, and to be honest, I have no interest." She laughed and dug ferociously into the ice cream vat.

"Guess I'm hoping that someday a rich guy'll come in here and whisk me away."

"You laugh," I said, "but if that's going to happen to anybody, it'll be you. Don't let this go to your head, but when you walked out of that curtain, I nearly fainted."

She snorted. "You're sweet."

"I'm not kidding."

Watching Dani's arm flex and her ponytail waggle through the glass, I imagined a story about a rural community where all the young women are stupidly gorgeous, causing men to wonder, *"Are they putting something in the water around here?"*

Hmm, I said to myself, *what if a community actually <u>did</u> put something in the water to make all of their women gorgeous? Why would they do it? What would happen?*

> Dani lives in a blink-and-you'll-miss-it hamlet surrounded by corn. But instead of Vermont, it's Iowa.
>
> Because of the secret chemical the town elders pour into the water supply on Mother's Day each year, all of the girls in the town grow up to become gorgeous young women. By the time they reach their late teens and 20s, they're prime genetic material, which explains the dearth of older women in town—they all marry rich men and move away.
>
> Each year, the community holds a grand bazaar in which potential suitors engage in a three-day competition to win the eligible girls. Men come from all over the world to get a chance to whisk away one of the gorgeous creatures.
>
> There are background and credit checks, feats of strength and skill (including the carnival high striker with its heavy mallet and bell), and a battle royal between the suitors with clown-sized boxing gloves.

In addition to a "courtroom" where the community publicly cross-examines each suitor, there are polygraph tests, compatibility tests, kissing booths and a talent competition.

On the final afternoon of the grand bazaar, each young woman chooses a lucky suitor, and a justice of the peace marries them.

I could see Dani here drawing a hell of a large pool of men to compete for her. Too bad stuff like that only happened in movies.

"Don't worry, Dani," I said. "The right guy will come along."

"I hope so." She wiped her brow with her forearm, nodded at me. "Nice suit, by the way."

"Thanks."

"Kinda hot for one, though, don'tcha think?"

"Yeah," I said, "but I'm trying to sell some paintings and I need to look respectable."

At the front of the store, the screen door creaked open. Doug and Goatee shambled in and browsed the T-shirts.

"Unlike these guys," I said.

Somehow their showing up in this general store when I was here seemed inevitable, as if it had been predestined at the beginning of time. Dani peeked over the top of the case, spotted them and rolled her eyes.

"Oh, Jesus," she breathed.

"You know them?" I asked.

"Yeah, unfortunately."

She finished with my second ice cream and rang me up. After I paid and she gave me change, I handed her a five-dollar bill.

"A tip, Dani. Lincoln's my favorite president by the way."

She smiled. "Thanks. You wouldn't believe how cheap most people are. Nobody ever gives me a tip."

"It's my pleasure. But you've got to tell me...what does 'Double Cherry' mean?"

She was about to tell me when Doug and Goatee bellied up to the ice cream case. She turned to them and scowled.

"What do you two losers want?" she said.

"Not sure," Goatee said.

They were drumming on the glass, gazing at the ice cream when Doug noticed me in his periphery.

"Hey, what are you—"

I wagged a finger at them. "You guys better stop following me."

"Ch'yeah, right," Goatee said. "It's like totally the other way around."

"Dani," I said, "these two have been following me all day."

"Doesn't surprise me," she said.

While Dani leaned forward and rinsed off the ice cream scoop, Doug and Goatee stood on their tiptoes, craned their necks over the case, and leered into her cleavage. If they had been peering over the side of the Grand Canyon without anything to hold onto, they would have plunged to their deaths. I, too, had admired Dani's DOUBLE CHERRY chest, but I was debonair enough not to breathe out of my mouth while doing it. Besides, now that she'd told me her dream—to have a rich man walk in here and whisk her away—I felt somewhat protective of Dani.

"Guys," I said loudly, "it's not polite to stare at a woman's breasts."

"We weren't," Doug said.

Dani tossed the scoop in the sink. "That's it! I've warned you two before. I want you out of here."

"But we didn't—"

"Frank!" Dani shouted at the back curtain.

I held up my ice creams. "Good luck, Dani. I hope you meet your prince someday."

"Thanks. Bye."

Outside, Alexas had a map spread out on the engine hood of our car. A retired couple stood beside her as she pointed on the map. I handed her the cup of chocolate chip.

"Thanks," she said. "What were they doing, *churning* the ice cream for you?"

"Sort of."

"Honey," she said, gesturing at the retired couple, "this is Rose and Carlton Smith. They were looking for Middlebury College and the art museum." She opened her blue eyes wide. "They collect Kinkades."

"That's correct," Carlton said. "Alexas tells us you have some extras?"

"We do," I said.

The screen door on the porch opened. A man shouted from inside.

"I don't want you two in here—ever again!"

"Screw you, Frank," Goatee said.

"Yeah," Doug said, "go bone one of your cows, Frank!"

"Oh, my!" Rose said.

Doug and Goatee galumphed down the steps and shuffled across the sandy lot. Doug shot me the finger. I shook my head.

"You *know* them?" Carlton said.

"No way," I said. "I caught them shoplifting and told the manager."

"Good man. Dirty hippies. They're everywhere, seems like."

"They sure are."

Doug and Goatee got into their SUV and roared out of the lot, kicking up stones and dust. Alexas squinted at me as if to say, "Chris...what *really* happened in there with those two?"

I took out my brochure of Kinkades and handed it to Carlton. He had a shock of silver hair, closely cropped on the sides and back, making him look a 70-year-old Jack Kennedy. He removed a pair of glasses from a pocket protector, slid them on and studied the brochure. His eyebrows arched.

"You still have these?" he asked.

"We certainly do," I said.

"Why are you selling them?"

"Well, they're duplicates and—"

"We don't have the space," Alexas added. "Small apartment, no walls...you know how it is."

"Yes, we were young once," Rose said. "Weren't we, Carlton?"

He passed the brochure to Rose. "Here, Mother, take a look."

"Oh, my goodness," she said.

My predatory instinct kicked in. I flashed my eyes at Alexas: *Mother? Goodness? Damn, Alexas, did you hook into a couple of live ones!*

"So, Rose," Alexas said, "what do you think?"

"Oh, they're wonderful. I'd love to have them, but money's a bit tight right now."

"Maybe we could work some kind of trade," Alexas said.

"Carlton," I said, "are you a retired engineer or computer programmer?"

"Engineer. How'd you know?"

I nodded at the pocket protector. "Don't see many of those nowadays. What'd you do, civil? Electrical?"

"Aerospace," he said quietly, as if even muttering it, he was revealing state secrets.

"Carlton worked for NASA," Rose chirped.

"Amazing," Alexas said.

"Just another flight engineer," Carlton said. "Lowest man on the totem pole actually."

"Still, that's incredible," I said. "Where were you, Canaveral?"

"Nope, Houston," he said. "But not in Mission Control. I was one of the guys in the back, working out solutions to things."

"Bet you're awesome with a slide rule."

Carlton nodded. "Well, I guess I am at that."

"Were you there during Apollo Thirteen?" I asked.

"Yup, and we were pretty busy, that's for sure." His tone made it clear this was all he would say on the subject.

Alexas raised her sunglasses on top of her head. "So what made you two decide to retire in Vermont?"

"Rose was from here originally," Carlton said. "She inherited her parents' farm, and about ten years ago we converted it into a bed and breakfast."

"Hold on," I said. "You're telling me you have a B and B. In Vermont."

"Sure do," he said.

Carlton walked over to a Honda SUV, rummaged in the back seat and returned with a pair of glossy brochures. The Apollo B & B: a big colonial farmhouse, fully renovated, with a red barn and horses to ride. A trout stream ran through the property, and to reach the place you crossed a covered bridge. A picturesque New England village was less than a mile away. They had hiking trails and bicycles you could borrow.

"Wow, it's amazing."

"We serve a light supper, too," Rose said. "Most places, you don't get that."

I glanced at the prices: $300–400 per night. I'd always wanted to spend a week in Vermont from late September to early October, but ever since Alexas and I had quit our six-figure jobs in Manhattan, leisurely vacations were a rarity. But here I saw an opportunity: we could take a nice vacation in October, the month of our wedding anniversary, without it costing us a cent. It was perfect.

"Rose, Carlton," I said. "How about this? You can have all of our Kinkades in exchange for a week at your B and B."

"When?" Rose asked.

"The first week of October," I said. "I think the color is going to be spectacular this year."

Carlton put his hands on his hips, stared out at the cornfield across the road and slowly nodded.

"Yes, yes, I can see that. How about it, Mother?"

"I'd have to check the book," Rose said, "but I think we have room that first week. It's Columbus Day weekend that's always the problem."

"I don't know…it hardly seems fair." Carlton waved the brochure. "These Kinkades are worth a lot more than a week with us. How about we make it ten days?"

Alexas loathed B&B's. Years earlier, she had said, *"I don't like being trapped, having to listen to their stories about every single knickknack. Those places give me the creeps."* Now I could see the conflict in her face: the desire to get rid of the Kinkades once and for all versus the dread of staying at a B&B with two strangers for ten days.

"A week will be plenty," I said. "So do we have a deal?"

"If the book says we have room," Carlton said, "then we have a deal."

III

As I'd predicted, the ride up to Vermont on that last day of September was glorious. Two weeks of late summer rain, followed by a sudden cold snap, had ensured stunning fall foliage. Even with my polarized sunglasses on, the gleaming colors around every turn were blinding, inspiring an idea for a story.

For months, everywhere around Millbrook I'd seen dozens of flyers for "LOST" or "MISSING" dogs; apparently, dogs disappearing in the area had reached epidemic levels. I'd always been fascinated by dogcatchers, ever since I saw an episode of *The Little Rascals*, in which the kids' dog Petey gets caught by the dogcatcher and taken to the pound. The story that was beginning to form in my mind would be entitled "The Dogcatcher." It would be about a 21st century man who puts a fresh spin on the antiquated profession of dogcatcher by doing it freelance and focusing on finding the missing dogs of rich people. He'd do some pro bono work, too, but because he did this for a living, he needed to make a buck. The hero's voice emerging in my head was redolent of Raymond Chandler's iconic private detective, Marlowe:

> It was one of those mid-October afternoons in the Hudson Valley when the foliage is so brilliant it hurts your eyes. I wore Armani sunglasses and, with the snap in the air, my Orvis leather flight jacket. Back in my closet, I had a great suit—a Hickey Freeman that cost me two grand—but in this business, first impressions are everything and the worn leather jacket says you'll *stick*.

I recited the passage to myself for a few minutes, playing with the syntax in my head, and when Alexas and I made a gas and rest stop, I wrote it down. I didn't know it then, but it would be another three years until I finished the story.

Halfway to the Apollo B & B, I got hungry. Ahead was a restaurant in a converted covered bridge. Enticed by the novelty, we stopped. The tables ran along the outside walls, where windows looked out on the stream and the mill falls below. We ate lunch and finished with coffee and pie. Upstream, a breeze rained fiery leaves from a sugar maple into the water. I drank the rest of my coffee and tossed the napkin on the table with a contented sigh.

"Is this great or what?" I said.

"Beautiful."

"I can't wait to see this place, Alexas. I know you hate B & B's, but I have a good feeling about this one."

"I'll just be glad to finally get rid of the Kinkades," she said.

"I know, right? Thank *God*."

A trio of Labrador retrievers—brown, yellow and black—trotted alongside the car as we crept up the driveway of the Apollo B & B. They weren't barking. It was a little unnerving, actually. Like when you meet quiet and polite 3-year-old kids, and you wonder, "Are the parents *sedating* that kid?"

Carlton came outside wearing a flannel shirt, followed by Rose in a quilt jacket. They paused on the doorstep as if posing for a Kinkade picture: *The Proud Innkeepers*. As we alighted from the car, Carlton came down to meet us.

"Beautiful dogs," I said. "And so well-behaved."

"Alexas, Chris," Carlton said, "meet Neil, Buzz and Gene. Neil's the brown one, Buzz is the yellow one and Gene is black. They're purebreds, all of them."

The wit of Carlton's name choices for the dogs wasn't lost on me: these were the first names of the astronauts of Apollo 11.

"Neil Armstrong, Buzz Aldrin and Gene Krantz," I said. "Cute."

Carlton rubbed his hands together. Rose patted her husband on the shoulder.

"He can't wait to see the Kinkades," she said. "He was up half the night measuring and installing mounts for them. With the alarms of course."

"Of course," I said.

"It's good to be careful," Alexas said.

I popped the trunk, where I had carefully packed the Kinkades, layered between blankets and pillows.

"Excellent packing job, Chris," Carlton said.

"My family moved a lot when I was a kid."

"Oh, military?"

"No, just nomads," I said.

Carlton stood dumbstruck for a moment. He looked me up and down, as though saying to himself, *"He seems well-adjusted. I hope he's not a damn hippie!"*

"I'm sure you have some interesting stories," Rose said.

"As a matter of fact—"

"I'll get these," Carlton said. "Mother, why don't you show them the room?"

I grabbed our suitcases from the back seat and hustled up to the door, where Rose and Alexas were already waiting.

"Rose was telling me that the original house dates back to seventeen ninety-six," Alexas said.

"Cool. Did George Washington sleep here by any chance?"

"Oh, no, I don't think so," Rose said. "I'll show you your room, and later we'll give you the grand tour."

She opened the red door and led us into a foyer at the foot of a staircase. The room on my left had been decorated as a parlor in Queen Anne style, and the walls sparkled with the unmistakable garish glint of fake gold leaf frames. Those had to be the Kinkades. Next to the fireplace was an armchair with an embroidered Kinkade picture. I stepped into the doorway for a better look. The Kinkades were displayed two and three high. Intricately positioned track lights shone down on the walls. On one wall alone, I saw a dozen Kinkades. *Jesus*. My chest felt tight all of a sudden.

"Chris, this way," Rose said.

The stairs had been modernized so they were wider and not as steep, but they still creaked like hell. At the top, Rose led us down the hallway past photos of the moon landing. At the end of the hallway, she stopped at a room with an "11" on it.

"We're giving you Apollo Eleven," she said. "It's the best room in the house."

"Oh, you don't have to do that," Alexas said.

"We want to."

She opened the door with a flourish and whisked us into an enormous suite that, while spacious and bright from the five big windows, suffered terribly from the competing decorating choices imposed upon it. It was as though three gangs of interior decorators were rumbling over disputed territory: the Colonial gang, with its four-poster bed, bureau, writing table and chair; the Space Age gang, with its framed prints and moon landing memorabilia; and the Kinkade gang, with its glowing cottages and lighthouses. *Clashing* didn't begin to describe the decor.

I went to the back window. There was a lovely rolltop antique writing desk, the kind I could imagine Dickens or Trollope writing at, with an even lovelier view outside. Clearly a non-writer had placed it here; all serious writers know that a beautiful view is the bane of writing.

A writer could get a hell of a lot of daydreaming done here, but not much in the way of words written. Outside, the lawn sloped gently down to the woods, where, in addition to the peak foliage, a stone wall ran the length of the tree line to a big lake. A pair of red canoes lay temptingly upright on a wooden stand. At the end of a long dock sat a pair of chaise lounges and a closed umbrella. The only writing a person might possibly do at this window would be about how desperately that person wanted to go outside.

"Terrific view," I said.

Alexas' cheek muscles quivered. She had a beaming smile on her face, but the effort behind it was noticeable.

"Yes," she said, "it's perfect."

"Well, I'll let you two relax," Rose said. "Bathroom's right through there. Extra towels, TP and such are in the linen closet. Why don't you two unwind a bit? The reception doesn't start until five, so you'll have a few hours to yourselves before everyone gets here."

"Reception?" Alexas said, a note of panic in her voice that only I could detect.

"The Thomas Kinkade Collectors' Society," she said. "We get together for wine and cheese, and since your paintings are adding a lot to our collection, we wanted to throw a little reception for you two. It's in your honor."

"I wish you hadn't done that," I said. "We didn't expect accolades."

"It's our pleasure," Rose said. "Freshen up and we'll see you soon. You'll enjoy meeting the other collectors. They're just like you two…wonderful people."

Rose closed the door behind her, and for a few seconds Alexas and I just stared at each other, shell-shocked. We were trapped, we knew we were trapped, and the worst part of it was, we should have seen it coming. Come on, seriously—a B & B named for a NASA program, run by two fanatical Thomas Kinkade collectors who, when we met them, had been seeking directions to an *exhibit* of the crap? As usual, I hadn't thought it through. I'd allowed myself to be blinded, blinded by a chance to dump the Kinkades and enjoy a week of October in Vermont, all in one fell swoop.

I dropped the suitcases next to the bureau and went into the bathroom. Immediately I knew Alexas would love it. Besides being about the size of our entire apartment, the bathroom gleamed of clean tile and porcelain. There were twin, wide-basin sinks, a corner shower and a massive claw-foot tub next to a window that looked out on the lake. A small flat-screen TV hung on the wall at the end of the tub.

"Alexas, before you say anything…come check this out."

She walked in. Her face transformed from a pout to a gape.

"How about that tub, huh?" I said. "Look, I say we suck it up for this Kinkade thing tonight, and then we'll have the whole rest of the week to enjoy ourselves. Okay?"

She nodded.

"Take a long bath and have a nap," I said. "I'm going out exploring."

"Okay. Have fun."

I went downstairs and out the front door. The three Labs lay on the grass. They perked up their ears as I walked by them snapping my fingers.

"C'mon, boys!"

They fell over themselves trying to get up and be the first one at my side. We rounded the corner of the house together.

The brown, or chocolate, one—Neil—loped up beside me, followed by the other two, who sniffed in circles around us. The air was crisp, and as I put my hands in my field coat pockets, I felt my Swiss Army knife and a lumpy bag of something. It was an unopened large bag of Combos®—cylindrical pretzels with nacho cheese filling—a relic from a year ago, when I was addicted to this stuff. I couldn't eat them anymore, but I didn't want to leave the full bag in my pocket; Alexas might find it and assume I was back on the junk food.

Neil, Buzz, and Gene were trotting alongside me now, panting happily, as I strolled down the long slope toward the lake. Maybe *I* couldn't eat the Combos, but the dogs could. Dogs were universal garbage disposals, weren't they? The moment I snapped the bag open, the dogs, continuing to trot alongside, gazed at me with pleading eyes.

I tossed a Combo to each of them. The pretzels disappeared into the deep grass. Clearly, being fed snacks from a bag, while on the move, was new for them. I put one in my palm for Neil. He sniffed, scarfed it up, and a millisecond later he was bouncing at my side.

By now, Buzz and Gene had circled back, and found and eaten the ones in the grass. They joined Neil at my hip. I took out a Combo, placed it on my middle finger like a boulder on a tiny catapult and flicked it in the air ahead of us. The breeze caught it. Neil and Buzz raced after the Combo, but it was Neil who correctly gauged its trajectory and jumped at the precise moment to snatch it out of the air. Poor Buzz. Neil was first on the moon and now first at this.

In quick succession I flicked three more, each in a different direction. All of the dogs astounded me (and themselves I think) with their incredible leaps, mid-air twists, and perfectly timed bites. But even with all the unusual excitement, the dogs still weren't barking.

Gene wasn't getting his fair share, so I got Neil and Buzz's attention and fake-threw a couple in the woods. A sucker play, but they bought it. While they disappeared into the trees, I dropped a handful of Combos at Gene's feet.

The bag was empty. I dumped the salty crumbs in the grass, folded the bag up tightly and tucked it in the back pocket of my jeans. When I turned around, the dogs were more amped-up than ever, darting back and forth in front of me, panting heavily, seeming to say, *"Wherethe-Combos? WheretheCombos? WheretheCombos?"*

"No more, guys. Sorry." I held up my hands, but as I returned them to my pockets, I felt one more Combo, hiding under the pocket flap. I took it out and held it in my fingertips.

"Ah-hah," I said. "*One* more, boys. Who wants it? Huh? Who wants it?"

As I got the Combo locked and loaded on my fingertip, the dogs could barely contain themselves. They were leaping in front of me, tongues flapping, drool flying. Then Gene barked, which got all three of them barking, and I knew that to quiet them I had to launch this sucker, which I most emphatically did.

The dogs raced across the few remaining yards of grass and galloped down the wooden dock. It was only then that I realized how close to the water we were. The Combo sailed on, seeming to gain altitude as though lifted by a thermal current. It carried the length of the dock, and plopped into the lake. All at once, the dogs sprang off the dock, splashed down and paddled straight for the Combo. It began to sink. But while Neil and Gene paddled in helpless circles, Buzz dove under and emerged licking his chops. Apparently Combos tasted great even sodden with lake water.

I reclined in one of the chaises as the dogs paddled to shore. They shook off and trotted toward me.

"No more, guys." I looked at them. "Oh, crap."

In ten minutes I'd managed to ruin three perfectly trained, clean, obedient, purebred dogs. It was the pet equivalent of turning three Eagle Scouts into crystal-meth addicts. They were sopping wet, muddy, and brazenly sniffing my coat pockets.

"No more," I said. "Sit!"

They lay beside my chaise, staring out at the lake. I didn't know how I was going to explain this. Somehow the truth—that I'd been feeding them Combos—seemed like a bad idea. *Maybe I was playing fetch with them. Yeah, I'd found a stick or a ball. Or, I'd had a ball with me. Where'd it go? Oh, it must've drifted out on the lake someplace. Yeah, that's better.* Nodding to myself, I took one more moment to enjoy the cool air, the placid water, and the foliage along the lakeshore, before heaving myself out of the chaise.

"Okay, boys," I said. "Time to face the music."

I was twenty feet up the lawn when I heard coughing on the dock behind me. Buzz vomited up a pile of Combos. As he sniffed in astonishment at what he'd done, Neil poked in with his snout and devoured Buzz's puke. It happened so quickly, there was no time for me to look away.

"Oh, God."

My stomach lurched. Luckily I hadn't eaten any of the Combos, or they would have been on the grass by now as well. As I walked down to the dock, Gene vomited. Once again, Neil darted in and vacuumed up the mess.

"*Gross*, Neil," I said.

Squatting at the edge of the dock, I splashed water onto the vomit stains. The dock was high and I had to lean out for the water, and as I was leaning, greedy Neil shoved his snout in my pocket, tipping me into the water. To say the water was cold was an understatement; in half a second it felt like all the heat in my body said, "Screw this," and left.

Throwing my arms onto the dock, I dragged myself out of the water and lay on my stomach for a minute catching my breath. I had to get the dogs and myself warm and dry, or the four of us would get hypothermia.

Well, maybe the dogs wouldn't (they were built for this), but I would.

I trudged up the hill, resolving to keep a close eye on Neil. With all of the Combos (a pound of them) now in his stomach, he was a ticking time bomb.

The dogs were loping up the hill toward the back door. As I followed them, I glanced up at the second floor and caught a glimpse of Alexas' face in the bathroom window. She was staring down at me and shaking her head. The dogs lay on the brick patio. I knocked on the back door. After a minute, Rose opened it.

"Oh, my, you're soaked!" she said. Then she noticed the dogs. "Goodness!"

"Yeah, we had a little accident," I said. "I threw a stick, it landed in the lake and they all went in after it. Then Neil bumped into me and knocked me in."

"Well, come in." She pointed to the right. "The utility room, all of you."

I went into a tiled room with a slop sink, tub, and clothes washer and dryer. The dogs followed me, hanging their heads, and lay on the floor. Rose disappeared for a moment, then came in and handed me a big towel. She glanced in the direction of the kitchen.

"I...I was in the middle of cooking," she said.

"Well, I'm soaking wet anyway," I said. "Why don't I give the dogs a bath?"

"You'd be willing to do that?"

"Sure."

"Oh, that would be wonderful," Rose said. "The shampoo, brushes and towels are over there. When you're finished, you can toss your clothes in the washer. I'll take care of them."

"Thank you, Rose," I said. "Sorry about this."

She shut the door behind her. I took off my field coat, removed my wallet, notebook and pocketknife, and put the coat in the washer along with my sweater and Oxford shirt. Once I'd dried off slightly, I looked down at the muddy dogs. They stood eerily still and stared up at me.

"Okay, boys," I said. "Here we go."

I decided there was no time to be thorough; this would have to be an assembly line operation. One by one, I hosed them down, scrubbed shampoo into their fur, and rinsed them off. The door opened and Alexas peeked in.

"I won't ask what happened," she said. "Need some help?"

"Yeah, could you dry them?"

She spread out three giant towels and gave them brisk rubdowns.

"Where's Carlton?" I asked.

"Hanging the paintings," Alexas said. "Why?"

I tossed the towels in the washer. "Does Neil look sick to you?"

"No," she said. "But I haven't been hanging around with them, so I have no idea what their normal behavior looks like."

"He looks nauseous to me," I said.

"What did you do?"

"Nothing. And why do you always assume I did something? It's annoying."

"It's you and dogs." Smiling faintly, she shook her head at us. "Anytime you get around them, you get them all riled up somehow."

"Can I help it if dogs love me? I'm like the cool uncle."

The dogs panted on the floor as I stripped out of my clothes and put them in the washer.

"Go ask Rose where the dogs go now," I said.

She slipped out, giving me a moment to remove the Combos wrapper from my jeans pocket and stuff it in the corner behind the washing machine. I put a towel around my waist. Alexas cracked the door.

"She says to turn up the thermostat and let them dry off."

"Got it," I said.

It was set to 68°F. With guests coming soon, Rose would want the dogs dry in a hurry. I turned it up to 80°F.

"Come upstairs so you can take a bath," she said, and disappeared.

"Be good, boys," I said.

On my way up to the room, I smelled blueberry pie in the kitchen and heard Carlton muttering to himself in the parlor. I crept up the stairs holding my towel and wincing at the creaking boards, then speed-walked down the hall to the room. I caught up with Alexas in the bathroom. The tub was half-full with steam curling around the faucet.

"Get in before you catch pneumonia," she said.

I dropped the towel and sank into the tub.

"It's perfect, sweet," I said. "Thanks."

She pulled a chair up beside me and gave me a washcloth. "So did you have fun?"

"You mean besides falling in the lake? Yeah."

"What aren't you telling me?" she asked.

I scrubbed my face with the washcloth and a bar of Ivory soap, rinsed my hair with the shower nozzle (recalling aloud a favorite line from *Lolita*: "*...the kind of place you know will have a rubber tube affixable to the tub faucet in lieu of shower*"), and got out of the tub. I grabbed a towel and dried off.

"That's it?" she said.

"I don't like baths. You know that."

"So, what happened with the dogs?"

"All right." I lowered my voice to a whisper. "I fed them something I probably shouldn't have, and now I think Neil's sick."

"What did you feed them?"

"Combos," I said. "An old package that was in my coat."

"How old?"

"A year at least."

"How big a package?" she asked.

"I don't know. A pound maybe."

"A *pound*?! God, Chris..."

"I know...I screwed up," I said. "Just keep an eye on Neil during this thing tonight."

Alexas heaved out a sigh I'd come to know very well: half exasperation, half adoration. I went into the bedroom to get dressed.

When I went downstairs to the kitchen, Rose opened the refrigerator—a commercial stainless steel job.

"Chris, how about a little snack?" she said. "You must be hungry after all that driving. Can I interest you in a piece of pie? I have fresh blueberry, apple or pecan."

"I haven't had pecan in years," I said. "Thanks, Rose."

"Hot or cold?"

"Cold."

"Whipped cream? It's fresh."

"You bet."

She put it on a plate and laid the plate at a breakfast table with a view of an active bird feeder.

"Coffee?" she asked.

"That'd be great."

"Help yourself. The giant gizmo over there."

It was one of those expensive Italian coffeemakers that ground the beans, brewed the coffee and dispensed it straight into your mug. There was a tree of Thomas Kinkade mugs. Cringing, I took a lighthouse one and made a cup of black coffee. I sat down at the breakfast table and had a sip.

"This is terrific," I said.

"Local roasters," Rose said. "Carlton has a friend who gets us a good deal on beans."

I gazed out at the foliage along the lake and on the distant mountainsides. I'd lived in New England or Upstate New York all my life and never seen foliage this vibrant. I could only imagine what Van Gogh might have done with this view, with every leaf on every tree surreally bright. The dream of a lifetime was being realized: a full week of strolling down dirt roads, photographing covered bridges and the autumn colors, canoeing the lake, breathing deeply of the cool, clean air, and reading at night by the fire. And the best part was, it wasn't costing us a nickel. Only a bunch of paintings with which, as Hamlet says, "I most willingly part withal."

Good riddance, Thomas Kinkade. Looks like I'll be having the last laugh after all, you schmuck.

"How's the pie?" Rose asked.

"Fantastic, thank you."

"Any ideas on what you and Alexas might like for breakfast tomorrow?"

I smiled. My grandmother Nan used to do this: ask me what I wanted for breakfast the next morning, before I'd even had that day's lunch. I used to say, "Nan, I can't think that far ahead," but eventually I figured out that her asking me created an opportunity to get exactly what I wanted.

"Know what we'd really like, Rose?"

"What's that?"

"Pumpkin pancakes and some really thick-cut bacon."

"I think we can arrange that," she said.

I finished my pie and sipped my coffee. I was watching a blue jay glare around on the bird feeder when Carlton walked in. He put his hands on his hips.

"Rose said you had a little trouble with the dogs," he said.

"Not really," I said. "We got wet, that's all."

"Well, they get overexcited with the guests sometimes. You have a dog?"

"No, but I enjoy them."

He nodded grimly. "Do you like trains, Chris?"

"Sure," I said.

Rose took my plate away. "Carlton, the man's on vacation! He doesn't want to see that."

Carlton opened a door, flicked a light switch and waved for me to follow him.

"You're going to like this," he said. "Bring your coffee."

By the time I reached the cellar stairs, Carlton was already at the bottom. I shut the door behind me and went down.

"One sec," Carlton said.

At the bottom, it was dim and quiet, and then Carlton said, "Okay, it's going to get really bright. Ready?"

"Ready."

Instantly the entire cellar was as bright as the surface of the moon. Carlton, wearing an engineer's cap, stood in the center of an enormous model train layout. Three trains wound through an intricate arrangement of hills, crossed a ravine, and crept through an old-fashioned village. The windows of the cottages and buildings all glowed yellow.

It was a Thomas Kinkade train set.

"So…what do you think?" Carlton asked.

"Wow," I said. "I didn't think Kinkade sold model train layouts."

"Far as I know, he doesn't. Built every stick of this myself. Only had the paintings to go by."

"Amazing. How long did it take you?"

"Six years. But I'm not finished yet. When it's done, I'm going to take photos of it, maybe see if Mr. Kinkade wants to buy it from me."

As a kid, I'd always envied a young friend, Howie Crothers, who lived next door to my grandparents, for his model train layout. I'd wanted a train set of my own, so I could build a world and give all of the plastic train people interesting backstories. But now, looking at Carlton in his engineer's cap as his trains whisked around the basement, I said a quick prayer of gratitude that Alexas had forbidden me from taking this up as a hobby. I suddenly realized that *this*—right here, with Carlton—was why she'd said no.

"Like to give 'em a whirl?" Carlton asked.

"No, thanks. Still got my coffee here. Mmmm."

Actually, my coffee was long gone, but I kept fake-sipping it to have an excuse not to do the trains. Upstairs, the cellar door opened.

"Chris," Alexas said, "you down there?"

"Yeah, be right up." I shrugged to Carlton. "The wife calls."

"I know how that is."

The passenger train eased up to the station platform and stopped.

"Thanks, Carlton," I said. "It really is something."

Upstairs, Alexas put a finger to her lips and led me back to our room. She closed the door behind us and leaned against it.

"I can't do this," she whispered.

"What do you mean?" I said.

"These people are weird, Chris. Rose wants me to do needlepoint with her. And guess what the pattern is."

I smiled. "A Kinkade painting?"

"It's not funny. This crap is everywhere."

"You mean like this?" I held up my Thomas Kinkade mug.

"I'm sorry," she said, her voice rising, "but anybody *this* into Thomas Kinkade has *got* to have something wrong with them."

"Shh, calm down, Bunny. What do you want to do?"

"I want to get out of here. Right now."

"But what about the vacation, the foliage?" I said.

"Some vacation…seeing a Kinkade everywhere we look. Besides, there's nothing to do here. We go check out the village, there's an hour. We go for a ride. There's another hour. And then what?"

"Well, we can't leave right now," I said. "They're having that reception for us."

"First thing in the morning then."

"Okay."

"*First thing*, Chrissy," she said. "No breakfast, no needlepoint, no stories about her stupid knickknacks."

I sat at the writing table and took in the view. It really was stunning. And a damn shame that it was wasted on collectors of kitsch. They didn't deserve this view. I did. Alexas came up behind me and stroked my hair.

"We accomplished our mission," she said, "which was to get rid of the paintings."

"But…I wanted to see the foliage."

"Tell you what," she said, kissing my head. "We'll find a cheap motel someplace and stay a couple of nights. I know how much you've wanted to do this. But trust me, Chris—you were going to get bored in a day or two."

"Yeah," I said. "We should probably get out of here before I accidentally break something or say something mean. All I know is, if any of these people tonight bash Edward Hopper or Andrew Wyeth or Maxfield Parrish or Thomas Cole or—"

"I doubt they know who any of them are." She patted my shoulder. "Okay, let's go get this thing over with."

We went downstairs and found Rose and Carlton in the parlor. There was a table set up with wine, cheese, fruit and finger sandwiches. I took a glass of white wine and gave Alexas one. She sat in a rocking chair near the roaring fireplace, but I remained standing.

"So, Chris," Carlton said. "You did a good job with the dogs' bath earlier."

"It was nothing. They were very well behaved."

He whistled and the dogs trotted in. Buzz and Gene were perky, but Neil was pretty listless.

"Boy, Mother," Carlton said, "Neil doesn't look so hot tonight, does he?"

"Tired probably," she said.

"Yeah," I said, "he was really running around out there."

The doorbell rang.

"They're here!" Rose announced brightly.

She scurried into the foyer with Carlton on her heels. Alexas stayed in the rocking chair near the fireplace. The dogs, evidently used to these receptions, lay quietly at her feet.

I watched Neil. He kept licking his mouth and swallowing. Otherwise he didn't move. I knelt down and scratched him behind the ears.

"Hang in there, buddy," I said. "Just a little while longer."

"How's he look?" Alexas asked.

"Like a dog that ate a pound of regurgitated Combos."

Rose and Carlton came in with eight other men and women. A fat guy in a too-tight navy blazer and hunting boots stomped into the room.

"So you're the ones that gave Carl all those great Kinkades! Next time you get a surplus, call me first! Jim Barker!"

"Chris." I shook his hand. "And this is Alexas."

"Nice to meet you," she said.

Jim went to the table with the poured wineglasses and handed one to each of the guests as they walked in. Rose waved for Alexas to join her near the doorway. She walked over, and Rose introduced her to a woman coming in. They shook hands and the woman continued into the room.

"Oh, Carlton, a fire!" the woman said. "Thank God!"

She tossed her shearling coat over a chair back, took a glass of wine from Jim and hurried over to the fireplace, where she minced her heels in place and made exaggerated shivering sounds. She was a striking woman in her mid 30s, trim and Yoga-firm, whose tousled brown hair and capricious sips from her wine told me I was in the presence of a master-level Hot Mess.

Over the years, myriad halfhearted petitions to my Creator to keep these women the hell away from me, a sensitive Pisces, had gone ignored. Tragically, I've always been a connoisseur of, and sucker for, hot messes, and when this one of blue-ribbon vintage canted her sculpted backside *par excellence* to the fire, and I unconsciously gulped down my wine at the sight of it, I knew I was doomed. Holding my now-empty wineglass, I walked over.

"Cold out there?" I asked her.

"Yes, and it's supposed to get down into the teens tonight," she said.

"Damn. That's too cold for early October."

She sniffed. "Got that right. I'm Ashley."

"Chris." I offered my hand. Instead of shaking it, she simply held on to it.

"Oh my...so warm." She squeezed it, then switched hands. "Do you mind?"

I glanced over my shoulder. Alexas was talking with a man at the *hors d'oeuvres* table.

"Nope," I said.

She put down our wineglasses and warmed both of her hands on mine.

"This is nice," she said. "I can't thank you enough."

"Tsk-tsk. Ever heard of gloves, Ashley?"

"*Yes.*" She tilted her head defiantly and waggled her hair.[13] "But...then my hands wouldn't be getting warm now...would they, Chris?"

"Hey, Ashley," I said. "Did you know that Thomas Kinkade has become such a pervasive force in the

---

13 A signature Hot Mess mannerism.

culture that the term 'Kinkadian' has entered the popular lexicon?"

"*Lexicon?*" she said. "What?"

Alexas approached, shaking hands with the other guests. Several of them were wearing their TK Collector's Society pins over their hearts. One woman touched hers and spoke to Alexas.

"Why aren't you wearing yours, dear?" she asked.

"Oh, I forgot," Alexas said. "Left it in my jewelry box at home."

Rose hooked Alexas' elbow and led her to a painting on the other side of the room. I let go of Ashley's hands.

"There you go. I think they're warm enough now."

"For *now* maybe." She plucked the sleeve of my tweed jacket. "But don't go anywhere."

Jim walked over clutching the necks of two bottles—red and white wine—in one of his pudgy hands, and a couple empty glasses in the other. Apparently he had appointed himself sommelier for the evening. Any glass that went below the halfway mark got topped-off. He filled a glass with white and gave it to me.

"What chapter did you say you were with?" Jim asked.

"Millbrook, New York," I said.

"Never heard of it."

"Well, we're a tiny chapter. There are only four of us so far."

"Uh-huh." Jim raised his voice to Carlton, who was across the room. "Hey, Carl! Which ones did Chris and Alexas bring you?"

Carlton picked up a large remote control that looked a lot like the one attached to his model train layout. He pressed a couple buttons, flicked a couple switches, and the lights dimmed. Then several spotlights came up, warmly lighting the Kinkades we'd given him and Rose.

"Marvelous," purred Ashley.

At my feet, Neil coughed and lay still. An elderly man across the room turned and addressed me.

"These really are terrific." He stood about six inches away from a painting, studying the canvas as if it were a Renoir. "They're something, quite something."

"I love the Boston one, Rose," said a woman beside her.

"Yes, it's *wonderful*, isn't it?"

While everybody else admired the paintings, I admired in a daze Ashley's improbably firm ass—a paragon of sinuously tight perfection the likes of which I hadn't seen since high school track and field, on the posterior of a comely female teammate, a triple-jumper with the befitting last name of Butler. Seeing Ashley, her butt canted saucily toward the fire, gave me a new idea for "The Dogcatcher."[14] I imagined her as the client whose dog is missing, myself as the dogcatcher, and the two of us in her living room discussing the case. I took out my pocket notebook, turned my back to Ashley and scribbled down part of a scene:

> "So, *you're* the dogcatcher," she said.
> "I am."
> "Would you care for a drink?"
> "I'd love one—after I've found your dog."
> "All business. I like that." She smirked at my veter-

---

14 "The Dogcatcher" appears in my short story collection *The Man, The Myth, The Legend*. You may now return to "The Thomas Kinkade Affair." Thank you.

inarian bag. "Is that your little toolkit?"

"Yes."

"Can I see your tools?"

"Maybe later," I said.

She sipped her drink. After studying me for a moment, she went to the fireplace, bent over and jabbed the logs with a brass poker. The beauty of that woman's glutes defied all laws of mathematical probability. Turning around she caught me leering and smiled at me through a curtain of hair. She sat down again and crossed her legs, gesturing at me with the highball glass.

"Chris, what are you writing?"

Standing behind me, Ashley peeked around my shoulder. I put the notebook away.

"Nothing."

"Wait…are you a *writer*?"

I nodded. "Don't say anything, okay?"

"Why, are you *famous* or something?" She gaped at me like I was an open treasure chest.

"Hardly," I said.

Neil coughed again. This time Alexas heard it and gave me a look. She jutted her head at the door.

"Not yet," I mouthed.

Jim appeared at Ashley's side brandishing a wine bottle. "So, Chris…what do you do?"

I hated getting into what I "did" because the second I said I was a writer, someone would ask, "Oh…what have you written?" And by *written*, they meant published. Invariably I disappointed them by saying, "Short stories, some magazine nonfiction, a lot of newspaper stuff." Therefore, to avoid this conversational cul-de-sac, I simply emphasized the writing from which I earned most of my money—speechwriting. But I waited too long to respond. Ashley stepped up beside me and put a hand on my arm.

"Chris is a *writer*," she said.

"Oh, isn't that wonderful," said a woman nearby.

"Actually, I'm a speechwriter," I said.

Jim poured more wine into Ashley's glass.

"Politicians?!" he said. "Please tell me you don't write for Obama."

"No, it's corporate stuff mostly. For executives."

"I've never met a speechwriter before," Ashley said.

I gave her a wink. "Well, you have now."

As Ashley and I clinked glasses, I caught a glimpse of Alexas. She rolled her eyes at me.

"I imagine it's quite glamorous, isn't it?" Ashley said.

Ashley still had her hand on my arm. Maybe it was my imagination, but she seemed to be faintly massaging me with her fingertips.

"It can be," I said. "They put us up at some nice resorts, but it's a lot of hard work, too."

"Oh, I'm sure it is," she said.

"Hard work?" Jim said. "Are you kidding? I've done construction every day since I was sixteen. *That's* hard work."

"Harder physically, Jim, you're right," I said. "All I can tell you is, after a full day of writing, my brain is fried. I can't think or even speak very well. *That's* how writing is hard work."

Jim chuckled. "It's not the same thing. Try laying brick for a living, buddy."

This walking suet cake was starting to annoy me.

"Listen, Jim. My paternal grandfather and great-grandfather were stonecutters in granite quarries," I said. "If they were alive today, they'd want me using my brain for a living instead of breaking my back."

"You shouldn't say writing's hard work, that's all."

He gave me a simian smirk that reminded me of a short, fat kid who, along with his unibrow Count Chocula-lookalike sidekick, had bullied me all through sixth grade. I gritted my teeth and took a deep breath. If Jim and I had been alone, I would have thrown my wine in his fat face and kicked a 60-yard field goal into his balls—presupposing my European walking shoe could find them between his fleshy thighs. But with all of these people around, physical violence was impossible. I decided to take another, crueler, approach.

"Jim, you talk like you have a lot of writing experience," I said. "I mean, to be able to say with such authority that it's not hard work. Tell me, what's the last thing you wrote?"

"Oh…well…uh…"

"Written many stories, Jim? Novels? No?" I snapped my fingers. "Ah, you're a theatre guy, a playwright!"

"No," he said sheepishly. "There's not much need for writing in what I do."

"So how do you know it isn't hard work?" I said. "But enough about writing. Let's talk art. Besides Kinkade, who are some of your favorite painters, Jim?"

He shrugged. "Oh, a lot of them."

"Name a few."

"I can't think of them off the top of my head."

"Kinkade's the only painter you know, isn't he, Jim?"

He blushed, looked around to see if anyone was watching.

"Hmm, I thought so," I said. "Hey, I've got an idea… why don't you go be fat someplace else?" I pointed. "I think that corner's big enough for you."

Ashley giggled.

"Asshole," he said. "You're lucky I like Rose and Carlton."

"And *you're* lucky I took my medication today." I glanced at the fireplace, licked an eyetooth. "I'd like to ram that fire poker through your neck."

His face blanched with shock. He walked away glancing over his shoulder at me. Ashley's hand trembled on my arm.

"My, you certainly told him off."

"Yeah, I guess," I said. "But I really shouldn't do that. I always cause myself trouble, and later on I feel guilty."

"Forget it, Chris," she said, rubbing my back. "He's an idiot. Why Rose and Carlton invite him to these things, I'll never know."

Sipping her wine, Ashley glanced around the room and surreptitiously eased her hip to the side so her tush touched my leg. *Hell-lo.* It felt as hard as an unripe nectarine. I was seriously tempted to give it a test squeeze.

For God's sake, Chris…you and hot messes—what is your damage?

Ashley nudged me with her butt. *Jesus.*

"You and Alexas are a cute couple," she said.

"Thanks. A lot of people tell us that."

She leaned into my shoulder. "So, tell me…does she share?"

"Excuse me?"

"You heard me."

She looked at me while seductively swirling her wineglass. Across the room, Carlton dinged his wineglass with a fork.

"Okay, everybody, I'd like to propose a toast. To Chris and Alexas, for generously parting with these lovely Kinkades."

"Here, here!"

Everyone raised their glasses and drank. Everyone except Jim, that is, who sulked in the kitchen doorway.

Then Neil got unsteadily to his feet. He coughed again and padded over to a chair with Thomas Kinkade upholstery. One by one, everybody noticed him and went quiet. For a second it looked like he was sniffing the cushion and then his head lunged forward and he spewed out the contents of his stomach.

"*OH…MY…GOD!*" Rose shouted.

"Whoo, that's a *doosey*," Ashley said.

Across the room, Alexas gently put down her wineglass and slipped out to the hallway. Sensing I would be leaving presently, I stepped away from Ashley. Carlton rushed over to the chair.

"Oh, Neil! Neil! Look what you've done!"

Carlton reached for his remote and turned on all the lights. Slowly he approached the puke-covered chair. He stooped and examined the chunky pile.

"Are these *pretzels*? Rose, did you change his dog food?"

"Of course not, Carlton!" She ran into the kitchen.

"Actually, Carlton," I said, "they're Combos."

"What?!" He stood up, red-faced. "What the hell are 'Combos'?"

"They're these hollow, cheese-filled pretzels. I had some in my jacket when I was walking with the dogs."

Rose came back with a roll of paper towels and started scooping up Neil's vomit.

"You fed my purebred Labrador retrievers *Combos*?!" Carlton said. "What the hell is wrong with you?!"

"It didn't seem like a big deal," I said. "Most dogs can eat anything. I didn't know yours had a special diet."

Jim leaned against the doorjamb eating a finger sandwich.

"Hell, anybody with *sense* knows you don't feed dogs junk food," he said.

"And anybody with *taste* knows Thomas Kinkade isn't art," I retorted.

The entire room turned and stared at me.

"*What* did you say?" Carlton said.

Alexas appeared in the foyer archway. Behind her, our bags were lined up beside the front door. She gestured at the door, but I wasn't ready to leave. Not *quite* yet. I nodded and she went out with half the bags.

There was a dam in my chest, a dam holding back all of the hatred and venom I had for Thomas Kinkade, and that dam was about to burst. A quote by Mark Twain flashed through my mind: *"We regret the things we <u>don't</u> do, more than the ones we do."*

"Well, Chris?" Carlton said petulantly. "What do you have to say for yourself?"

"Carlton, everybody," I said, "I sense you're all good people—well, except maybe Jim over there. Anyway, Carlton, Rose…first, I'm sorry I fed your dogs Combos. It was stupid of me. I think you two are warm and generous, and Alexas and I thank you for your hospitality. I also want to thank you two for taking the Kinkades off our hands. You see…we *hate* them. We weren't able to sell them. Hell, we couldn't even give them away. But you took them, and we thank you for that.

"Now, I'm not an art expert, but I know enough to know why Thomas Kinkade is bad. While he probably started out competently enough, he never evolved. He found a couple of things that he did reasonably well and kept doing them, over and over and over again."

I swept a hand around the room. I was suddenly a museum docent.

"Consider the sameness of the compositions. And I'm not talking about a signature style or an artistic fingerprint that declares it's that artist's work, like how every Van Gogh is recognizable as one of his. I'm saying that Kinkade's stuff simply all looks the *same*. Lighted windows. A misty, ethereal glow. It's boring. As someone pointed out at the Middlebury exhibit this summer, Kinkade's work seeks only to anesthetize the viewer, to hypnotize the viewer into a false state of contentment.

"Consider, too, the lack of restraint in his work." I pointed to a San Francisco street scene. "Could he possibly have gotten *one more* street car, one more window, one more anything into that picture?"

"He has a point," Ashley said.

She winked at me. The rest of the room turned to her aghast.

"I'm begging you," I said. "Stop buying this factory-produced crap. Please. There are so many artists out there who need support. Start buying work that *you* like, and stop needing somebody else's stamp of approval before you buy it."

Alexas stepped into the room. "Rose, Carlton, I'm sorry it didn't work out, but thank you. You have a lovely place. Chris, I'll be in the car."

She took our remaining luggage and left. I poured myself a full glass of Chardonnay, downed it in two swallows and went to the door. Still dumbstruck, everyone followed me like zombies to the foyer archway. I stood at the front door.

"Rose," I said, "your pecan pie is amazing."

"I'm glad you liked it."

I opened the door. "Oh, and Ashley?"

She stumbled into the foyer, one arm in her coat, and clutching a wine bottle in the crook of her other arm. Her eyes glinted with a look I'd seen in the eyes of so many hot messes: a look of amused self-confidence, that her leaving with me was a *fait accompli*.

"Yes, Chris?"

"That ass of yours? *Fabulous*. Whatever you're doing—StairMaster, Pilates, yoga—keep it up."

She was frozen—mouth agape, coat half-hanging off her, wine bottle starting to slip—when I stepped outside and shut the door behind me. The car was parked at the end of the walkway, and Alexas was behind the wheel with the engine running. I jogged down the walkway and got in.

"So," I said. "Ready, Bonnie?"

"Sure, Clyde.[15] But what about *Ashley*?"

"What about her?"

"You two were *pretty* friendly in there," she said.

I shook my head. "Hot mess, Bunny. Doesn't count. You know the evil spell they cast over me."

She sighed and kissed me. "Yes, I do."

"I'm sorry, sweet," I said.

As Alexas pulled the car away, I caught a glimpse of them inside the house, crowded around the living room window, staring out at us.

For some reason, where we were in Northern Vermont, motels were scarce. We meandered along mountain roads for an hour before we found a place near an out-of-season ski resort. It looked open. The lights were on anyway.

"Look…'Restful Motor Court,' " Alexas said. "How about it?"

"I don't know," I said. "Looks a little Bates Motel-ish to me. What's with that house on the hill?"

"They've got a vacancy. Let's at least go inside and check it out."

She parked beneath the porte cochère, and we went in together. The man at the counter was older, with heavy jowls. Judging by the amount of Brylcreem in his salt-and-pepper hair, he was singlehandedly keeping afloat the company that manufactured that antiquated grooming product.

"Need a room?" he asked.

---

15 This only works because my middle name *is* Clyde.

I stopped in my tracks. There, on the wall behind him, was a giant Thomas Kinkade: a village full of glowing cottages.

At that moment, I knew there was no way of ever beating Thomas Kinkade. The only way he was going down was by his own followers eventually committing mutiny against him; bearing torches, they would steal him from his bed one night, tie him up in a Kinkade cottage someplace, then decapitate him with a gilded guillotine. But on this night, weary beyond measure, I wanted nothing more to do with Thomas Kinkade.

"Alexas," I said, nodding at the painting.

"Ugh. No way."

"Screw this place. Let's go."

"Hey!" the man said.

I walked out, my arm firmly over my darling wife's shoulder, grateful to have her, and delirious that those damn paintings were out of our lives forever.

3

You Know What's Coming Next

Of all days for this to happen.

Already late for my urologist appointment, I stumbled up to the reception desk and was greeted by a breathtaking 20-something blonde, all legs and curves. She stood at a filing cabinet, pulling files, looking bored. She wore stiletto heels, a black pencil skirt, and a baby blue silk blouse. As she moved, the V of her blouse leaves vacillated between intriguing and slutty.

FACT: No man wants to have to talk to a young woman this attractive when his appointment is about the malfunction of that most mysterious piece of uro-sexual impedimenta, the prostate.

I hadn't felt dread like this in 20 years, when I bought a *Playboy*[16] at Store 24 in Boston and, despite my attempts to get the male clerk with the acne-scarred face, the hot girl rang me up.

"*Good* morning," the receptionist said.

"Hi. I'm here for my nine-fifteen appointment."

---

16 Unfortunately, it was an all-photos special issue—*Redheads*—so I couldn't claim I was buying it for the articles.

"That's *fine*." She sat down and typed on a computer keyboard. "Could you please confirm your date of birth for me?"

I told her.

"Not that it's really necessary," she said. "You're the youngest patient we have today. Probably the youngest we'll see all week."

"Great," I said, "is there a door prize?"

She gave me a squint-eyed, tight-lipped smile that, in my younger and more vulnerable years, would have instigated a vigorous lunchtime tryst in the parking garage. Still smiling, she pinched a sample cup off a shelf with her fingertips and playfully put it into my hand. The cup had a red screw top and a label with my information on it.

"Apparently…we need a urine sample," she said. "The bathroom's down the hall. When you're done, put the cup in the little door in there." She smiled again. "Good *luck!*"

When I got there, I saw a water cooler tucked into the wall beside the bathroom door. Cheered by its tacit encouragement, I drank a few cups before going inside and unscrewing the sample cup.

And then I waited.

The sample cup had one measuring line written on it: 100 ml. This is less than half a cup of coffee, but considering the present stinginess of my bladder, it might as well have been a gallon. It didn't help that I was notoriously impatient about such things—things like urinating.

"Come on," I said, looking down. "Let's go!"

I closed my eyes and thought of water—of garden watering cans, of trickling fountains, of mountain snow melts forming springtime freshets, flowing fast and heavy and pure. For a moment I considered turning on the faucet for inspiration, but I didn't want people outside to think I was finished and to start knocking. That would break my concentration. Besides, the sink was three feet away, and I'd learned the hard way a long time ago not to walk and urinate at the same time.

After waiting a minute, relaxing my bladder and visualizing, I finally got a steady stream going, although it was hardly laser-like, as it had been in my youth. When you're 11 years old and the urine shoots out of you so strongly that you could subcontract your junk for hydraulic mining, you can't imagine a day in the future when you'll reminisce about the good old days: when the urine flowed continuously and effortlessly, like those waterfall lemonade dispensers in mall food courts.

As the cup filled, I began to have high hopes, but then my stream stopped. I gave it another few seconds and checked the cup. Not even past the label. A disappointing performance, but it would have to do.

In case I'd forgotten what to do with this Tupperware container of my own urine, a giant sign above the toilet with an intimidating, left-pointing red arrow clarified matters: "Put Sample Inside Door!" Screwing the cup closed and zipping up, I went over to the door and opened it.

There was another door inside; together the two doors seemed to form an airlock for urine. For some reason this was unnerving. A small sign on the shelf between the two doors read "Leave Sample Here. Thank You!"

Given how much work went into producing it, I was reluctant to part with my sample. The sole marking on the cup of 100 ml made me worry that my paltry 40–50 ml wouldn't be enough. Steeling myself with a deep breath, I knocked on the inner door, inadvertently punching it wide open. The door smacked against a metal cabinet, making a terrible clang. A vision of myself in a bizarro version of the movie *Charlie and the Chocolate Factory* flashed into my mind: me being scolded for straying from the tour. I peeked through the inside door. A lab technician walked in a stoop toward the opening.

"Leave it on the shelf," he said.

"But it's less than half," I said.

"Leave it on the shelf."

I craned my neck for a better view. Cups of urine, in the full spectrum of yellows, festooned a countertop. I spotted a familiar piece of lab equipment.

"Hey," I said, "is that a gas chromatograph?"

"Leave it on the shelf!"

"Fine!"

I washed up. The second I opened the bathroom door a nurse led me to an exam room. She glanced at my file and clucked her tongue.

"Oh, my," she said. "You're not even forty?!"

"Is that a problem?"

"The doctor'll be right with you, sir."

The steel door clicked shut with a finality that only Edmond Dantes being locked up in the *Chateau d'If* could appreciate. I had no idea what I was supposed to do next. Usually they leave one of those so-called garments (a hospital "johnny") with instructions to change into it and wait for the doctor. But the only two items in my purview were a economy-size tube of what was clearly *lube*, and a box of latex gloves designed for "increased tactile sensation." And, as an added indignity, the gloves weren't white, but periwinkle. Seriously…*periwinkle.*

There was, however, a telephone by the door. For a second I wished I knew somebody in Kuala Lumpur. I didn't know exactly where that was, but I sensed it was far, far away, in the Pacific someplace, and I wanted to stick them with a big phone bill. I nixed the idea, though. The doctor would certainly arrive before I figured out how the phone system worked.

I put my bag on a chair and checked the cabinets for a gown. Nothing. There were only tubes and tubes of lube, stacked up like cordwood. Faced with the reality of why I was here, I decided there was no use delaying the inevitable. I stripped to my underwear, plopped my clothes on the chair and stood there for a moment, looking around at the 8'x10' room. I realized that, at least in a small way, my view of the world was about to change.

While driving Alexas to work that morning, I had barked about everything. Stupid stuff, like how the new cook at the diner couldn't make a scrambled egg: "He *needs* to turn that griddle down!" I'd been dreading this appointment for a month, ever since the morning when I woke up, shuffled into the bathroom needing to urinate, and *nothing came out*. Convinced it was an anomaly, I'd waited another half-hour before trying again, and even then it took me five trips to completely drain my bladder. The next day, I went to my primary care physician.

"You're a little young," she said, "but it could be an enlarged prostate."

"What does *'enlarged'* mean?" I asked.

(Later on I learned that this is one part of the male anatomy where bigger is absolutely not better.)

"I'd like you to have a cancer screening," she said. "And there's a specialist I want you to see. He's very good."

He might be very good, this specialist, this urologist, I thought, staring at the tube of lube, *but he's kept me waiting in here for ten minutes without any clothes on.* Breathing deeply, trying to keep myself calm, I glanced around the room, looking for a way to exact some revenge.

In a moment, he'll have me in the most humiliating position a man can be put in. Some minor act of sabotage is called for, if for no other reason than to preserve some dignity in my own mind.

Nothing in the room could be broken without it being obvious, but there *was* a full box of latex gloves on the counter. I put my ear to the door. Hearing nothing, I dug into the box and removed all of the gloves but *one*. I stuffed them in my jacket pocket, jumped back on the exam table and swung my feet nonchalantly back and forth. Three seconds later, the door whipped open and a diminutive man with white hair walked in carrying a laptop computer.

"Oh," he said, "you're undressed."

"I thought that was the idea. There was no gown, so—"

"Your PSA test results were okay," he said.

"Are those antibodies or something?" I asked.

"It stands for Prostate-Specific Antigens."

Forever a perfectionist, even about trivial matters, I said, "And mine were point-two-nine out of, what, four? That's really good, right?"

"It's consistent with men your age."

He read something on his computer screen and clucked his tongue.

"When did you start taking the saw palmetto?" he asked.

"Actually, the day after I first had trouble. My wife—"

"I don't believe in that stuff, you know."

"What, marriage?" I said.

"No. Saw palmetto."

"Come on, Doc," I said. "It's a remedy thousands of years old. All of those Native Americans must have found *something* good in it."

"Well, we can discuss it another time. I have quite a number of patients to see today, so for now, please take off your shorts and sit on the table. I'll be right back."

He left.

So this is it, Chris, the moment you've been dreading.

I removed my boxers and sat bare-assed on the tissue paper draped over the examination table. Naked from the waist down, covering my privates with a forlorn pair of Fruit of the Loom, I had a glimmer of the unease women must feel when they visit gynecologists.

The trouble is, nothing in our culture prepares men for this. Take movies, for instance. You never see Clint Eastwood put in this position: bottomless in a cold examination room, waiting to have a stranger probe a part of his anatomy that even *he* isn't familiar with. I began to fantasize about the doctor forgetting me, making me wait beyond my pre-set limit of 10 minutes, at which point I would jump off the table, dress in a huff and punch that antisocial lab tech in the neck when he tried to stop me from leaving.

The doctor returned and opened his laptop on the counter. He pulled the last glove from the box, shook the empty box, frowned and threw it away. My revenge was sweet, but, like a mint consumed at a diner cash register, the sweetness was short-lived.

"Okay." He slipped the glove on his hand and snapped it tight. "I'd like you to lie flat on your back. We're going to start with a physical exam."

In typical doctor fashion, he opened with that mysterious rapping on the abdomen. In this maneuver, the physician places a hand on you and knocks on that hand with his other hand, as though he's knocking on a door but deadening the sound because he doesn't really want anyone to answer. Nobody, not even doctors, knows what this procedure is meant to accomplish. If a voice answered "Who's there?" they'd know the patient had a problem. Otherwise, I'm convinced this is just a flashy filler move designed to make the $1,700 exam last longer than two minutes.

He moved on to my bladder, pressing really hard for some reason, and asked, "Do you feel the need to urinate when I do *this*?"

I told him no, but briefly thought how great it would be if his relentless pressure forced urine out of me, like wine from a compressed wineskin.

"Moving on to the penis," he announced.

Really? I'm glad you told me because otherwise I'd never know what was happening.

"Normal-shaped opening," he said.

And that's when I noticed he was wearing a Bluetooth earpiece. I was relieved to know that the creepy play-by-play wasn't for my benefit. His words showed up on the computer screen as text.

"Pretty sophisticated setup, Doc," I said. "The voice-to-text and all."

He didn't answer. He was rolling my testes around in his fingertips with his eyes closed, like a safecracker working a dial on an unfamiliar vault.

"Testicles fine," he said. "No abnormalities detected. Now, please stand up, and when I tell you, cough."

The Old Cough Test. I coughed twice while the doctor jabbed his fingers underneath my scrotum. Suddenly I longed for my junior high school physical exams, administered by the school nurse, the fresh-faced and angelic Miss O'Malley.

"Fine." He turned to the computer and punched a few keys. "Okay, Mr. Orcutt…you know what's coming next. Turn around and lean over the table with your elbows down, like this."

He did an "air" version of the maneuver beside the table. As I bent over, there was a blur in my periphery. A box of Kleenex slapped down on the table in front of me.

"For wiping up the excess jelly afterward," he said. "May want a few of these as well."

Whack! A box of baby wipes landed on the table.

"All right," he announced, "cold jelly!"

He applied it, and, yes, you could say it was cold; it was like having that area sprayed with liquid nitrogen.

"So, Mr. Orcutt," he said casually, like we were seated beside each other on a shuttle flight. "What kind of work do you do?"

Of all the tricks doctors have at their disposal, mental distraction has to be their favorite. I suppose if you're about to do something that will make a patient *very* uncomfortable (in some cases violently so), the best thing you can do is get him thinking and talking about something else. In my case, I loved how the guy waited until I was in this humbling position before asking me what I did for a living.

I started to tell him. He said, "Hmm, sounds interesting," and then something the diameter of a late summer gourd plowed into the place where the sun has never shone.

For years I had laughed at a scene in the movie *Trading Places*: the private detective, Clarence Beeks, is knocked out, taped into a gorilla suit and locked in a cage with a live gorilla. When the real gorilla gets horny and enters Beeks from behind, Beeks' eyes pop out of his skull.

Today, however, I wasn't laughing.

What was happening was very uncomfortable. Uncomfortable in the same sense that sticking your arm down a dark hole is uncomfortable, except this time, rather than entering it, you're on the receiving end. I became my prostate, silently yelling, "Hey, what the hell!? You're not supposed to be in here!"

How long did the doctor stay in there, you ask? Long enough to read *Moby Dick* in braille.

Finally, without fanfare, he withdrew his finger. Thus endeth the "digital rectal examination." Stupid me—when I originally heard this term, I thought, *"Good, they finally updated this test. Now they'll insert something like a fiber-optic cable!"*

Uh, no. When they say "digital," they mean exactly that—a *digit*.

"Smooth, symmetrical, no bumps," the doctor said. "You're good."

Lightheaded, I stood up slowly. The doctor left, giving me time to breathe again and use the paper products. I needed something pleasant to look forward to. The second I got out of here, I was driving over to Dunkin' Donuts and wolfing down half a dozen sugar-raised.

Out in the waiting room, the blonde receptionist smiled and took my co-pay.

"Seems I'm fine," I said. "False alarm, I guess."

"Well *that's* good," she said. "You looked a little worried when you came in."

So, what would I tell another man about this procedure? Simple. I'd tell him it sucks.

"Prepare yourself," I'd say. "Imagine the worst humiliation you could possibly experience, then imagine that same humiliation if you were unclothed and violated. That's close to what it feels like."

Later that evening, Alexas asked me, "But aren't you glad you did it?"

"No," I said. "It happened. Let's leave it at that."

The truth is, while I was relieved the test came back negative, I was eager to put it all behind me.

4

ABSENTMINDED

Shortly after we were married, my wife began to say I was absentminded, but I vehemently disagreed. In my opinion, that term described people like Professor L., a former literature professor of mine turned mentor and friend—a man who not only misplaced things in his apartment, but also routinely tripped on sidewalk cracks whenever he took a walk in Boston. Surely, I said to Alexas, I couldn't be that bad.

"No, you are," she said. "Trust me on this."

"Am not," I said.

She said something else, but I ran out of the room with my hands over my ears and humming loudly so I wouldn't hear it.

Ten years later, however, when I couldn't find one of the eleven books I'd been reading, and I eventually discovered it in the freezer, I realized she was right: I *am* absentminded.

Once, I left my stainless steel mug at the diner and never noticed it was gone. Then, early one Saturday morning—before the obnoxious, Wellie-wearing weekenders mobbed the place—Alexas and I went down to the diner for breakfast. When the waiter, Kenny, walked over with coffees for us, mine was in my stainless mug.

"Holy crap," I said, "I left that here?"

"Yeah, you do it all the time," Kenny said.

I looked at Alexas for corroboration.

"He's right," she said. "You do."

"The absentminded professor," Kenny said. "I keep waiting for him to leave his wallet. Heh-heh, just kidding."

After the revelation at the diner, I started to notice my absentmindedness more often. Besides misplacing things—including typical items like keys, glasses, wallet, and favorite pens, as well as not-so-typical things, like my car in unfamiliar parking lots—I frequently lost my words. Of course, when I say I *lost* my words, it's not as if the words got kicked under the couch or fell behind the condiments in the refrigerator. They didn't, and I know they didn't, because I would have seen them there the next time I went searching for my belt. The words weren't gone; they were in me; I could feel them inside, wanting to come out, but they were slipperier than they'd ever been; I couldn't get *hold* of the pesky buggers.

I was in the kitchen making soup when the subject of my absentmindedness came up again. Alexas described what I was like when I "lost my words."

"You'll be in the middle of a conversation," she said, "usually describing something in great detail, when you just freeze up. You're like a paused DVD. Sometimes you even wiggle back and forth with your mouth open."

I opened up some jars of spices and shook them in. "Oh, Jesus. Really? I don't look retarded, do I?"

"No, people can tell you're thinking intensely about something, searching for the perfect word."

"*Le mot juste*," I said. "Flaubert's advice to Maupassant."

Alexas sat at the kitchen table, crossed her legs and gazed out the window at our neighbor's construction project: the rebuilding of a 100-year-old garage.

"Anyway," she said, "they're usually fascinated by you for some reason, so they keep listening, but it can cause some awkward moments."

"Like…?"

"Like last week, at the hotel in Boston," she said. "You were telling the concierge that story about the Red Sox–Yankees game, and you completely spaced out in the middle of it. He was patient, but I could tell he was worried something had happened to you."

"What, like I had a stroke?"

"Exactly."

"Did I finish the story?"

"No, you mentioned how you liked the Doubletree's policy of giving guests cookies at check-in, and he interpreted that as your asking for a cookie, so he went and got you one. You thanked him and walked away."

"But I don't do that a lot, do I? It's only once in a while, right?"

"No," she said, "it's pretty much all the time."

I stared down at the three jars of spices in my hands. The tops were off all three, so I couldn't tell which ones I'd put in the soup, even when I inspected the broth.

"Hey," I said, "which of these did I add?" I showed her the three jars: rosemary, cayenne pepper and onion salt.

"Add a little more pepper and rosemary," she said.

"But which ones did I add?"

She sighed. "You see? See what I have to deal with?"

But losing track of the ingredients I used while cooking wasn't as bad as what I call my "grocery store wakeups." Similar to the alcohol-induced blackouts and alleyway wakeups I experienced as a college student in Boston, my grocery store wakeups go like this…

At least once a week I wander into our village grocery store, Marona's, and come to in a random aisle, clueless as to how I got there or what I came for. Apparently, I stand absolutely still, straining to recall what we need back at the house, which leads me to wonder *when* I left, and I get stuck in an endless loop until Caroline walks by and says, "Hey, Chris…how you doing?"

It's as if she knows not to bother asking me the standard questions—"Can I help you?" or "Can I help you find something?"—because she knows I don't have a clue. In fact, it's as if she knows I'm stuck in an endless loop, and, like an old skipping LP record, if she simply nudges me I'll find my way again. I'm glad she doesn't ask, "So, Chris…whatcha up to?" I have no idea what I'm up to; for all I know, I might have just robbed the bank.

Then there are the conversations I have in my *mind*, so later on, when I "re-broach" the subject with someone to whom I'm sure I mentioned it, I start in the middle. The result is, the other person (usually Alexas) is completely lost.

I suppose this tendency comes from working alone on a daily basis. When you spend as much time in your own head as I do, your thoughts tend to become cyclical. Complicating matters is the fact of being a fiction writer, where my characters are voices in my own head. What happens is, when I'm having a conversation with myself about a subject, one of these voices fills in as the foil or antagonist. When I'm only in my own head, this isn't a problem. The trouble comes when I have to talk to other people, and I launch into the conversation somewhere in the middle, without giving the person any background. Example: what happened between Alexas and me after the cat's vet appointment.

That morning, I had taken our cat, Sweetie, for her checkup. While waiting, I sat next to a sobbing woman whose dog had been hit by a car. The vet gave the woman a terrible choice: either spend "at least" $3,000 to patch the dog up (without any guarantee he'd recover), or have the dog put down. The vet left her to think about it. Nobody was around to comfort the woman, so, most reluctantly, I found myself gently rubbing her back and consoling her. I finished with Sweetie's appointment before the woman made her decision, so for the rest of the day I wondered what happened. That evening, as Alexas and I were reading in bed, I said aloud, "Alexas, do you think they put down that dog?"

"No, I'm sure the dog's fine," Alexas said. "The shelter wasn't giving him back to the owners until he had all his shots and a checkup, right?"

I put my book down. "What are you talking about?"

"The dog we rescued last week—the sheltie. What are *you* talking about?"

"The dog at the vet today. I told you—the one that got hit by a car. The vet said, 'Unfortunately it comes down to a question of economics.' Remember?"

"Nope. I think you had this conversation in your own head, Chrissy."

"No way," I said. "I told you all this."

"No, dear, you *imagined* you told me all this. There's a difference. One's real and the other's"—she pointed at her temple—"in your *mind*."

"Grrrr. Don't talk to me."

"You're absentminded, that's all," she said. "It's no big deal. Einstein couldn't dress himself. At least you've got *that* going for you."

"I'm not absentminded," I said. "Those people are always doofuses."

"Einstein was a doofus?" she asked.

"No, but I'm no Einstein."

"I think you are."

"How am I absentminded then? And don't bring up my losing stuff because everybody does that."

She sat up in bed and turned to face me, ticking items off with her fingers.

"All right, besides misplacing things and freezing in the middle of conversations, there are the frequent incidents at Marona's—"

"You mean my wakeups? I know about them. And they're not that frequent."

"Fine. Sometimes you start cooking, and I can see it. You get an idea, so you wander off to your office with the food still on the stove."

"I've only done that once," I said. "Maybe twice."

"Okay, here's one." She gave me the tolerant smile of a kindergarten teacher. "You call me at the office to ask me what day of the week it is. And if you know the day, you don't know the number."

"The only reason I don't know the day of the week," I said, "is that in my world—wake up, write, go to sleep—every day is the same. That's an unfair example because my routine doesn't vary much, you know that."

"True, but most people know what *day* it is."

"Whatever. Anything else?"

She thought for a moment. "Okay, I've got another one. Ready?"

"Yeah." I was starting not to enjoy this, and Alexas was starting to enjoy it too much.

"People's names," she said.

"Everybody forgets names."

"But you go to the same places every day. Like the post office. For the longest time you couldn't remember Kenda's name, and you kept sending me in there under some contrived, *Seinfeld* pretext to find it out."

"I had an index card with all their names on it," I said. "I kept it in my wallet. I had one for the library, too."

"What happened to them?"

"I lost them. But that's not the point. The point is, by making those cards, I showed myself as not being absentminded."

Alexas smiled. "All right…how do you explain the random disrobing?"

"What the hell are you talking about?" I said.

"Pajamas in the bookcase, hats in the bathroom, socks draped over the tops of doors."

"I'm drying the socks. They're wool usually, so I can get more than one wear out of them."

"There's nothing wrong with your being a little absentminded, honey," she said. "That's why you have me."

"No, we have each other because we're both crazy."

"Bleh," she said.

I kissed her goodnight and went to sleep. The next morning, we went to the diner for breakfast. Kenny was already putting our coffees on the table as I slid into the booth. Alexas leaned over the table and whispered to me, "Honey, your fly's down."

"That's funny," I said, sipping my coffee. "It reminds me of the story of President Lyndon Johnson and the Italian ambassador. So…President Johnson was going to see the Pope for the first time. The Italian ambassador had heard that Johnson was a Texas redneck, and he was afraid the President would embarrass him, so he starts going on and on about proper etiquette, table manners, titles of nobility, all of this stuff, right? And Johnson listens to all of it. So, they're in the limousine, and the car pulls into the Vatican, and the ambassador—who's basically breathless now because he's been talking so long and so fast—the ambassador stops as the car pulls up and says, 'So, Mr. President, do you have any questions, sir?' 'Just one,' Johnson replies. 'What's that, sir?' And Johnson says, 'Are you going to zip up your fly?' Isn't that great? I think parts of it are apocryphal, but—"

"Christopher."

"Yeah?"

"You need to zip up your fly," she said.

I took a deep breath, nodded gratefully, and zipped up.

After breakfast, we kissed goodbye on the sidewalk. As I watched her drive off to work, I realized for the first time how right she was about my being absentminded, not to mention how lucky I was to have her. This realization was underscored when I went to the post office and found in my post office box a solicitation from the Alzheimer's Association, Hudson Valley Chapter. Clearly, the forces of the universe were conspiring to tell me that I was indeed absentminded.

So now the question was, what to do about it? Workarounds like the index cards were effective only for a short while. The more I thought about it, trying to be less absentminded was going to be too difficult.

I decided to go the other way: from now on, I would embrace it.

The next day, I got my first chance to work the absentminded angle. I was driving up to Hudson, NY to have lunch with an author pal of mine, Dave King. It was a weekday, late morning, in mid October, around the time of the elusive peak foliage. As I was driving, I noticed these tiny black specks on the road. Nearing each one, I saw that they were woolly caterpillars, either committing mass suicide or making a dangerous migration to the other side of the road. What was so special about the woods over there? I couldn't help but be awed by their bravery.

I began to gently swerve the car so that my tires straddled them. At 55 mph on a two-lane road, it wasn't easy, but I couldn't bear the idea of killing them, any of them, for the same reason that I always watched my footsteps carefully when I walked around the village so I wouldn't step on ants.

As a higher-order being capable of governing his actions and protecting helpless creatures, I considered it my duty—in a truly Kantian sense—to slalom safely over each caterpillar. Because if I didn't (therefore failing to set a good example), who else would?

This, I reasoned to myself, swerving across the double-yellow line to avoid one of the intrepid little guys, was a perfect example of Immanuel Kant's Categorical Imperative. I wasn't swerving around the caterpillars because I'd gain something by sparing them; I was swerving around them because sparing them was good in itself. If I were to express my actions as a maxim, it would go something like, "One should always avoid killing innocent, defenseless creatures." Kant would say that my predicament, and the maxim I'd formulated, constituted a Categorical Imperative because it would be okay if it were a universal law of nature.[17] "One should always avoid killing innocent, defenseless creatures" was a maxim that to act on was good in itself and therefore *should* be a universal law of nature.

As I understood it, Kant would say that if a person were confronted with a situation where he wasn't sure what the right thing to do was, he should ask himself this question: Would you be comfortable having the maxim of your action become a universal law? In this

---

17 I was aided in clarifying these thoughts while driving because at a village garage sale the day before I stumbled upon a book entitled *The Range of Philosophy*. Among other readings, the book included a nice refresher essay on Kant's ethics: "Kant: The Right and Our Duty."

case, I *would* be comfortable with the maxim I'd formulated becoming a universal law; but considering my own safety and that of other drivers, I would want to modify it thusly: "One should always avoid killing innocent, defenseless creatures, so long as in the act of avoiding killing the creatures, one does not endanger other people or creatures."

Philosophy is about splitting hairs, an intellectual exercise I'd enjoyed deeply in college. Although I still occasionally read some of the old masters (e.g., Plato, Kant, Mill, Russell), I missed the hair-splitting.

In this case, there was some question as to whether my gently weaving over and between the caterpillars posed some risk to other drivers, but I was exceedingly careful, and when in doubt—when faced with a choice of potentially squashing one of the little guys or hitting a tractor-trailer head-on—I cut a narrow margin, missing the caterpillars by inches.

Glancing in the rear-view mirror after a long straightaway, during which I had successfully swerved around no fewer than 50 caterpillars, I was pleased to see the car behind me doing the same. In my own small way, I was effecting change on the planet. By modeling respect for life—even the lives of "insignificant" caterpillars—I was persuading others to do it too. As Gandhi taught, "We must become the change we want to see in the world."

I passed yellowing cornfields gleaming in the sun, and a big orchard farm stand, where, on my way home, I planned to stop and buy a peck of Cortlands and a gallon of cider, and continued down the road, weaving around the caterpillars. When I glanced in the rear-view mirror again, a state police cruiser was roaring past the car behind me. Every single light on the thing was flashing. It was after me. I hadn't been speeding, at least not much, so it had to be the weaving. I pulled onto the shoulder, rolled down my window and shut the car off.

In the past, anytime I'd been pulled over, my *modus operandi* for dealing with the situation was simple: say nothing and hand the cop my driver's license and registration. Over the years, I'd discovered that no apology or explanation would change the outcome, so rather than demean myself by trying to talk my way out of a ticket, I would accept it as a *fait accompli* and retain my dignity.

But this time, as the trooper got out of his car and adjusted his hat, I decided to change my strategy. This time I would play up my absentmindedness. This time, instead of coming off as haughty or hostile by my silence, I would humble myself and be as meek and cooperative as possible. As he approached my window, I put my hands at exactly 10 and 2 on the steering wheel, feigning nervousness by letting my hands tremble a bit.

"License and registration, please," he said.

He was a young man, maybe in his mid-20s. I handed my paperwork to him.

"Sir," he said, "do you know why I stopped you?"

"No. I wasn't speeding, was I officer?"

"Have you been drinking, sir?" he asked.

"Absolutely not, officer," I said. "I stopped drinking years ago."

I opened my eyes wide and affected an expression of self-disgust I'd practiced in the mirror a few times, and topped it off with a tiny head-shake.

"Officer," I said, "was it the weaving?"

"Yes, why?"

I was faced with a choice. Either I could mention that I was a writer—pointing to my digital recorder on the passenger's seat and saying I'd been dictating something and gotten distracted—*or* I could tell him the truth. Besides being true, the truth showed I had morals and a respect for life. Maybe after dealing with countless selfish, lying douchebags, the hard-hearted trooper might be touched by someone honest trying to do a kind thing.

"Well, officer," I said, "this might sound ridiculous, but…it's the caterpillars."

"The caterpillars?"

"Yes, the ones all over the road," I said. "I don't want to run any of them over, officer, and I'm afraid I got so caught up in steering around them that I forgot where I was. You see, officer, I have a tendency to space out thinking about something else. Like today, I was thinking about the philosopher Kant and the Categorical Imperative. I'm really, really sorry."

He held up my license. "Anything on here I should know about? Any tickets, suspensions, that sort of thing?"

There had been a speeding ticket three years ago, but I had gotten it plea-bargained down.

"God, no," I said. "There was a stop sign or something a while ago, but that was like this—another lapse of concentration, I'm afraid."

"Okay, I'll be back in a few minutes," he said.

He returned to the cruiser, where I could see him punching my info into the computer. I gazed out at the sparkling foliage. No matter what happened, I'd handled this well. Instead of being a silent prick (thereby guaranteeing myself a ticket), I'd given myself a 50-50 chance of beating the rap.

Still, even if he did give me a ticket, I was glad I'd spared those caterpillars. I know most people would say, "*Dude*, they're only caterpillars! Get a life." But that's precisely my point. They're only caterpillars. Nobody else is looking out for them, so somebody needs to. And while I was sure some of them wouldn't make it across today, I wanted to believe that a few made it to safety and would live to complete their metamorphosis.

And what a feat if they made it! To cross about 24 feet, or 288 inches, of death! Given how slowly they moved (certainly less than 1 in./sec.), it was a miracle any of them made it across any road.

Staring out the windshield, I saw another caterpillar crawl over the lip of the blacktop from the sandy shoulder and begin his long and dangerous trek. After a moment, he passed in front of my engine hood, so I couldn't see him. I sat up in my seat and peered over the hood, but I still couldn't see him. He had to be underneath the tire. The trooper returned and peered down into my window.

"Mr. Orcutt?"

"Sorry, officer. One of them just crawled in front of my car."

He handed back my paperwork.

"I'm not giving you a ticket," he said.

"Oh, thank you, officer. Thank you. I—"

He held up a hand.

"Your license was clean, and…well…I think you were honestly trying to avoid hitting those caterpillars. I've seen them myself and I try to avoid them when I can, so I respect what you're doing." He took a deep breath. "But…I wouldn't be doing my job if I didn't give you a warning. You need to refrain from weaving on the road, sir. Not only is it dangerous, but the next person that pulls you over probably won't be as understanding."

"Thank you, officer," I said. "And I want you to know that I'm going to make an effort to be less absentminded when I drive. The other day, back in Millbrook, I swerved onto the shoulder because my mind was elsewhere, and I almost drove onto the golf course, so I know I definitely need to work on this."

"Pull out first," he said. "I don't want another car hitting you."

He started back towards the cruiser when I called out the window, "Officer?"

"Yes, Mr. Orcutt?"

"One of the caterpillars went in front of my car while we were talking. Could you make sure it's not under the tires before I pull out?"

With a faint smile, he checked over his shoulder for traffic, then leaned over and peered under the car.

"You're good," he said. "He's right in the middle. Pull straight out and he'll be fine."

"Have a good one, officer," I said.

"You too, Mr. Orcutt."

As he dusted off his hands and strolled back to the car, I pulled slowly ahead. Then, in the rear-view, I noticed the cruiser also straddling the caterpillar as the trooper followed behind me.

At lunch with Dave King, I told him about the traffic stop and explained my theory: that in terms of manipulating people into doing your bidding, the male equivalent of the blonde bombshell was the absentminded professor.

"I came up with it on the way over here," I said. "I've always been absentminded, so now I'm making it pay."

He laughed. "You may be right about that."

"I'll be conducting experiments between now and our next lunch. I'll let you know what happens."

"Provided you don't forget," he said.

"Right."

Emboldened by my success with the state trooper, that evening I told Alexas of my plan.

"Getting out of that ticket told me something, Alexas."

"What's that?"

"Instead of getting upset when I lose something, or can't remember, I need to embrace it."

"Okay."

"*Okay?*" I frowned. "What does that mean?"

She shrugged. "I think it's cute. But I also think it's only going to interest you for a couple of days. After that, you'll get distracted by something else and you'll forget all about this and go back to being plain-old absentminded."

"You're saying that I'm too absentminded to sustain a plan that capitalizes on my being absentminded?"

"Yup, pretty much," she said.

"You're wrong. This is going to be my new thing."

She smiled. "Have fun."

Provoked into action by Alexas' skepticism, the next morning, when I left the house without my wallet, I decided to use what formerly would have been a nuisance as an opportunity to test my theory. I had just finished my breakfast at the diner. As Heather walked over and refilled my coffee, I made a show of looking for my wallet.

"Forgot your wallet, Chris?"

"Yeah, I'm sorry. Could I pay you later?"

"Sure."

When I finished my coffee, I crossed the street to the bank and went to a teller I recognized.

"Hi," I said.

"Good morning, sir. How can I help you?"

"I need some cash."

"Okay, do you have a check or a withdrawal slip?" she asked.

"Nope. Forgot 'em."

"Well, do you know your account number?"

"Nope, no idea."

"How about your driver's license?"

"No it's back home with my wallet," I said. "I can give you my address, how about that?"

"I'm not supposed to do this, but I *do* recognize you." She looked around and pushed a form toward me. "Okay, fill this out with everything you know, and I'll fill out the rest. How much will you be withdrawing?"

"Oh, I don't know…six, seven hundred maybe."

She winced. "Gosh, I'm not sure if—"

"I'll come back later with my license. Besides, where am I going? I walk by your window twice a day, every day. You could always grab me off the street if I was trying anything."

She smiled. "I suppose we could. All right."

So that was how I left the bank with $700 (of my own money, of course). I went across the street and paid Heather, but I never did go back to the bank and show them my license. What I was learning was, folks look out for the absentminded, like they do for toddlers and old people. To test my theory once more, later that afternoon I went to the library to pick up some books, purposely "forgetting" my library card at home.

"No problem, Chris," Ann said. "We know who you are."

"Thanks."

"Oh, dear. It says here you have a dollar fine. Would you like to pay that now?"

"That must have been on Columbus Day," I said. "I returned some books, but I forgot you were closed. I'm really sorry."

"Okay, we'll let it slide"—she winked—"this time."

That day, I started writing this piece about being absentminded. In the weeks to come, my continued experiments of making my absentmindedness "pay" became more and more outlandish. Yet all had the same result: people took pity on me and let me get away with stuff.

I crossed the Hudson River one afternoon on the Bear Mountain Bridge, claiming not to have cash for the toll, and although I offered to give the matronly tollbooth operator my name and address, she said brightly, "Don't worry about it, honey. Hope you find your wallet!" At Best Buy on a busy Saturday afternoon, I got a young salesman's attention in the camera battery section by walking along the row, looking between my camera and the batteries, and grimacing. There were at least eight other people waiting, but my obvious pained, confused expression attracted help first. Absentmindedness, I noticed, trumps anger and impatience every time. And for my *pièce de résistance*, I went to the post office one morning in my pajamas, robe and slippers.

When I was a boy, my maternal grandfather "Ab" would go to the Corner News Store on Sunday to pick up the papers, routinely wearing his slippers, and his white terrycloth bathrobe over a pair of paint-stained pants and a flannel shirt. He didn't do it to be eccentric or anything; this was his ensemble around the house, and, like his grandson, he could be a bit absentminded, often forgetting what he was wearing when he ventured off his property. When I got to the post office, people who knew me barely raised an eyebrow at my outfit.

"Just roll out of bed, Chris?" Mo asked from behind the counter.

"What?" I feigned surprise at my robe and slippers. "Oh, God, I can't believe—"

"Relax, what can I do you for?"

"I can't remember. I don't even know why I came down here."

"Well, you've got a package anyway. Wait a sec."

She disappeared in back and returned a minute later with a plastic bag that rattled.

"My medication," I said. "But not for this. Not for the forgetfulness, I mean."

"Whatever, Chris. None of my business. Now, go put some clothes on before you catch cold. Next!"

As I continued to document my newly embraced absentmindedness, I realized that I could continue in this vein of capitalizing on it *ad nauseam*, but to what end? And, as far as this piece was concerned, where was it going? How would I finish it?

For a long time I've been enamored of the Latin proverb *solvitur ambulando*: "It is solved by walking." To work out this problem, I went on one of my semi-legendary long walks, taking in the foliage on Altamont Road, through the tunnel of stately oaks and maples; past the horse farm where, in 1987, two guys I know once hid a stolen Pepsi machine; past the pastures with donkeys and the signs that read "Do Not Feed Donkeys—They Bite"; past Mary Tyler Moore's old house; down the rock cut for the old railroad; and finally, across the golf course, the old Bennett College grounds and the village green to Marona's. As I crossed the green, I started to remove my gloves.

What if I ended this piece this way? I have another one of my "grocery store wakeups" in Marona's and elicit the help of a girlfriend from high school whom I occasionally bumped into in the store. She helps me remember why I'm there—to get stuff for a special anniversary dinner. The ex-girlfriend helps me pick everything out, and she pays because I forgot my wallet. Or maybe she reminds me of what day it is—my anniversary—and I realize I haven't bought anything for Alexas, so she drives me to the mall where she advises me on a nice scarf or a piece of jewelry. Of course this would be entirely made up because—

"Excuse me," said a woman in front of Marona's, "did you drop a glove? We were inside"—she nodded at the store—"and Cille thought she saw you drop one."

I checked my pockets. Sure enough, one had fallen out. I turned around, and there it was: standing on its end with the fingers sticking into the air, like somebody had been buried alive and was clawing his way to the surface.

"Thank you so much," I said. "If it weren't for people like you, I wouldn't have gloves."

"No problem," she said and went back inside.

I retrieved it, making sure both gloves were now tucked securely in my coat pockets, and went in the store.

"Thanks, Cille," I said. "You know, I'm seriously considering getting some of those mitten clips that little kids have."

"Well," she said sagely, "if you lose your gloves a lot, they probably wouldn't hurt."

Now, why was I here? Right, lunch. I wanted tacos. We had everything necessary at home except the ground beef, so I bought a pound of it, along with some Marona's homemade sweet sausage for dinner. I paid (I *did* have my wallet) and walked home.

Back in the apartment, I threw off my coat and dropped the ground beef in a frying pan. I put the taco shells in the toaster oven, on low bake. Sliding them in, I noticed that the tops scraped the upper element, but I was certain that, like on regular stoves, when in bake mode that element wouldn't go on. Out of habit, to suck the cooking smells out of the apartment, I opened the window and turned on a fan sitting on the table.

It was going to take the beef a few minutes to start cooking, so I decided to go check my email. I'd left the computer on, in sleep mode, and when it came up

I launched my mail program only to discover nobody liked me. At least today they didn't. I glanced at Sweetie, asleep in her basket by the window. Seeing her reminded me that I needed to give her her antibiotic.

Recently she'd developed a minor infection on her posterior from these bizarre, dormant scent glands not draining, so I had to give her an eyedropper of liquid antibiotic twice a day. And right now was the ideal time to administer the medicine: with her asleep and then groggy when I roused her. I went out to the kitchen, got the vial from the refrigerator and shook it up. The beef was only beginning to sizzle, so I had time. Squeezing 1ml into the eyedropper, I crept back to the office with my hands clasped behind my back.

Dum-de-dum. Just strolling around the apartment, Sweetie. Nothing to worry about.

When I got in the room, the cat looked up at me sleepily from her basket. I approached her slowly, pet her head for a few seconds, then wrenched her head back firmly and gently, and jammed the eyedropper between her back teeth. Instantly her eyes widened to chasm-like proportions. Cats have this trick they pull on us humans: they exaggerate their eye expressions so we think they're in desperate pain, when in fact they're only mildly put out by the situation.

"I'm sorry, Sweetie," I said softly, "but it's for your own good. Papa has to do this."

Holding her head still with one hand, I squeezed the eyedropper. She squirmed and her mouth opened, but when I removed the dropper, I saw she had swallowed the medicine and was licking her chops.

"Good girl," I said. "You see, that wasn't so bad, was it? Papa hates to do it, Sweetie, but you can't fool around with antibiotics. Believe me, Papa knows."

Papa did know. Petting the cat's head, I thought back to the summer between high school and college, when my friend Carl Kropp and I did so-called landscaping for a very nice gay couple who paid us each $7.00 an hour (*good* money for a kid in 1988). That summer, I punched a guy in the mouth with a sweet left hook, taking most of his already rotten front teeth out, and developing an infection in my hand as a result. The problem was (besides the ensuing legal problems), I'd been given an antibiotic to take, and only a couple days after I started taking it, I went to my friend Jason's house for the weekend and forgot to bring the antibiotics. *Well...*by the end of the weekend, my left hand had swollen to the size of a catcher's mitt. It was a disturbing deep red. I was put in the hospital, where for ten days they pumped a powerful antibiotic cocktail through my veins. The masochistic surgeon, who would be performing the amputation if it came to that, drifted in each morning and stood at the foot of my bed like the Grim Reaper. He gave me one task: to soak my hand in iodine and continually probe the open wound in my knuckle with a long, wooden Q-Tip saturated with the fiery antiseptic.

"Really dig it in there," the doctor ordered. "It's got to hurt, son. You look like you work out. Well, young man, this is truly a case of 'No pain, no gain'!"

So I did as ordered, every couple of hours, while watching Bob Ross painting shows, and every night I went to sleep worrying that the surgeon would waltz in the next morning, examine me, and tell me my hand would have to come off. Day by day, I watched the line of redness creep imperceptibly up my wrist, until it seemed to hit a high-water mark. In the meantime I speculated on whether, if my hand were amputated, I would still be attractive to girls. Maybe girls would enjoy the novelty of sleeping with a one-handed guy. Maybe they'd give me a nickname: One-Hand Chris, Stumpy, or, The Handyman. Missing a hand would certainly be a conversation-starter with them, that's for sure. And at least it was my left hand, not my right, so I wouldn't have to re-learn how to write.

All of which is why I was overjoyed the morning the surgeon came in, fingered his mustache, and said, "Well, it looks like you'll get to keep your hand." Maybe I'm misremembering it, but I could swear I detected a soupçon of disappointment in his voice.

"I've got to be honest with you," the doctor continued, "I thought it was too far gone. But it appears all that probing you did with the iodine solution paid off. But remember"—he gripped my arm and shook me violently—"from now on, if you have an antibiotic, take it every time, and take *all* of it! Okay?!"

I nodded vigorously. Back in the present, I pet the cat again.

"So you see, Sweetie," I said, "that's why you have to take the medicine."

She blinked at me. I kissed her head and smelled smoke.

Damn...the tacos!

The apartment was full of smoke as I ran out to the kitchen. The smoke alarm hadn't gone off because, after so many false alarms, I'd removed it months ago.

In the kitchen, I took the pan with the beef off the stove and shut off the burner, and that's when I noticed that it wasn't the *beef* that was burning; it was the taco shells. They were in flames inside the toaster oven. I looked under the sink for the fire extinguisher and didn't see it. Without thinking, I went to the toaster oven, opened the door and blew on the shells as you would birthday candles for an octogenarian. The flames on the now-blackened shells flickered out for a split second, then ignited again. And now, because the toaster door was open and I had blown in oxygen, the flames were monstrous and malevolent, curling out of the top. If I didn't do something, in about three seconds the entire kitchen and maybe the house would go up.

In the half-second or so that I stared at the burning toaster oven, a remarkably long string of thoughts flashed through my mind: our renter's insurance, how much it covered in damage, and whether I'd remembered to send in the latest premium; the time Ab had caught his bathrobe sleeve on fire and I pulled the robe off him; the time my sister Mandy had been making French fries and caught the kitchen on fire, the fire department was called, and I ran into the burning kitchen to rescue our cat; my frequent admonitions to Alexas never to leave a kitchen when the stove was on; and how similar this rapid but crystal-clear string of thoughts was to people's descriptions of their entire lives passing before their eyes when they were dying. All of this went through my mind in less than a second, along with the thought of, "You dumbass…*do* something!"

Grabbing the toaster oven by its sides, I yanked it off the counter so the plug came out of the wall socket. Now it was unplugged, but I was holding, at arm's length, a flaming cauldron. I glanced at the open window. I could throw the entire oven out on the back lawn, and I was about to do so when I remembered there was a pile of dry leaves down there. My next thought was, "*WATER, MORON!*" Dumping the toaster oven in the sink, I shook out the burning shells and sprayed them with the sink nozzle. When the flames were completely out, I was left with a pile of taco shell cinders and a smoke-filled apartment.

I put the extinguished toaster oven on a cutting board and placed it next to the window with the fan to suck the smoke out, then opened the bedroom window across the apartment and set up another fan blowing into the kitchen to create a draw.

A bit shaken, I glanced in the refrigerator, hoping there was a bottle of wine or beer in there. Finding nothing, I went downstairs and sat on the front porch steps. I was waiting for the smoke to clear out upstairs and for my heart to stop racing.

Once I could breathe again, I realized that, by my foolish attempts to capitalize on my absentmindedness, I'd tempted fate. This tendency toward absentmindedness was dangerous, and I'd been wrong to try and benefit from it. From now on, I resolved to be more mindful.

That is, right after I called Alexas to tell her what had happened, and to ask her what day of the week it was.

5

THE REDHEAD IN THE EMERALD SLICKER

To me, she would always be *the* redhead.
For a few brief weeks in 1994, I loved redhead Anne Bernay, and she loved me. She loved me and believed in me as a writer.

It was May, and I had no idea what I was doing with my life. All I knew was that I wanted to write. Since graduating from college in Boston two years earlier, I'd been working in Upstate New York as a reporter for a weekly newspaper. Then—very briefly—a waiter, a substitute teacher, and a Radio Shack salesman. Then a reporter for a daily newspaper.

A few months earlier, my musician friend Tony Scotto and I had decided to move to Boston. Our brilliant plan amounted to this: he would get a day job that enabled him to gig at night; I would wait tables and write stories while applying for reporting jobs at *The Boston Globe* and *The Herald*.

Like many plans made by two 24-year-old artists, ours disintegrated soon after we arrived. Tony and I had a temporary falling-out, and I was forced to find another place to live. Luckily, another friend, Jason Scott

Sadofsky, came to my rescue by inviting me to share his studio apartment in Cambridge.

Besides waiting tables 4–5 days and/or nights a week, I was writing short stories every day. Since the studio (366 Harvard Street) was so tiny, and since Jason's snoring rivaled the sawmill that Hemingway lived above in Paris for a while, each morning I had to leave to get the quiet I needed to write. I walked down to Harvard Square to the Au Bon Pain café and set up among the chess players, the students, and the homeless newspaper hawkers. And there, I wrote.

(Right about now, you're probably asking, "What does all of this have to do with Anne Bernay? Who is she?" Well, as Polonius says to Queen Gertrude in my favorite play, *Hamlet*, "Stay awhile…I will be faithful.")

I wrote every morning inside the snug café, or outside if the weather was nice, from 7:00 until 11:00 a.m. Afterwards, on days when I wasn't waiting tables, I was free to do whatever I wanted. I went to the Boston Public Library and checked out books. I went to lunch with former professors. And a couple of times I put on my suit, sat in the lobby of the Copley Plaza Hotel, and eye-flirted with the beautiful rich women, nurturing fantasies of becoming a kept man to finance my writing.

Now, about my day job, waiting tables. I was a terrible waiter. I mean the worst. I tried, believe me, but the job required skills I simply didn't have. Like multitasking. When given more than three tables, I would panic. Thankfully, the female waitstaff all liked or pitied me, and they frequently helped me out. One of them, Helen—a pretty and ambitious girl from Ireland—said to me in her enchanting lilt, "Oh, Christopher Clyde…don'tcha know you can never work in service? Always thinkin' about somethin' else 'yuh are!" And she was right. Often during a shift, I would go in the walk-in refrigerator to write in my pocket notebook, completely ignoring my customers.

Still, even with the help of my fellow waitstaff, the pressure got to me, and it came to a head the day after the Boston Marathon. I'd been working double shifts for ten days straight, with zero time to write, and I was scheduled for another double that day. I told the assistant manager that I needed a break.

She refused. We argued. I quit.

And when I walked out of there with my meager tips for the day, I met a homeless man and took him to dinner.

With my afternoons and evenings now free as well, after my morning writing sessions at Au Bon Pain I began taking longer and longer excursions around Boston. My adventures ranged from stumbling into an outdoor photo shoot for a New England Patriots Cheerleaders calendar, to watching a street fight (more of a bare-knuckle brawl) on a South Boston sidewalk, to attending a philosophy lecture at Harvard by the brilliant Robert Nozick, to going to a Red Sox–Oakland A's baseball game in which I saw the "Bash Brothers" hit back-to-back homeruns over the Green Monster, to hitchhiking to Hyannis and being taken to lunch by the woman who picked me up. At the end of each day, I made my way to a different bar around the city and wrote in my notebook about my adventures.

And it was at one of those bars, on May 10, 1994, that I met Anne Bernay.

At rush hour that evening I saw a covey of attractive, laughing young women flocking into Bertucci's, a brick oven pizzeria near Faneuil Hall. The women's shoes echoed on the cobblestones, and when I got a whiff of their perfume in the salty air from the harbor, I followed them inside.

I sat at the bar jotting down my day's observations: anything unusual that had happened or that I'd seen, heard or smelled. It was practice in the art of observation. I sat drinking 20-ounce drafts of Sam Adams Boston Ale and tried to recapture any moments that had struck me in some way. One was from a few nights earlier, when I'd been walking back to Cambridge:

> Saw a couple eating dinner on the MIT bridge tonight. He wore a tux and she an evening gown, and they had a complete dining table set up on the sidewalk with a light blue tablecloth, silverware, candle in a hurricane lamp, and cobalt blue place settings.

When I finished with my observations exercise, I ordered another beer. Down the bar, three women my age were smoking, and a miasma of cigarette smoke hung in the air around them. For some reason, the smoke cloud triggered a memory of my first job, at 14, as a busboy and dishwasher in an Italian restaurant and pizzeria.

Turning back to my notebook, I drifted into the memory, smiling at surprising details like how, late every Thursday afternoon, the owner, Sonny, would clean out the register, bundle up the cash in a paper bag, and host a dozen dark-suited men in a closed dining room that evening. The restaurant was right off the Taconic Parkway, about 80 miles north of New York City. Having seen *The Godfather* a few times, even at age fourteen I had imagination enough to know the dark-suited men were mobsters paying Sonny "a visit."

Three pages into the story, I ordered another beer and looked around. The smokers were gone. In their place was a woman with creamy skin, pale blue eyes, and heart-stopping red hair. She wore an emerald slicker, which I only mention because it perfectly complemented that hair: full, thick, and with loose curls that grazed her shoulders, forming little cursive J's, O's and S's. Here was the quintessential redhead. My breathing faltered, but I covered for my nervousness by drinking half my beer.

A piña colada sat on a napkin in front of her. She was staring at the glass, twirling the stem in her fingertips. I went back to writing and put down two more sentences and half of another when I noticed her watching me. She must have known that I was on to her because she quickly turned back to her drink, making her curls jiggle.

Then she took a sip of the piña colada, swallowed hard, and said, "So…what are you writing?" I closed my notebook, stopping in mid-sentence (to this day, that entry remains unfinished).

"I was remembering my first job," I said. "As a dishwasher in a Mob restaurant."

She giggled. "Well, that explains it."

"Explains what?"

"Why you were so intense about it. What else do you write?"

I gave her my spiel, and in retrospect I probably laid it on a bit thick. I talked about being a "former" newspaper reporter (I'd left the paper only two months earlier), and mentioned a magazine piece I had coming out soon about a champion tennis player's experiences at Wimbledon. All the while, she looked unblinkingly at me with those pale blue eyes and shook her head as though in a daze.

"Wow," she said when I finished, "you've got a lot of guts. Do you do other work to earn a living?"

"Like a day job?" I said.

"Yes."

"I did, but I quit it. Long story."

She peered down at her drink. "I wish I were a writer."

"Ah, you wish you *were*," I said. "The subjunctive mood. Nice."

"I majored in English," she said, arching her eyebrows.

"Where?"

She told me, adding, "I wrote some stuff for the magazine, too, but I haven't done anything since."

"It's never too late," I said. "What do you do now?"

"I'm a proofreader in a law firm." She looked down at her drink again.

"Hey," I said, "at least you *have* a job."

"*You* have a job," she said. "You're a writer."

I wanted to leap out of my stool, take this woman in my arms and kiss her, but I thought that might be a bit much. Instead I grabbed my things, including my beer, and moved down to the stool beside hers. I gestured to the bartender for two more drinks and put a twenty on the bar to cover them.

"You didn't have to do that," she said.

"How else am I going to have my way with you, if I don't ply you with alcohol?"

She giggled, crinkling up her nose. "You're cute."

"You think I'm kidding," I said. "Can't you tell I'm one of those guys that needs to get girls drunk first?"

"I seriously doubt that."

"Chris Orcutt," I said.

"Anne Bernay."

We shook hands, and I raised my beer. Her eyes widened.

"A toast?" she said. "To what?"

"To beautiful Boston redheads in shiny emerald coats."

She smiled and clinked my glass with hers. She wasn't wearing a wedding ring.

"So, Chris," she said, "why are you here all alone?"

"Do you want the long version or the short version?"

"Well, if it were any other guy, I'd want the short version, but I like listening to you."

"Good," I said with a wink, "I'll give you the epic version."

Now…I could tell you about how that evening, after meeting at the bar, Anne took me to dinner at a Tex-Mex restaurant in Cambridge, and how we walked to the quad at Radcliffe College, sat on a bench and held hands. The air was warm and the lawn was lush, and several old maples in the courtyard stirred in the shadowy breeze.

I could tell you how we met in Harvard Square a few days later, how she picked me up in her Volkswagen Cabriolet with the top down, and we played tennis at the courts over at the business school, and it began to rain. We kissed in the rain, remembered we'd left the top down and ran back to the car.

I could tell you how we went to dinner in the North End, and how the old Italian couple that owned the restaurant thought we were married and gave us a table in the brick courtyard outside and brought us a complimentary bottle of Chianti. I could tell you how Anne and I painted a picture of a life together, and how we took walks in the Public Garden, and how I met her for lunch a couple times outside the law firm where she worked. I could tell you how she was with a man she didn't love, and how in a few short weeks we fell for each other. I could tell you about all of those things, but I won't. Not here. Not now.

What I want to tell you about are the things Anne said to me—words that have sustained me while writing in relative obscurity for over 20 years. She truly was an angel, and she came along when I most needed one.

During our dinner in the Italian restaurant, I told her about my new day job as a parking valet, remarking that it was pathetic compared to her boyfriend's work as a lawyer. But instead of scoffing at or belittling my new job, she said something I've never forgotten.

"Chris," she said, "don't let those little shit jobs get you down. You're above all that crap. You're a *writer*. Just think of those jobs as experience for your writing."

After our dinner in the North End, Anne's life was hell. She and her boyfriend had a big blowout, during which she considered moving out and getting her own apartment. I tried hard to convince her to do it. At some point during this escapade, she came by Jason's place and read through some of my writing. I walked around the neighborhood while she read. When I returned, she put down the pages slowly and turned to me with a smile—a smile that I still remember because it was tinged with awe—and said, "Chris, whatever you do, just keep writing."

Looking back on it now, there was finality in that statement. I think she had made up her mind about the kind of life she wanted, and while she admired me and my willingness to live as an artist, I think she knew that she didn't have it in her to make the necessary sacrifices.

She asked to borrow some of my pages to show her college friends, and the reverence with which she asked and slid them into her bag told me I didn't need to worry about them. Besides, I wanted her to take them. I wanted to guarantee that I saw her at least one last time.

A few days later, we met in the Public Garden. The ducks were out, as were the swan boats, and the flowers were in bloom. We walked together holding hands, but as soon as someone approached us on the path, she let go of me because she was worried about bumping into people she knew.

And once again, Anne said something that has stayed with me, kept me going all these years:

"I told my friends I met a writer," she said. "They asked me if he was the real deal. And I said, 'Yeah, he is. He really is.' "

6

A Sorry Mendicant

I believe it was the novelist Virginia Woolf who once said that a blocked writer, or one searching for ideas, is "a sorry mendicant who goes begging through the hours."[18] Whoever said it, I agree with the sentiment. Writer's block is not pretty.

Robert B. Parker, late author of the Spenser, PI novels, once said in an interview that he didn't think writer's block existed. He thought it was laziness. And while that might be true of some writers—that they aren't really blocked; they simply don't want to work—such has never been the case with me.

When I'm blocked it's because of fear: fear that what I write won't be good enough. I've learned that writer's block is likely to take hold over me whenever I forget that writing is a *process* of creation and revision, and that almost never is the first version of what I want to say the best it can be.

---

18 When I was fact-checking this book, I couldn't find the source of this quote. It's possible that a writer other than Virginia Woolf said it, or I might have dreamt it, or I might have said it myself and then doubted I could have ever uttered something so wise about writing, and therefore incorrectly attributed it to Mrs. Woolf.

I can't speak for all blocked writers, but when I'm blocked, I seek out conflict with people and institutions, and I channel my creative tension into distractions, raising my procrastination from writing to a rarified art form. Over the past 25 years as a writer, I have manifested my writer's block in countless ways. I have taken day-long, meandering car rides, and, if another driver's driving has annoyed me, I have followed that person for hours, across state lines in some cases. I have researched pencils, going so far as to investigate what became of the lead formulas of superior brands that no longer exist. I have visited my library's used book sale and stolen back books that I donated because they didn't put the books in their collection like I asked them to. I have also stolen copies of my *own* books from library used book sales, when I've discovered they were copies I inscribed to specific readers, and the readers hadn't valued them. I have started national campaigns to boycott candy bar companies when they changed their packaging from traditional paper and foil to Mylar. I have written rants on social media websites, about politics or American history or English grammar, or sometimes about social media itself. I have written letters to the editors of daily newspapers, or pretended to be a college student and written satirical pieces for college newspapers. I have savored afternoons drinking beer in bars with names like "Hurricane" and "Ice House," flirting with attractive female bartenders, watching soccer (which I loathe) and correcting the grammar of men who speak rudely to the waitresses. I have feuded with a local thrift store because they refused to exchange a $3 denim shirt I'd bought that didn't fit me. I have called the office of Connecticut Senator Lieberman and argued with his underlings about his policies, even though I am not now, nor have I ever been, a resident of Connecticut. I have invented an alter ego, Dakota Perez, and persuaded small-town journalists to write articles about "my" exploits.[19]

The German Christian theologian and philosopher Meister Eckhart said that God gives to each one of us what is best for him. I believe this is why God has not given me a silver Aston Martin V12 Vanquish, nor a bourbon-drinking 25-year-old mistress in the form of "red-headed, deep-breasted, slender and indolent" Clarissa from John Cheever's story "The Chaste Clarissa." God knows that neither the Aston Martin's 568 horsepower, nor the deep-breasted redhead reclining languorously in the passenger seat with a bottle of Maker's Mark Kentucky Straight Bourbon in her lap would be best for me. Not at all. And if I had writer's block at the same time? Forget about it. I wouldn't self-destruct; I would spontaneously combust.

There are three types of people that others should never mess with. The first group—violent, recidivistic felons—is self-evident. Then there are old people. Old people, seeing their mortality out in front of them like a highway rest stop on the next hill, tend not to mince words. In fact, they often tacitly express an attitude of *"Yeah, well, I may be going down, but I'm taking a few of you sonzabitches with me!"* Of course not all old-timers have this attitude, but some do, and you know which ones they are. They're the crotchety old douchebags,

---

19 For an example of one of these articles, check out the webpage for this book on my website.

the sour-faced curmudgeons, and they're mean because they're running out of time.

Finally there are the blocked writers, who have the opposite problem as the old folks. Blocked writers, and all artists to some extent, have *too much* time, that's our problem, which is why civilians should never mess with one of us who is blocked. We're in pain because we can't do what we want to be doing, yet we still feel the desire, the tension. It's like a teenage guy getting the chance to bed his generation's premier sex symbol, and at the moment of truth a *crane* couldn't get his equipment to rise to the occasion. It's torture, and we have to take our pain out on somebody. Why not the propane company? Or the cable company? Or the people who make your bank checks, because after a month of sitting in a drawer unused, you notice that the design you chose, "Antique," sucks.

So, box in hand, you put on your coat and walk down to the Bank of Millbrook, a sturdy brick building that looks like what a bank should look like—a lesser palace of the Medici. They'd recently installed Palladian-style windows, which lent the building a reassuring air of cachet and prosperity.

I went inside, winked at the tellers, and shambled back to the customer service office, where Jacqueline ("Jackeh-LEAN") smiled and ushered me into her glass cubicle.

"So, Chris, what can we do for you today?"

"Well, I got these checks." I put them on her desk. "And I don't like them."

She picked them up and appraised the top check in the light from the window.

"I see what you mean," she said. "They're very plain, aren't they?"

"Yeah," I said. "They're called 'Antique.' More like *'Boring.'*"

She chuckled. "Well, let's order you some new ones, shall we?"

She pulled a couple of well-worn laminated sheets from a drawer. "Now, do you want to stick with 'Checks for Less,' or would you like to step up to the 'Deluxe' ones?"

"I want the yellow ones like my grandparents used to give me," I said. "If I remember correctly, in the right light, they shone like gold."

"That's sweet," she said.

"I'm not kidding. The yellow ones. I want them."

"I believe they're Deluxe."

"Okay."

"They're going to be more expensive."

"What, five bucks more?" I said.

"Eighteen."

"Total?"

"No, eighteen more," she said. "Twenty-six total."

"Twenty-six dollars for *checks*?"

"I know, it's a lot."

"Are these special checks? Like a lot of research and development went into making them?"

"I don't believe so."

I considered this. Could I really afford to waste $26 on pieces of paper that served no purpose except as a way of parting me from my money? Not really.

But I wanted those yellow checks.

"I've got to look at these for a long time," I said. "Let's go with the yellow ones."

"Super!"

She pulled the "Deluxe" catalog off a shelf behind her. The pages, I noticed, weren't nearly as well-worn as the old "Checks for Less" laminates. Jacqueline opened the catalog, and for the next ten minutes, we leafed through while I commented on each design.

"Who gets the animal ones?" I asked. "Zookeepers?"

"You'd be surprised," Jacqueline said. "A lot of people get the horse ones, especially around here. Cats and dogs, too," she added brightly. "Do you have a cat or dog?"

"A cat," I said. "But she's a bitchy little bore. I don't want to look at her on a *check*."

"Okay." She flipped the page.

"Hold it," I said.

Right in the center of the next check was a 12-point whitetail deer.

"Who gets these?" I asked. "Deer lovers?"

She looked around and whispered to me. "Hunters."

"You'd have to *really* love hunting," I said.

"So, no?"

"No."

She flipped the page to the Looney Tunes™ collection.

"And who buys these," I asked, "cartoonists?"

"You'd be surprised. A lot of people your age."

"I did love Bugs," I admitted. "And Yosemite Sam. 'My biscuits is burnin'!' "

"Wow, good impression," she said. "You sound just like him."

"We all have our gifts," I said. "I do an even better Kermit the Frog."

"Really? My daughter loves Kermit."

The way she said it, I think she was hoping I'd launch into my Kermit impression, but I didn't feel like it. Always leave them wanting more. We flipped through the rest of the checks, and I shook my head at each one. When she reached the end of the book, she closed it and said, "So…what do you think?"

"Nah," I said. "Let's go with the cheap ones. In blue this time."

"Very well."

She carefully returned the "Deluxe" catalog to the shelf behind her and grabbed the "Checks for Less" laminates. Instead of being in a classy catalog, they were in grubby, dog-eared laminates held together by a single binder ring. She placed them on the desk in front of me and pointed at a bunch of graphic icons, grouped into categories: Careers, Hobbies, Sports, and Transportation.

"How about a little logo on your checks?" she asked. "Make them a little prettier."

"You think so?" I said. "I think they're going to make them look a little dorkier."

She plowed ahead. The woman was determined to put a logo on my checks.

"What about your profession?" she asked. "You're a novelist, right?"

"Yes," I said. "Do you have a typewriter?"

She consulted the pages. "No, there doesn't seem to be one."

"How about a pencil?" I asked.

"No, that's not on here either. How about a computer? Would that work?"

"No thanks. Can I take a look?"

"Certainly."

I scanned the pages intensely, but nothing appealed to me. The fact was, I didn't want to see any of these blocky figurines and Lego-like vehicles on a regular basis. In fact, after only a minute of this, my interest was rapidly waning. Sure, the little people on bicycles, the ones running and swimming, all looked like they were having a great time, but were they *really*? Or were they just ink slaves, condemned like Sisyphus to the same activity, check after check, year after year? My new checks would start at #2200. How long would it be before the little man and woman hiking got sick of each other, and one pushed the other off a cliff? Two hundred checks later? Five hundred? Maybe they'd been having trouble in their relationship long *before* check 2200, and one would murder the other by 2250. You never know.

The simple fact was, I wasn't obsessed enough with anything—at least not with subjects that appeared on checks—to have images printed on a two-year supply. Now, if they had a collection called, say, "Great Battles and Generals of WWII," that would be another matter altogether. Patton atop a Sherman tank, surveying the battlefield with his enormous field glasses. D-Day. The Eagle's Nest. The Enigma machine. Tiger tanks, V-2 rockets, MG-42s, with facts and figures about each weapon. Every person who touched the check would learn something about WWII, and it would keep the vets' heroism and sacrifices alive.

There were only three other subjects that interested me enough to see them printed on checks. One, film noir. Have famous stills from the best noir films printed in the corner of each check (use a different movie for each check, and only allow movies to repeat once per book), with witty dialogue from the film underneath. And if "Checks for Less" needed to bring in somebody as a consultant, I'd do it, and I'd only want a lifetime supply of checks for my services. I'd give them great scenes and lines like Barbara Stanwyck and Fred MacMurray in *Double Indemnity*, when they meet secretly in the grocery store, Stanwyck wearing sunglasses when she says (over the canned peas), *"No one's pulling out, Walter. It's straight down the line for both of us, just like we planned."*

My second obsession, which I would also enjoy having on my checks, is typewriters: different models of typewriters on the checks, with factoids about each model. But checks that I'd really look forward to using would have my ultimate obsession printed on them—redheads. Redheads going back 40–50 years were fine. Classic redheaded sex kittens like Ann-Margret, Claudia Cardinale, Luciana Paluzzi, and Jill St. John, as well as 21st century hotties like Leanna Decker, Isla Fisher, and *Sports Illustrated* swimsuit model Cintia Dicker.

"Chris?" Jacqueline said.

"Yes?"

"Do you want a logo on the checks?"

"No, Jacqueline. Plain blue is fine."

"Duplicates?"

"Yes, duplicates."

It was after Alexas got home and I'd given her a recap of my argument with the propane company. She was in the shower when she called out, "I've got it!"

I ran into the bathroom, which, given the size of our apartment at the time, took all of two seconds.

"Got what?" I said.

"I think I know why the propane is getting used up so fast," she said.

"Why?"

"Well, it's been really cold for the past couple of weeks, right?"

"Yeah."

"Maybe the hot water heater has had to burn more propane to stay up to temp or keep from freezing, you know?"

"Makes sense," I said. "I don't know what else would explain it, but then again I don't know anything about heat dynamics."

"What did the delivery guy say?"

"I don't think he's an expert in heat dynamics either, dear."

"I know that, silly," she said. "What happened when he showed up?"

"I stuck my head out the back window when he was filling the tank, that's what happened," I said. "I think it freaked him out. I mean, because we're on the top floor and suddenly this guy with uncombed hair is hanging out the window above you, questioning what you're doing."

"I can imagine." She peeked out of the opaque blue polyester curtain. "You probably looked like Beethoven."

"God, I hope so," I said. "Anyway, I'm like, 'But you guys were *just* here.' And he says, 'You were down to thirty percent, sir. She took another twenty-five point-one gallons.' Seriously—'*she* took,' like the tank's a Navy vessel. And the jerk actually said, '*Point-one*,' can you believe it?"

"I believe it. Then what happened?"

I took a pair of tweezers out of the medicine cabinet and proceeded to pluck the cricket hairs off my earlobes. I call the minuscule, stiff black hairs "cricket hairs" because if the ridges of my finger brush against them, they make an annoying "zzzt-zzzt" sound in my ears like a cricket.

"Nothing happened," I said, plucking a hair. "I told him to go ahead and fill it, and then I called the company and got a girl on the line. I must say, she was *incredibly* knowledgeable about propane. She's giving me all this stuff about how the computer estimates our usage and crap like that, and I finally say, 'Look, doll, it's been less than a *month*.'"

"You didn't really call her 'doll,' did you?"

"You're damn right I did—like a film noir antihero." I plucked another hair and put the tweezers back in the cabinet. "She didn't say anything, so I don't think she cared. Meanwhile, 'You guys were just here' is even better. Like they're this band of renegade propane tank-fillers who top off tanks unnecessarily, then hustle back to the hideout, cigars clenched in their teeth like Hannibal on *The A-Team*, and go, 'All right, who's next?'"

"You're so *weird*," she said from behind the curtain. "But back to the water heater. I'm not sure, but I think if we get one of those blanket thingies, it'll reduce our consumption."

"Dammit, now I've got to worry about the water heater being cold? It's all alone down there, dark and cold and—"

"*Stop* anthropomorphizing the water heater," she said. "It's fine."

"All right," I said. "So you think this blanket will work?"

"It should."

"Let's do it then. Right now! Is Home Depot still open?"

"It's eleven o'clock, sweetie," she said, "and they're 20 miles away."

"There's got to be *some* place we can get a blanket for a hot water heater tonight."

"It's time for bed."

"What if we wrap it in a sleeping bag," I said, "or a couple of old blankets, and secure it with duct tape?"

"It's late, sweetie. Besides, I think these things have to be fire retardant or inflammable or something."

"Inflammable means the same thing as flammable, but that's whole other thing," I said. "Okay, it's too late tonight, but we're doing this. I *hate* these propane bastards. *'Lah-dee-dah, we'll come every twenty-six days, every three if we feel like it.'* "

The water in the shower shut off, and the curtain opened. Alexas stepped out with a towel around her torso.

"Shhh," she said. "Chrissy?"

"Yeah?"

"You're having arguments in your head again. Nothing's wrong. Nobody is fighting with you."

"You're right," I said.

"We'll get a blanket for the hot water heater, and everything will be fine."

"Okay. Thanks, sweet."

"Talking you off the ledge," she said. "It's what I do."

"Operation Qwerty" began with a phone call Friday, mid-morning. During the five minutes that my anti-communications defenses were down (I'd forgotten to take the landline off the hook), the painter who lived across the street, Dwight Anderson, called me.

"Hey," I said. "What's up?"

"I was out on my morning constitutional," he said, "and as I happened by little Uncle Al's,[20] I spied a portable typewriter case on the porch. Knowing how much you appreciate them, I stopped to take a look."

"What brand is it?"

"I didn't notice."

"Did you open it up and test it?" I asked.

"Yes."

"How's the action on that keyboard?"

"It seems excellent," Dwight said. "But I'm hardly an expert on the machines, the way you are."

"But it has all of its keys," I said.

"Of course."

---

20 The thrift store in the Village of Millbrook that I'd been feuding with for a year.

"Well, I ask because a lot of older ones are missing a key or two. What brand is it? Underwood? Remington? Smith-Corona? Olivetti?"

"I didn't notice," Dwight said. "It was very clean and sleek and really quite lovely. You should get down there and grab it before some other collector does."

"I don't know, Dwight," I said. "If I bring another typewriter into this apartment, Alexas might divorce me."

"Hmm…yes, I see," he said. "It would put you in a bit of a fix, wouldn't it?"

"Yeah."

"Well, it's down there, and people really aren't supposed to leave donations on the porch, especially since they don't reopen until the middle of January sometime and—"

"Wait a second," I said. "You mean they're not even *open*? This typewriter is sitting outside?"

"Exactly. The person who left it there *clearly* didn't value it, and I know the ladies at the store aren't going to know what to do with it anyway, so *you* should go rescue it."

"You mean steal it. That's larceny you're talking about, my friend."

"Look, it's going to *rust* out there, right?" he said. "They don't open for another two weeks. Besides, if anybody questioned you about it, you could tell them you didn't want to see such a nice typewriter go to pot."

"How big is it?" I asked.

"Oh…about the size of bread box."

"I don't have a bread box, Dwight. You know our toaster oven? Is it about that size?"

"Yes, that sounds about right," he said. "It's all enclosed in a dapper little case with its own handle. Really quite stylish. I would have picked it up for myself, but I already have one. Look, I have a client coming in a few minutes, so I have to ring off. *Ciao!*"

He hung up. I stood frozen with the receiver still in my hand and gazed across the office at a photo of John Cheever sitting somberly in front of a typewriter. He didn't have any answers for me. I hung up the phone.

This didn't feel right. This was exactly the kind of seemingly innocuous situation that leads straight to a jail cell.

Stealing a used typewriter from the porch of a thrift store.
In broad daylight.
What good could come of this?

Ah, but you see, it's precisely this kind of risky, stupid activity—the manufactured drama, the false mission, the impromptu caper—that appeals to the blocked writer. He cries out for the adrenaline rush, the creative defibrillator. And the looming possibility that he might get caught, combined with the addictive thrill of getting away with a victimless crime, compels him to do it.

Hell, the blocked writer isn't doing anything important now anyway. In my case, I was in the middle of writing a speech for an executive of Pepsi Bottling Group (not even a company that produced *sugar* water; they produced High Fructose Corn Syrup water). Because this kind of writing required zero creativity on my part, I never got blocked writing it; there was no end to the poetry I could shape from all of that stultifying corporate-ese. Anyway, it wasn't as if I had anything *better* going on, so I threw on my overcoat (a thrift store one, ironically), grabbed my L.L. Bean tote bag and went out the door. The snow banks were high on either side of the sidewalk. I swung the tote bag in my hand and thought about the new typewriter.

Maybe <u>this</u> typewriter will be the golden key to unlock your writing, to keep you from ever being blocked again.

Halfway down the street I remarked to myself that I'd never been a very good thief. A horrible one, in fact—having been busted *twice* for shoplifting before the age of 16. *Why was I doing this then?* I think I wanted to get caught. Being arrested, fingerprinted, questioned…at least then I'd have something to write about.

I passed Rocky's Pizza and rounded the corner onto Front Street. Just then, a state trooper whisked by, the studs on its snow tires scratching the pavement. I rolled my eyes to God. *Come on, seriously?* Was this a sign that I should abandon my plan? Maybe. Fueled by writer's block, however, and bent on self-destruction, I marched on to Uncle Al's.

It was -5°F that January morning, and every time I breathed in through my nose, I could feel the hairs in my nostrils freezing up. The cold and some spitting snow explained why the street was desolate, but when I got to Uncle Al's and went up the porch steps, in my periphery I noticed a Land Rover. It was backed into a parking spot across the street with its engine running. Someone was inside. If I took the typewriter now, I'd be in plain view of whoever was in the vehicle. I'd have to wait.

In the meantime, I opened the case and looked over the machine. It was an Olympia SM-5 or 6, with decent chrome, but several of the keys stuck. Still, it was worth rescuing. I closed the case, hopped down the stairs and walked the 50 feet to Marona's. The occupant of the Land Rover, an older woman in a powder blue down jacket, followed me.

To erase any suspicions she might have about me, I held the door open for Land Rover Lady, complimented her pretty jacket, and once inside stood dumbly in the checkout area. Standing here for a moment was part of my plan. I wanted to come up with an excuse to leave that wouldn't arouse the suspicions of Land Rover Lady, who had observed me earlier coveting the Olympia.

What if she left here, I thought, *and decided to check Uncle Al's porch and found the typewriter missing? What if she was the one who had donated it? The woman would probably be able to give a good description of you. Relax*, I told myself, *you give people way too much credit for their observation skills.*

The checkers, Cille and Caroline, looked up from their registers.

"Hi, Chris!"

"Good morning, ladies."

Since it was Friday, the rich trophy wives were up from Manhattan, playing country mice. One of them—a 30-something woman, tan and trim, with the legs of a thoroughbred filly—smiled intriguingly at me. Winter, spring, summer or fall, I had only ever seen her in Marona's in a short white tennis skirt. I smiled back at her.

"You all look lovely today," I said.

"Stayin' out of trouble?" Cille said.

I narrowed my eyes at Tennis Lady. Still smiling at me, she picked an invisible piece of lint off the pleat of her skirt. I took a breath through my teeth.

"Trying to," I said.

"You okay, Chris?" Cille asked.

I patted my coat pockets. "Sorry. Forgot my wallet."

"Happens to you a lot," she said.

"Yeah," I said. "Be back in a bit."

I left and walked briskly back to Uncle Al's, noticing for the first time that the building's other tenant, with a window looking out on the porch no less, was a small law office. The blinds were up and the lights were on inside. The idea of stealing the typewriter in plain sight of lawyers made me nervous. *However,* I mused, *if a cop happened by and caught you in the act, proximity to the law office would make retaining counsel a lot easier.*

I bounded onto the porch in two quick steps, snatched the typewriter by the handle and returned to the sidewalk. In three seconds, I had gone from innocent to guilty of petty larceny. Now I tried to slip the case in my tote bag as I walked, but it was a tight fit and I had to stop walking long enough to shove it in. Even then, its rounded silver case peeked out of the top. All I could hope was that the person who had donated the typewriter was long gone, and that I could cover the 100 yards to my house before the trooper made his second pass through the village.

Even though I sensed that this particular typewriter wasn't going to remain in my collection, that the most it could hope for was the typewriter equivalent of a homeless shelter (a warm, dry office; some dust removal spray; and maybe, if I was feeling generous, a little sewing machine oil), keeping it, if only until Uncle Al's reopened in two weeks, still felt like stealing. So I began to rehearse what I'd tell the trooper when he inevitably showed up. He'd knock on the downstairs door, and when I opened it he'd say that he'd received a report about a stolen typewriter, at which point I'd invite him into the narrow hallway and wave at the typewriter case in the corner.

"You mean *this* typewriter?"

I'd go on to explain how, as a collector, I couldn't stand to see this delicate piece of machinery rust outside for two weeks until the shop reopened. The cop, now believing he'd found not a thief but a kook, would nod reflexively at me, as one would humor a schizophrenic, thank me for my time and back warily out the door.

I made it back to the house and set the Olympia on the kitchen counter. So, after going through all of that, I wasn't even interested in testing out the typewriter. In fact, the whole caper was never about the typewriter. It was about my being blocked and my need for something—*anything*—to fill the creative void, if only for half an hour.

One blocked morning, I was in the diner when I met a silver-haired master cabinetmaker named Ron. He lived in Washington state but was in Millbrook for a while because his sister was dying. Ron had made (at his sister's request) a casket for her.

And here comes the inciting incident, the disturbance to the status quo, the spark of conflict in anticipation of which we blocked writers literally rub our hands together.

Ron told me that the funeral director had tried to talk him and his sister out of a handmade casket, claiming that the handles tended to break off and the "bottoms fell out of them." I coughed into my coffee cup, very nearly spilling it on the table.

"*What?*" I said. "Are you kidding me?"

"Yeah, that's what I said." Ron raised his eyebrows. "I don't know if it's an urban legend or not, but according to him, it does happen."

"Sure it does," I said. "And I bet his saying that had nothing to do with losing a five- or six-thousand-dollar sale."

Ron shrugged. "I don't know. That's what he was saying, that's all."

I said that Ron should ask the funeral director if the handles and bottoms coming off were phenomena isolated to handmade caskets, or would Ron and his sister be safe buying one at Walmart, a company which recently (in keeping with the class act that they are) had gotten into the casket business. I added that Ron should also ask the funeral director which casket he would have more confidence in: one lovingly handcrafted by a single master cabinetmaker, or one hastily assembled by a cabal of disgruntled Chinese prison labor?

Ron chuckled. It warmed my heart. Making this obviously distraught guy smile was my greatest comedic accomplishment in months. I kept going.

"I'd also love to ask this funeral director how many funerals he's presided over where he's actually observed the bottoms falling out of caskets, or the handles shearing off. What an emotionally blackmailing scumbag. These guys profit off other people's misfortunes."

"I know," Ron said. "It's *got* to be an act with them. I mean, there's no way they can feel *that bad* with everybody, every time."

"Exactly."

As I said earlier, when I'm blocked, I fight. And it's not unusual for me to *pick* fights with people I don't know. It's got to be disconcerting for these people, especially on days when my hair is long because I haven't had it cut in months, and it's fly-away because I forgot to put product in it. Now that I think about it, "disconcerting" isn't strong enough; it must be downright *terrifying* for these people, which is fine by me.

A few days after meeting Ron, during my usual backyard to parking lot cut-through on my way to the diner, I spotted the funeral director. A fat, turkey-shaped man, he was leaning against a newly-washed hearse, smoking a cigarette and chatting with another man—a ghoulish-looking gray-haired man—who was also smoking. Usually there was no action back here, especially in the morning when I took this shortcut, but today, there they were, blocking the gap in the fence that led to the diner.

Something that continually surprises me about myself is my ability to experience vicarious outrage over the injustices experienced by others. My sense of empathy for people, for all living creatures, and even sometimes for inanimate objects, operates at a keen pitch all the time. I think of it as emotional tinnitus, and frankly it's exhausting. There is no end to the number of windmills this Don Quixote is capable of jousting.

So the funeral director and his ghoulish assistant (this I deduced from the ghoul's stooping, servile posture) were in my way. Now, I could have turned around and gone down the alley to the street so I wouldn't have to pass them. Or I could have politely asked to pass through the gap in the fence. Those would have been reasonable, conflict-free solutions to this problem.

But as a blocked writer, I didn't want a conflict-free solution.

I wanted confrontation.

For a brief moment I worried that Ron hadn't given me the whole story, or that he'd been in the wrong to begin with and was trying to make the funeral director look bad. But as I drew closer to the funeral director and saw the lines etched in his face—lines caused by a lifetime of feigned sympathy and emotional blackmail—I knew that Ron the Cabinetmaker had told me the truth. I *had* to confront this guy.

I know he was only trying to earn a living, but there's something unsavory, and a little bit douchey, about morticians, who only make money if someone dies. This begets a question: what do they do the rest of the time? They seem like people who would do a lot of ice fishing, which annoys me. I think ice fishing is the dumbest activity ever conceived by man. *It's winter, dude!* LEAVE THE FRIGGEN FISH ALONE!

Anyway, I was really bothered by what this undertaker had said to that poor cabinetmaker from Washington state. I didn't want Mr. Formaldehyde here thinking he'd gotten away with anything.

From time to time, when I'm happy and creative and brimming over with largesse, I'll assume a pseudo-superhero role I call *Helperman*, who helps strangers. But when I'm blocked, angry and capriciously irritable, I assume another role: *The Confronter*. When I was three feet away from them, I stopped and put my hands in my pockets.

"Hi there," I said.

"Hello," said the funeral director.

There are three keys to successfully confronting a scumbag. One, surprise: Do it when they least expect it. Two, public humiliation: Inasmuch as possible, do it when there are people around, and the more people the better (in this case, the ghoul wasn't much, but he'd suffice). Three, proximity: Get uncomfortably close to their personal space without invading it.

"You're the funeral director, right?" I said.

"I am." He puffed on the cigarette.

"I'm curious about something," I said. "I heard you recently told a man that homemade caskets are no good because they fall apart, and that you've seen 'a lot' of accidents with them. Is that true?"

"Excuse me, do I know you?"

"No. So tell me…what happened? Did the bottoms of the things fall out and you had cadavers rolling around or what?"

"I'd like you to leave," he said. "This is private property."

"So what the man said is true, isn't it?"

"Please leave, young man."

"You should be ashamed of yourself," I said. "That man made a special casket for his dying sister, and you told him it was no good because you'd be out...what? Five, six grand, right?"

"He asked you to leave," the ghoul said.

"No, that's okay," the funeral director said. "I'm curious why he's so outraged about something that is none of his business."

"I'll tell you why," I said. "Because I hate injustice, and I hate con men and emotional blackmailers. As far as I'm concerned, you're like those blacktop companies that sucker old ladies into having their driveways sealed, then take off with the deposit."

The funeral director shook his head. "Don't think you're jumping to conclusions about this? You only spoke to one man, right? How do you know he was even telling the truth?"

"Don't try to confuse me, mister, make me doubt what I heard. Because he's a cabinetmaker, and when we shook hands, I could tell he was honest, and he had no reason to lie to me. But I'll tell you this: I better not hear about you pulling something like this with anyone I know personally."

"Is that a *threat*?"

I love when guys like him say that. Of course it's a threat. They always say it so snottily, as though they've caught you in something, like they keep a lawyer's phone number on speed-dial for just such an opportunity: *"Mr. Smith? Somebody threatened me! I want to sue!"*

"Watch yourself, Butterball," I said. "And step aside. You're in my way."

I brushed past them, went through the fence, down the street and into the diner. Kenny, having spotted me through the window, had already placed a cup of black coffee at my seat at the counter. As I took a sip, I noticed I was breathing heavily. This was a tad worrying. What if being The Confronter caused me eventually to have a heart attack? Or worse, a stroke? As Tony would say, "lotsa luck" trying to write with half my body paralyzed. It was undeniable: my blood pressure was up from browbeating the funeral home director. And what had my outrage accomplished? Nothing. That guy would always be an emotionally blackmailing schmuck.

On the other hand, I *had* achieved some emotional catharsis. I had a theory about people who suffered heart attacks and strokes, and who contracted diseases like cancer: The bottling-up of anger and other negative feelings festers inside a person and actually causes these illnesses. Of course I had no scientific evidence to support my hypothesis, but I was convinced: Keeping all of that negativity inside for long periods can't be good for a person. I sipped my coffee and stared out the window at Franklin Avenue.

Besides, my behavior when blocked could have been a lot worse. When Mark Twain was blocked, he became the target of the financial schemes, fancies and half-baked plans of friends and associates, most of whom were blocked creatives themselves. Once, he was approached by the struggling owners of the Paige Compositor. No doubt, in Twain they saw a sure-fire sucker: a writer with lots of extra cash, and who was eager to immerse himself in something, *anything*, besides his work. That little distraction bankrupted Twain, and he had to spend the next several years touring the world to pay off his creditors.

Then there was Ernest Hemingway. During the early years of WWII, burned out and blocked after writing *For Whom the Bell Tolls*, he asked the U.S. Navy to outfit his fishing boat, *Pilar*, so he could patrol the waters between Cuba and Florida, hunting for German U-boats. Hemingway was given extra gasoline rations, as well as grenades, depth charges, machine guns and ammunition; but instead of searching for U-boats, he used the gasoline to go on long fishing trips and the machine guns to shoot sharks.

Maybe I wasn't as bad as Hemingway or Twain, but I still needed to find better activities, better diversions, for when I was blocked. I'd been pretty athletic in my youth: baseball, tennis, hiking, camping, mountain climbing, fishing, biking, weightlifting, you name it. Maybe it was time to take up sports again. Maybe get back into cross-country skiing, and, in the spring, learn golf.

Kenny walked over and refilled my coffee. "Whatcha up to, Chris? Writin'?"

"Nope. Not today."

He nodded at my Boston Red Sox cap and gestured at the far end of the counter, where two guys with Yankees caps were sitting.

"Boy, you don't want to go down there," he said.

"Why not?"

"Those guys were trashing the Red Sox. They said Ted Williams was overrated."

"Oh, *really*...?" I picked up my coffee and stood. "Introduce me to them, Kenny."

7

ACCIDENTAL INVADERS

It was a cold October dawn, and the first light in the bedroom was a gray fog. My mouth was dry. I reached for my water glass, took a sip, and spied something floating on the water. Actually, whatever it was, was swimming in circles an inch from my mouth. I ran into the bathroom with the glass and flicked on the light switch.

It was a ladybug.

The cranky part of me wanted simply to pour the thing down the sink and go back to bed, but something about its frantic, six-legged dog-paddle tugged at my heart.

It was scared.

I suppose I'd be scared, too, if *I'd* fallen in a narrow, steep-sided column of water 100 times deeper than I was tall.

"Okay, buddy, hold on."

I closed the sink drain and carefully poured out the glass through my fingers. The ladybug clung to the rim of the glass. When I finally shook him out, he landed on his back on the sink counter, looking as dead as a bug could look this side of being squashed.

Having reached middle age without deliberately touching an insect, I had no intention of breaking my streak now. I flipped him over with my toothbrush. On his shell were six tiny black spots. He staggered forward like a man crawling toward a desert mirage. After a couple of inches, he stopped and turned his microscopic head to me. Something in the cant of his head said he was annoyed.

Not a lot of gratitude here.

"Oh, well," I muttered to myself. "Jesus healed ten lepers and only one thanked Him."

The ladybug might have been ungrateful, but I still didn't want anything bad to happen to him. In his exhaustion, he might tumble onto the floor, where the cat would get him. What he needed was a safe perch. Tricking him into crawling back onto the toothbrush, I ferried him up to a little ledge beneath the big globe lights on the vanity. Soaked and cold, he would appreciate a warm refuge.

After a few steps beneath the lights, his antennae stirred. He pulled his legs and head beneath his shell and settled down for a nap.

At breakfast, I regaled Alexas with the tale of my heroic deed.

"He was drowning in my water glass, and I gave him new life." I waved my hand in the general direction of the bathroom. "He's under the vanity lights now, recovering."

"Awww, you're sweet," she said. "But how do you know it's a *he*?"

"I don't know, it just is. All insects seem like males to me."

"Well, I think you're a male chauvinist. And I'm sure the girl ladybugs do, too."

I gazed out the window at the deep blue sky. Great weather, I'd saved a bug's life, and it wasn't even eight o'clock yet.

"You know, Alexas, of all the bugs in the world, I like ladybugs best," I said. "They're welcome here anytime."

For the next two days, every few hours I tiptoed into the bathroom and nudged the ladybug with whatever was handy: my pencil, a comb, a bookmark. At first he responded with a reassuring wave of his antennae, but this soon degenerated into his wagging only one antenna and eventually his curling both into what I can only describe as a scowl.

I stopped checking on him.

The next morning we awoke to a windowsill full of ladybugs. Two, three dozen at least. With the outside temperature dropping each night, I'd been cracking the window at bedtime for cool, fresh air, and a caravan of insects had infiltrated the opening. They filed along the sill, up the wall, to the ceiling. On their spindly legs they managed to carry what looked like giant, rounded steamer trunks containing everything they owned.

A pair clung to the window, basking in the morning sun and flicking their antennae against each other's like girls playing patty-cake. Clearly, God had made the little bugs cute so people would be reluctant to kill them.

"Alexas, aren't they adorable?" I said. "I could watch them all day long."

"Adorable is one word for them."

I opened the closet, moved the vacuum out of the way and pulled out a clean shirt. I was putting it on when I noticed that the hollow between the window and the screen was littered with the husks of dead ladybugs. They had fallen from above and landed flat on their backs. Meanwhile, the caravan continued up to the ceiling.

"Alexas, look at this. What's going on?"

"I don't know. Maybe it's a seasonal thing, like a migration or something."

"No, I know what it is."

"What?"

"The one in the bathroom talked," I said. "He was still there last night, right?"

"Absolutely. If it's the same one. He was crawling around on the mirror when I last saw him."

I went into the bathroom. Exactly one ladybug was perched on top of a shower curtain ring. I couldn't see the telltale six spots on his back—he was too high up—but I knew it was him.

"Told your buddies, didn't you?"

He didn't say anything.

"Look, we don't mind, but this can't get ridiculous. Okay?"

He wagged his antennae.

"All right. So long as we understand each other."

Did ladybugs have some way of communicating to their homeless brethren that Alexas and I could be trusted to provide a warm, safe haven? Maybe, like ants, they left a chemical trail that the other ladybugs followed. Or maybe they had developed a system of symbols like the hobos used during the Great Depression to give directions and warnings to other hobos. This idea would occupy my imagination for the rest of the day.

I had begun writing this book in the summer, and somehow, even in the midst of this autumn chaos with the ladybugs, I continued to work on it. Although I say that I "somehow" continued to write, the fact that I was able to block out reality and indulge my imagination really didn't surprise me. Over the years I had written through arguing neighbors, barking dogs, dinning study halls (while a high school history teacher), droning leaf-blowers, and a throbbing week-long tooth abscess.

But this book, the one you're reading now, was giving me trouble. This was the first time I was attempting to write about my own life, about things that had really happened to me. I found myself going so deeply into memories that I was disturbed by some of the things that had happened, or I questioned whether the events actually *did* happen, and was jolted out of my writing trance.

I put down my pencil, got out of my office chair and went looking for Alexas. The Muse. Whenever I got stuck in my writing, I only needed to talk to her for five minutes, and magically whatever problem I had, or thought I had, would vanish in her presence. In the movie *The Muse* with Albert Brooks and Sharon Stone, Brooks says of Stone (the Muse) to a friend, "She doesn't give me the ideas. She just points me in the right direction." And that's exactly what my Muse, Alexas, always did for me.

Out in the hallway, drill sounds resonated from the kitchen. On Saturday mornings while I wrote, Alexas—ten times more mechanical than I—did home-improvement projects around the apartment. This morning she was drilling holes in the walls for shelves. I leaned miserably against the doorjamb. Spotting me, she stopped and put down the drill.

"Bunny," I said, "do you have a second?"

"Of course." She smiled at me while wearing a pair of safety goggles. Ordinarily, wanting her undivided attention I would insist she remove the goggles before I started talking. Today, though, they lent her an air of technical expertise, which for some reason I found strangely reassuring.

"Okay, here's the problem," I said. "I've had a lot of experiences, but once I write about them, I start to question whether they actually happened. I'm not sure what's fact and what's fiction anymore. It's maddening. See what I mean?"

"I do, but look at it this way," Alexas countered. "You have plausible deniability for your entire life."

"Hmm…plausible deniability," I said. "I guess that's pretty good."

"Are you kidding? That's *great*."

"Want to hear some titles I'm considering for the book?" I asked.

"*Yes!*"

I laughed and kissed her.

"All right," I said. "The first one is *Alien Girls*, based on the story of the girls who gave me those crazy pants, remember?"

"Hmm, okay," she said. "What else?"

"*Revenge Fantasies.*"

"Oooh, I like that."

"It's the title of one of the pieces. But I don't know if I want to include it or not. I'm not as angry and vengeful as I was when I wrote it a couple years ago."

"I've got one," she said. "How about *A Portrait of the Artist as a Middle-aged Man?*"

"I don't know," I said. "There are probably about six people out there—all English Lit professors—who will get the James Joyce reference. I want the title to be something about writers and how we're always getting into trouble. Something like that. I'll figure it out. Anyway"—I nodded at the bedroom door—"how are our little friends doing?"

"There are a few more of them," she said, "but nothing we can't handle."

"Who knows…maybe they'll end up in the new book."

"Maybe." She kissed my cheek and picked up her drill. "Get back to work, honey."

"Yeah, all right." I sighed and shuffled back to my office and my book.

On a crisp late October afternoon, during my final bike ride of the season, I nearly caused a terrible accident.

I was speeding down a steep hill, tucked into the handlebars while pedaling furiously, when something crawled across my glasses lens. I swerved instinctively and was greeted by a van honking behind me. The van lurched into the oncoming lane, where another car approached, then swung back into our lane. As the two vehicles passed each other in a jousting blare of horns and the Doppler effect, I pulled my bicycle to a stop on the shoulder. My mouth was bitter with the taste of adrenaline. I was shaking. I yanked off my glasses. Of course, it was a ladybug. Must have crawled into my helmet, the little bastard. I blew on him, not softly, and he flew off lazily into the meadow.

Before bed that night, as I was putting on my sleeping socks, I looked up at the corner of the ceiling. What had started as a tidy Bedouin bivouac was now an unsightly refugee camp. A hundred or more of the insects were gathered, the livelier ones flitting about like troublemaking teenagers, buzzing their wings as if to say, *"Hey, guys, guys, guys, guys! Look, look! I can fly…I can <u>fly</u>!"* Then there were the elderly and infirm—the ones dragging themselves along by only their two front legs. Even if they were all harmless, I was uneasy about having insects congregating where I slept. Alexas was reading when I nudged her.

"Bunny," I said, "there's no chance they'll, like, crawl in our ears or anything when we're sleeping, is there?"

"No, Chrissy," she said. "Don't be ridiculous."

It didn't seem ridiculous to me. If I were a ladybug, what would I be looking for? A cozy, sheltered spot to hibernate, right? Well, I could imagine one of them crawling across my face, reaching my ears and saying, *"Hmm, a warm empty hole. What's in here…?"*

I put in a pair of earplugs. Alexas sighed.

"They're not going to go in your ears," she said.

"I know they're not." I tapped an earplug.

After a spate of cold weather, that night was hot and the air a dead calm. I awoke at 2 a.m., sweating. A trickle of sweat rolled down my arm. It rolled, and rolled, and rolled, a lot longer than any droplet had ever rolled down my skin before. But now that I was wide-awake, I realized it wasn't a drop of sweat at all. I could feel six tiny but distinct impressions as it moved.

Ladybug!

I swiped at it in the darkness. It hit the floorboards with a click.

"What's wrong?" Alexas groaned.

"Nothing, just hot in here. Go back to sleep."

The fact was, the little bug had unnerved me. I took a shower, then cleared the entire area around the bed of ladybugs while Alexas buried her head beneath the pillow.

Over the next week, as I worked on my laptop in the bedroom, I observed the slow dissolution of the refugee camp. Factions broke off and established independent colonies around the room: a few on top of the mirror, some on the blinds, a coterie on the shelf above our bed.

These guys, however, didn't worry me. I could *see* them. It was the plucky, venturesome lads crawling into places unseen, the wayfarers traveling to the edges of the known ladybug world—the *Magellan* ladybugs—that made me wonder, with eyebrows clenched, what to do.

As I was staring at the closet, one of them brazenly crawled up the door. Indeed, he was unusually speedy, the Usain Bolt of ladybugs. Still, I was faster.

"Where do you think *you're* going?" I said.

I placed a bookmark in front of him, but he was having none of it. One of his buddies had already been tricked by this gambit, and word was out that a ride on the bookmark bridge only leads to the same boring points of interest you've already visited. Tired of being bested by an insect, I gently flicked him off the closet door and onto the bedspread, where he kept crawling.

I shook my head and smiled. I really did admire their pluck and resilience.

At the two-week mark, however, they were becoming an annoyance. I was in the shower, reaching for the shampoo, when a small gang of them eyed me menacingly from the loofah. In bed, I picked up a book; half a dozen were holding what looked like a zoning board meeting on the front cover. "Guys, come on!" They adjourned and filed off. One morning I even went beltless until lunch because one of them was sleeping on it. But what could I do? Anytime I looked at them, all I could think was what remarkable creatures they are.

Between TV programs one evening, a fast-talking newscaster blurted out a teaser that got my attention: *"Are ladybugs taking over New Jersey? News at eleven!"* As usual, they were trying to get people to tune in by spreading fear. I wanted to stay up to watch it, but long ago, annoyed by their use of scare tactics, I had vowed *never* to watch. Still, I was more curious than ever about this strange phenomenon, so I got on the internet.

I learned that the ladybugs I was dealing with were actually *Asian* ladybugs, and that for some unknown reason, they were attracted to light-colored houses. After reading articles about homes infested with *thousands* of them, I realized that Alexas and I were getting off easy. Yet, somehow—was it subliminal?—I ended up on a website for a pest-removal company, whose content was both informative and oddly comforting:

> Asian ladybugs…are accidental invaders…. Accidental invaders do not feed or reproduce indoors. They cannot attack the house structure, furniture, or fabric. They cannot sting or carry diseases. Ladybugs do not feed on people, although they will occasionally pinch exposed skin. Ladybugs may leave a slimy smear and they have a distinct odor when crushed.[21]

Basically, the article said, ladybugs only become a problem if you kill them. I watched one crawl toward my laptop for a moment, then ran out to tell Alexas about what I'd learned.

"Listen," I said, "whatever you do, *don't* kill them."

I explained about the smear and the odor.

"I wasn't planning on it," she said, "but that's good to know."

Her reaction didn't surprise me. Alexas had become accustomed to my no-kill policy with spiders in the apartment. So many webs festooned the corners of our bathroom ceiling, it looked like the cave in the opening of *Raiders of the Lost Ark*. When I returned to my laptop, the ladybug I'd seen near it was gone. To this day, I'm convinced he crawled into the fan vent and never left.

Obviously I was cooped up and not thinking clearly. What I needed were fresh air and foliage. Throwing on

---

21 Source: http://www.pestproducts.com/ladybugs.htm

my field coat, I walked out past the golf course, up Altamont hill and back, and didn't think about ladybugs *once*. Returning to the village, however, it was as if the damn things were excreting a mind-control pheromone because suddenly all I could think about again were ladybugs. What about other light-colored buildings in town, like, say, the post office? Were the ladybugs, at that very moment, assembling on the counter in formation and conspiring to invade our mail? And what of my second office, the Millbrook Diner? Would the ladybugs be attracted to its gleaming chrome façade? What exactly *was* their position on shiny aluminum siding?

Dropping into the bank, I mentioned our ladybug problem to the gals in customer service.

"They can be real pests, can't they?" Kathy said. "Do you have them now?"

"I do."

"It's a shame they're so cute," Wanda said. "I hate to kill them."

"We've all been there," Jacqueline said. "To vacuum, or not to vacuum, that is the question."

I sighed. "Yeah, I guess it is."

It was Friday evening, about 10, and I had pulled off a coup by getting Alexas to watch the movie *Aliens* with me, and right before bed no less.

Putting on my pajamas, I reflected on the movie and its parallels to our situation. Like the ladybugs, the aliens were unwanted visitors that infested human space. But unlike the tiny bugs that inched charmingly along our walls, the aliens used humans as living hosts, had blood that dissolved steel, and they killed everybody.

Meanwhile, look at these cute ladybugs, I thought. *Clustered together for warmth. They're not doing any harm. It's not like they're <u>aliens</u> or anything.*

As I was slipping under the covers, though, one particular ladybug worried me. He was hanging on the ceiling, directly over my mouth. I kept thinking about the possibility that when I fell asleep and my mouth inevitably went slack, the ladybug might, in an example of horrible irony befalling its benefactor, choose that exact moment to die, plunging the six-plus feet straight past my parted lips, and I'd swallow him. Even worse, I'd wake up and realize too late that the crunch in my mouth was not a broken tooth or a piece of cashew, but the shell of the ladybug that had been hovering over me. I rolled out of bed, grabbed my pillow and a blanket, and headed for the couch.

I awoke with a fist-sized knot under my shoulder blade. There was no coffee in the house, I had seven overdue library books to return, and (*oh, lovely*) there was a ripping rainstorm outside. I got dressed, but I couldn't find my umbrella so I had to jog to the diner clutching the books under my coat like I was going into labor with them. After eating breakfast, I tried to wait out the rain. I hung around the diner through so many free coffee refills that even Thanasi's saintly patience wore filo-thin. Finally I gave in and hoofed it, wind-whipped and book-pregnant, up to the library. I dumped the books on the counter.

"Sue, I owe you guys some money."

"Wow, you hardly ever return books late." Her brow furrowed. "You look a little peakèd, Chris. Is everything okay?"

At hearing this, the knot in my back flared up again.

"I haven't been sleeping very well. My upper back is acting up for some reason."

"Lot of worries?" she said. "Things hanging over you?"

I thought about last night's ladybug.

"Yeah," I said, "you could say that."

When I got back to the house, Alexas was making the bed. The heat was on and the bedroom was warm for a change. I stood in the doorway, dripping, and gazed at the swarms of ladybugs around the room. Now that I was really looking, there had to be close to a thousand in here alone. And who knew where else they might be lurking?

"Jesus," I said.

Alexas arranged the pillows on the bed and spread out the quilt at the end. She walked over, put a hand on my back and rubbed.

"Chrissy, I know they were cute at first, but there's a *lot* of them now. They're taking over."

As always, I was impressed with Alexas' composure in a crisis. I nodded.

"Yeah, at first they seemed grateful," I said, "like they were saying, 'Thank you, *thank you* for the warm home for the winter!' But now look at them…acting like *we're* the tenants and they're the co-op board." I shoved my hands in my coat pockets, which were soaked. "Were you going to vacuum this morning?"

"I was. Why?"

Maybe I was imagining it, but I could swear I saw a glint of glee in my beloved's eyes. I glanced at the ladybugs. At some point over the past month, I had convinced myself that they could understand me. I gestured at the closet, where the vacuum cleaner was.

"But wait until I'm in the shower. I can't watch."

"Don't worry," she said. "I'll take care of it."

I took longer than usual preparing for my shower. Perhaps I was silently saying goodbye. I also wanted to give the ladybugs a few more minutes of warmth. This, I reasoned, was their equivalent of the condemned man's last meal. What treat might the ladybugs have requested? A certain microscopic insect delicacy? A blade of juicy grass?

I had just stepped into the hot spray when, out in the hallway, the vacuum switched on. Like a stone tossed in a pond, a feeling of regret plunked in my chest and sent ripples of nausea all through my body. The roar of that Hoover upright, and the doom it meant for those harmless ladybugs, triggered a litany of questions. If they couldn't harm me, what was I afraid of? Did I really have to kill them? Maybe I could have collected them in a jar and released them outside someone *else's* light-colored house. A few candidates came to mind. But no, that simply would have been delaying the inevitable. If the owners of the next house didn't kill them, the cold would. Still, shouldn't I have given them a chance, a chance at life? Who were *we* to kill them anyway? And were they truly becoming a nuisance, or was it the uncertainty they created—the uncertainty of "Will they crawl in my ears tonight?" and "What if they become too numerous for us to handle?"—was this uncertainty making me fearful, and so I was doing the thing that we humans usually do when confronted with things we're afraid of—*we kill them?*

As the hot water beat down on my shoulders, from the bedroom came the vacuum's terrible screeching and sucking sounds: the edging nozzle scratching at the baseboard. I knew that despite their hardiness the ladybugs were being ripped from their perches into a black, dusty void. I thought of the judge in the Clint Eastwood movie *Hang 'Em High* and the expression of helpless resignation on his face when the gallows doors crash open. I had sentenced the ladybugs to death and was similarly troubled by it; but as in the case of the hanging judge, it was too late to change anything now.

After my shower, I dressed and went into the bedroom. Alexas was coiling up the vacuum cord. I hugged her for a long time and she hugged me back. No words were necessary. Glancing at the vacuum canister, I thought about recovering any survivors, but I dismissed the idea. Even if still alive, they would be maimed, or, at the very least, really pissed off.

The bedroom walls seemed naked now. And then a lone spider crept out from behind the mirror. Hesitantly, like a soldier at Bastogne emerging from his foxhole after a heavy shelling, he walked in circles, probably wondering what the hell had happened to the cobwebs he'd worked so hard on, not to mention the delicious winter menu he'd been planning.

And then, as I was watching the spider, a ladybug took off from behind the window blinds and flew in figure-8's around the room. He flew and flew, eventually covering the whole room, then started over. Clearly, he was searching. I didn't have the heart to tell him that all of his friends and relatives had, on my orders, been mercilessly vacuumed up.

He was still flying around as I shut the door.

8

Nobody Says Anything

Would somebody else please say something? Why am I always the one who has to speak up, who has to confront the rule-breaker, the queue-jumper, the noise-polluter? I'm begging you—stop waiting for the other guy to do it, because invariably that guy is me, and I'm worried that one of these days I'm going to hit upon a psycho and get myself shot. So, *please*, will you start taking some of the load off for me?

You could start at the movie theater. When the sound is too loud (or not loud enough), or somebody's talking on a cell phone, or a couple has brought their three screeching toddlers to a violent R-rated movie, I'd appreciate it if *you* summoned the courage to speak up.

For example, take the time I was in a movie theater, watching *Indiana Jones and the Kingdom of the Crystal Skull*. A father had brought his two tween girls and a newborn to the movie, and they were sitting right behind me. After suffering through 10–15 minutes of the baby's crying, hoping they'd realize they were in the wrong movie and would leave of their own volition, I turned around in my seat and said to the admittedly put-upon dad, "I'm sorry, but you *have* to do something about that baby. This is a critical part of the film and we can't hear it. Please!"

He took the baby out, and while I got a nod of thanks from the couple across the aisle and a reassuring pat on the knee from Alexas, I felt like crap. I wished I hadn't had to be the one to ostracize the poor bastard.

However, in this kind of situation, the philosophy of utilitarianism reigns supreme. "The greatest good for the greatest number," as Jeremy Bentham put it. This made a lot of sense, and in the context of the Indiana Jones movie, the greatest good for the greatest number meant getting the screaming baby the *hell* out of the theater. Then again, you have to question a philosophy advocated by a guy (Bentham) who, after his death, had himself stuffed and put in a glass case, and his preserved body wheeled out once a year to attend a board meeting of University College London. John Stuart Mill is the far better poster boy for utilitarianism.

At another movie a couple of weeks later, when the picture froze during the previews, I just sat there.

"I'm not doing it," I said to Alexas. "Not this time." I tapped the thick biography of John Steinbeck I was reading. "I'm sitting right here and enjoying my book."

"You shouldn't," she said, flipping through *Entertainment Weekly*. "Let somebody else handle it for a change."

Then I repeated the personal mantra I'd come up with recently: "It's not my problem."

"Mm-hm," Alexas said.

So I sat there. I checked my watch. Two minutes passed. Then five. I glanced over my shoulder. Nobody moved. Nobody even showed signs of moving. Some stared dumbly at the blank movie screen. Some wolfed popcorn. Some hunched over their chairs looking oddly at their groins. No, wait…they were texting. Ten minutes passed. I lost my place in my book and turned to Alexas.

"Nobody's going to say anything, are they?"

"I'm sorry, Chrissy."

"Goddamn sheep," I said.

I got up, swept my gaze across the crowd and raised my palms to them.

"No, no, don't get up," I said to the seventy, eighty other moviegoers. "I've got it!"

I marched out to the concessions stand in the lobby. A uniformed teenager leaned over the concessions counter. Big surprise: he was staring at a smart phone.

"Hi," I said. "The projector's stopped in theater seven. It's been about fifteen minutes."

The kid continued to stare at the phone screen, his thumbs dancing on the glass.

"Uh-huh," he said. "Somebody'll get to it in a minute."

"Who's *somebody*?" I asked. "Did someone report it already?"

"Um, I don't know."

At this point, most people would give up. Most people would shamble back to the theater hoping the message had gotten through. But I, Chris Orcutt, am not most people. I take these small slights personally, viewing what others might consider a minor inconvenience as being emblematic of a much larger issue. To me, situations like this one are merely the tip of a giant iceberg—an iceberg of rudeness, selfishness and incompetence—and I consider it my bound duty to do something about it.

I said, "Then how about, *kid*, putting down the friggen phone and *telling* somebody!? We've been waiting long enough!"

The kid's arm with the cell phone slowly went limp. Clearly, no customer had ever spoken to him that way before.

"Geez, sorry." He shuffled away.

"Thank you," I said.

By the time I got back to the theater, the previews were playing again. If any of the patrons saw me come in, they didn't say anything. No one applauded. If this were a scene in a movie, a jolly English guy in the back row would stand up with a flask of brandy and exclaim, *"Good show! Three cheers for Orcutt! Hip-hip…hooray!"* I plopped down in my seat.

"It just started," Alexas said. "Nice work, Chrissy."

"Yeah, nice work," I said.

Recalling how I'd spoken to the kid in the lobby, I regretted having paid extra for the unlimited popcorn and soda refills. Surely by now he had spread the word about me, perhaps even with a surreptitiously snapped cell phone photo. I was certain that if I went back to the concession stand, one of them would spit in our food.

All right, enough about movie theaters. There are plenty of other places where I could use your help.

Like the park. Where I live, in Millbrook, New York, there is an adorable park in the village called the Tribute Garden. It has picnic benches, a chessboard table, swings, slides and jungle gyms for the kiddies, and a quiet corner for people like me who want to read or write while gazing out at the rolling hillsides and thoroughbreds on the adjacent Thorne estate. Clean, immaculately maintained, and watched over by a stand of venerable old maples that give excellent shade on hot summer days, the Tribute Garden is everything you could wish for in a park.

That is, until some knucklehead comes along.

I was in my usual spot in the quiet corner of the park, sitting on my portable camp chair with my feet up on a picnic bench, wearing a fedora and safari jacket, and reading Hemingway's *Green Hills of Africa*. From time to time I would look up from the book and stare into the waving tall grass on the Thorne estate, and without any horses around I imagined myself as Hemingway, staring across the savanna. Somewhere out there in that tall thick grass awaits the angry male lion I wounded. With the breeze at my back, which means the lion is downwind from me and knows I'm coming, I can truly feel the thick-tongued fear Hemingway must have felt as he walked into the dense grass, waving tall and lightly rustling, and then, behind me and to my right…

BOOM!

I jumped half a foot in the chair and toppled backwards. My first thought was that someone had blown up the playground. On my back, I glanced upside-down in that direction. No one was screaming, no kids running in circles with their hands in the air. The kids and their mothers were fine, although some were craning their necks toward the field of the Catholic school next door. There was another boom. This one didn't sound as loud; this sounded merely like the sharp report of a gun. Rolling onto my stomach, I slowly I got to my feet and jogged to a spot along the fence.

Two hundred yards away, a man, boy and dog stood atop a knoll behind the Catholic school. The man fidgeted with some apparatus in his hand while the dog looked on intently, wagging its tail. Then the man stepped to one side and extended his arm. The dog froze.

BOOM! And the dog took off. A wobbly, beanbag-shaped projectile sailed across the field, and the dog chased after it. Now I understood: this was a hunting training device for the dog. I stood and went to the chain-link fence. My head just cleared the top of it. I stared at the man.

I couldn't believe it. I couldn't believe a guy could be so solipsistic and clueless that he'd actually think it was okay to discharge any kind of firearm on the property of a school, literally a stone's throw from a park where dozens of kids were playing. I could only imagine the creative rationalizations this clown had come up with:

"Well, school's out and no one's using the place anyway."
"This isn't a real gun. What's the problem?"
"The world's a violent place, so the sooner those tykes get used to the sound of gunshots, the better off they'll be."

In my periphery I noticed the kids and their parents stopping what they were doing. The gun went off again. I continued to stare, hoping that if the interloper saw a man in mirrored sunglasses and a fedora, it would be unnerving enough to drive him away without incident.

And it might have been unnerving enough, had he been able to see me. Standing against the fence with only my head and shoulders clearing the vines and thickets, wearing a khaki safari jacket, I was pretty well camouflaged. In order for this guy to see me, I'd have to move.

We predators are programmed to respond to movement; stop moving, and most of the time we won't see you. I waved my hands over my head like I was signaling for a rescue plane. He must not have seen me because as I was waving like mad, the gun went off again. The dog fetched the beanbag. Matt, the Tribute Garden caretaker, came running up the hill behind me.

"What's happening, Chris?" He was sweating. "Are those gunshots?! Should I call 911?"

"No, look," I said, pointing at the happy hunter.

"Oh."

"You know, Matt," I said, "I understand he needs to train his dog, but that's what gun clubs are for, right? I mean, how stupid *is* this guy? You don't fire a gun—even a fake one—in public, around kids."

"You're right."

I grabbed the picnic table and dragged it to the edge of the fence.

"Hey, what're you doing?" Matt asked.

"Standing on this so he'll see me."

"You gonna say something to him?"

"No, I'm going to try something else first. But if I do have to say something, you've got my back, right?"

"Sure, sure." He wiped his face with a handkerchief, stuffed it in his pocket. "Listen, I've gotta finish the mowing before the rain. Can you handle this?"

I sighed, climbed on top of the picnic table. "Yeah."

"Thanks."

He walked away. Turning my attention back to the man, I resumed my arm-waving. The picnic table had added two feet to my stature, putting me well in the man's view, but the bench itself was hidden by a low thicket. From his perspective, far across the field there was an eight-foot-tall stranger in sunglasses and a fedora waving at him. The man was in the middle of loading his next salvo when he stopped and yelled, "What's the problem?"

I didn't reply. There were any number of comebacks to his question; he had left himself wide open. Moreover, his asking "what's the problem" betrayed his own feelings about the matter: he knew that what he was doing was wrong. A variety of replies came to my mind:

"What do you mean, 'what's the problem?' You're firing a gun in the direction of children, that's the problem!" This one I dismissed immediately because it opened up for debate whether it was actually a gun he was shooting. From this point, the conversation would likely degenerate into semantics: Are a gun and a device that only *sounds* like a gun the same thing?

"You're a friggen' idiot, that's the problem!" Too confrontational, and possibly not true. For all I knew, the guy was in Mensa. Besides, this reply instantly escalated the conflict from a 2 to a 10, virtually guaranteeing that I wouldn't get the result I wanted, which was for the noise to stop. Also there were kids around, so I couldn't use foul language without risking becoming a pariah myself.

"There are children over here!" No good. He had his own kid with him, so he could argue it wasn't dangerous.

"We're trying to read over here!" Trouble was, there was no "we"; there was only me and my chair, or me and my book, or me and the flies; and, not being royalty, I couldn't rightly use the royal "we." And to say that *I* was

trying to read would only elicit a response of, "So? Why don't you read someplace else?"

"Could you please do that someplace else?" A polite reply, and with the right person—someone who appreciated civility—it could work. But with a likely knucklehead who hadn't thought through the situation, it would be interpreted as weak.

Standing on the picnic table with my hands on my hips, maple branches brushing my hat brim, continuing to stare across the field, I reached a decision: *The best thing to do here is say nothing. Let your silence and stature unsettle him for a while.*

Besides, yelling back and forth across a field is unseemly, not to mention notoriously inefficient. I'd been in long-distance shouting matches before. They were cumbersome, self-conscious affairs in which the act of broadcasting one's view and having to wait several seconds for a reply tended to erode one's confidence in one's position and reduce the entire situation to absurdity.

"Well?!" the man shouted. "What's the problem?!"

A breeze rustled the trees around me. It was difficult not to smile. The man's rising frustration and self-consciousness, the absurdity of the situation, and the certainty that my chosen gambit was going to work—all of these made my standing atop the picnic table and being thought a simpleton by the other people in the park curiously worth it.

"I'm talking to you!" he said. "Hey!"

No, you're shouting at me. A mosquito landed on my arm. I had decided that any further movement would detract from my ominous steady stare. Just as the mosquito was drilling its proboscis into me, I lowered my arm very slowly and pressed it against my shorts, squashing it. No one would appreciate my level of sacrifice for this cause.

"It's a free country!" the man yelled.

I couldn't believe my ears. Boy, did this guy know how to get under my skin; this very nearly provoked a response from me. "It's a free country" was to me what (according to Boswell) patriotism was to Samuel Johnson: "the last refuge of a scoundrel." I stood stone-still, not even bothering to wipe away the drop of perspiration tickling my temple.

"Jerk!" the man yelled. Holding the gun in one hand, he put his other arm over the boy's shoulders and walked toward the parking lot.

I waited until they were out of sight before getting off the picnic table. I returned to my chair, chugged half a bottle of water, put my feet up, and resumed *Green Hills of Africa*. A man wearing a Yankees baseball cap walked up from the public bathroom hut.

"Wanted to thank you." He nodded at the gender-neutral bathroom, where a woman led a little girl inside. "My wife and kid were scared to death. We thought somebody was shooting, you know?"

"So did I. Knocked me out of my chair."

The man shook his head, gestured out at the field. "I'm really glad you did something about that, 'cause I didn't want to have to fight. You know, with the family right here and everything."

"Sure."

He cleared his throat. "Anyway, I thought I'd tell you…I had your back…you know, if anything went down."

He actually said, "went down."

"Would you have, really?" I said. "What about the family?"

"Look," he said, "you don't have to get all high and mighty. Nothing would've happened anyway. He had his kid with him."

"Who are you, and why are you bothering me?" I said.

"What's your problem?" he said. "I came over to thank you and you're making a big freaking deal here."

"Get lost."

"Dick!" He walked back to the bathroom.

It gets tiresome being the lone enforcer of civility. There are way too many selfish jerks around for me to handle the entire workload alone.

I have been in public libraries when people's cell phones rang, and I had to be the one to point out the No-Cell-Phones rule and explain to violators the tradition of libraries as quiet sanctuaries where absolute silence is the rule—a lecture that every time I give it leaves me feeling more and more like a relic. I have been in expensive restaurants where diners have received more phone calls in 10 minutes than I get in a month, and had to explain to them the concept of personal dignity: that maybe they didn't want the rest of us to hear about the results of their blood test or the breakup of their relationship, and that they really ought to have these conversations in private, and how there used to be things called *phone booths* for precisely this purpose; and then to the younger offenders,

I had to *describe* a phone booth because many of them have never seen one.

"They were really cool," I say. "There was a phone inside, and you'd go in and close the door. Some of them even had a bench so you could sit down while you talked."

After blinking at me in disbelief, the young offender finally says, "A phone with a box around it? Come on, man, you're full of crap. Why didn't you use your *cell*?"

I have spoken sharply to idiot parents in the laundromat for allowing their restless, sugar-high kids to climb into dryers and take spins on somebody's leftover minutes. I have left doctors' offices unannounced when made to wait more than 30 minutes past my scheduled appointment time. I have upbraided the staff in urban voting locations for making the process, to my mind, incredibly complicated and time-consuming, not to mention outright uncomfortable for the elderly and infirm. And I have found and confronted a guy in my then-city neighborhood, who, every autumn, ran his leaf blower at 6:00 a.m.

"But I like to get started early," he whined.

"Tough," I said. "If I hear that goddamn thing again before nine o'clock, I'm coming back and smashing it with an axe!"

To a lot of people my behavior might seem outrageous, reminiscent of the plots of the TV show *Curb Your Enthusiasm* with Larry David, but I want to make something clear: I have never done what I do to imitate art. Also, as Alexas points out, many of the situations David's character gets into are the result of his being oblivious to social conventions. Almost never does David's character say or do what he does out of a sense of injustice. But I do.

Seldom, I've discovered, does life give us big moral choices to wrestle with. Rather, we're presented with daily, seemingly insignificant annoyances that are really small tests of our integrity. Most of us will never face a Sophie's Choice or an Abraham's Predicament. Instead, we get the neighbor who is contributing to high cable TV prices by stealing the premium channels and are unsure whether or not to confront him about it—or simply report him. We get the soccer mom or football dad, yelling vile, vociferous things at their child's 7-year-old opponents and are faced with the choice of standing up for the kids or allowing ourselves to be intimidated by the parent's bluster. I look at these moral and ethical dilemmas as training for the Really Big Stuff, if it ever comes along. These small conflicts are continually honing my sense of injustice and my desire to correct it.

The morning after the fake gunfire incident at the park, I was setting up my camp chair in my usual corner when Matt rode up on a golf cart.

"Hey, Chris?"

"Yeah?"

"I wanted to thank you. You know, for yesterday."

"It was my pleasure."

"He came *back*, you know. Yesterday afternoon."

"You're kidding," I said.

"Yeah, he pulled in, asked if you were an employee. I told him no, you're just somebody that comes here for the quiet. Told him we thought somebody was firing a gun and that I was about to call nine-one-one. He shrugged and walked away. I don't think he'll be back."

"Good," I said.

"Anyway, like I was saying, thanks. It's good to have you around. Nobody ever says anything. You're a rare breed, Chris."

I nodded. "Have a good one, Matt."

He drove away. I sat down in my camp chair with my feet on the picnic table, poured a cup of coffee from my Thermos and sipped it. The sun was warming the tall grass on the Thorne estate. A crow glided in and perched on a distant fence post.

I'd begun to question whether I wanted to continue my avocation as the Guy Who Always Says Something. For the moment, though, I was recharged. Like a hole-in-one does for a golfer's enthusiasm for the game, Matt's "attaboy" had given me enough recognition to keep going.

Maybe nobody else would say anything.

But I would.

9

Love Story to Sweetie

What can you say about a 9-year-old girl cat who died?

That she was bright-eyed. And beautiful. That she loved Breyers blueberry yogurt. And Cabot cheddar cheese. And me. That she was finicky, which I viewed as a sign of her gastronomic refinement. Once, when I offered her a piece of Jarlsberg, she batted it across the kitchen. My kitty liked her dairy piquant.

I never learned where I ranked among her favorite things. I might have topped yogurt and cheese, but certainly neither shrimp nor the summer sun patch by the sliding glass door. Many times, Sweetie was enjoying the sun patch when I called her to come lie on Papa. She appeared to work out a complicated cost–benefit analysis of leaving the warm spot, concluded it was best to stay put, and lay her head on the floor as final verdict.

We met—that is to say I bought her—in a pet store in ritzy Scarsdale, New York. "Critter Comforts," was the name. At the front of the store near the checkout was a fenced-in display of cats and kittens: rescued feral cats, discovered living underneath a local orphanage. It was a veritable bargain bin of house cats. A sign offered incentives (shots, food, toys) to buy one of these implicitly inferior animals, ones lacking papers, pedigree, provenance. But it wouldn't have mattered; I'm a sucker for the underdog(cat).

It was mid-morning, shortly after feeding time, and all of the mothers and kittens were piled on top of each other on carpeted perches, smushed against the wire fence. They were all dead asleep, except one: a gorgeous, green-eyed tabby with minute streaks of orange in her gray-black coat and the stripe pattern of a tiger. Unlike most cats, whose faces broaden out as they get older, Sweetie's always retained its youthful proportions: big eyes and a svelte mouth with a paper-white chin. She stood up tall, stretched and gazed at me, and as I reached over the fence, she leapt into my hands.

It was my one and only experience of love at first sight.

I walked her around the store ensconced in the crook of my arm, shopping for toys and feline accoutrements. I bought her a carpeted stump with a hollow den for sleeping. A carrier. Some catnip mice, and what would eventually prove to be her favorite recreational activity, the one at which she was an unmitigated natural: Feather-on-a-Stick. Feather-on-a-Stick was used for a game I invented: Bigjump. Upon my saying "Bigjump" in a sprightly and encouraging tone, Sweetie would jump to ever-increasing heights and claw the feather to the ground.

Of course the five dollars per spare feather was outrageous, later prompting in me a ridiculous desire to win the lottery so I could start my own feather-on-a-stick company and drive this price-gouger out of business. But for the moment all I cared about was showering affection on my new writing companion, so I bought everything, including food and food dishes and brushes and bitter apple deterrent spray, as well as extra feathers.

The cat was Alexas' idea. It was November 2001. After 9/11, I had taken a voluntary severance package from a Manhattan financial services firm, and with Alexas' blessing was going to focus full-time on my writing. Up to that point, I had wedged my writing into my days John Grisham-style: before work; on train and subway rides; during lunch alone in the gourmet corporate cafeteria; and in the middle of work meetings, pretending to take copious notes, but instead accumulating words toward a new novel.

Alexas had insisted on a companion for me partly because of the long hours I would be home alone during the week, but also because a couple years earlier I was diagnosed manic-depressive, specifically Bipolar II. Alexas had read a magazine article about the therapeutic effects of pets on the mentally ill. Getting a cat, she argued, would soothe my own savage beast by giving me something to care for.

And for several years this strategy worked, in the early months especially. Between writing stories and submitting them and getting the mail and burning the rejections and flushing the cinders down the toilet, I had kitten duty to attend to, which included being ubiquitous and forthcoming with copious no's when I caught her biting on electrical cords or scrunching into dangerously tight spaces.

Since my bipolar meds made me tired—even more so during a depressive cycle, which lasted from two days to two months—I took a nap every afternoon. Having always slept flat on my back, I allowed Sweetie to curl up in the V between my legs. Her naptime was invariably shorter, and within an hour I would be awakened by light, exploratory footsteps on me beneath the blanket that gradually worked their way toward my chest, until her sweet face burrowed out from the covers. She blinked, licked my cheek and curled up, purring (all 1 pound of her) atop my beating heart.

Feather-on-a-Stick, Bigjump, and aquarium fish-watching were her preferred activities in the early years, although we eventually had to get rid of the aquarium. She had figured out how to flip open the top hatch and catch herself a treat.

It was around this time that I started to understand the questions and responses implicit in Sweetie's meows. From the beginning she employed a full palette of cat communication techniques: sharp, plaintive meows with sustained, scolding eye contact (employed usually when I had done something wrong, like being away for several hours); bright, contented chirrups; and the calculatedly adorable "silent meow"—which she did whenever I was writing and she wanted attention. Also in her array of subtle tricks were the "tail hug," wherein she curled the tip of her tail into the crook behind my knee; the clawless paw-tap; the head-bunt; the flop-down; the eraser-bat (she did *not* like pink pencil erasers); the quiet stare, which by its unwavering intensity was her equivalent of shouting; and what I termed the "lah-dee-dah"—her brazenly sauntering across my desk in front of me, often while I stared out the window or at a sheet of paper in my typewriter. Sometimes she even went so far as to walk across the keyboard.

I should mention how she got her name. Easy: the day I brought her home, after I had observed her for hours and had noticed her sweet disposition, I said to my wife, "She's so sweet," to which Alexas replied, "That's it! Let's call her 'Sweetie.' "

And there you have it.

As with all pet owners, we had our share of close calls. Like the time Alexas and I were standing at our 3rd floor apartment window, which was open and sans screen, and Sweetie, spying her first bird in the tree outside, sprang for it. Miraculously, I caught her in midair. After that we never opened a window that lacked a screen.

Then there was the D.C. Incident.

Sweetie had been in our lives for two or three years when Alexas' mother invited us down to Washington, D.C. for a long weekend. I wasn't comfortable leaving Sweetie alone, we couldn't find pet care on short notice, and I was damned if my precious girl was going to be jailed in a kennel, so we brought her along. She had traveled with us before, but something about D.C. freaked her out. (Dubya was in office at the time, so we'll blame him.) The first day wasn't an issue because we arrived late in the afternoon, ate dinner, and went to bed. The next morning, however, Alexas and I rose early and took a ferry down the Potomac to Mount Vernon. Sweetie, of course, stayed in the hotel room, where Alexas had set up a food station and litter box.

When we returned late in the afternoon, Sweetie was gone. We looked everywhere in the hotel room, scoured the hallways and stairwells, called her name, summoned the manager, and cross-examined the maid (we had left a prominent DO NOT DISTURB sign on the door)—all to no avail.

Finally, about three hours later, after searching and worrying and imagining frightful things, like her being thrown down the laundry chute with the dirty linens, I realized where she was. In my greatest Sherlock Holmes moment ever, with Alexas, my in-laws, the manager and the maid rapt before me, I strode to the hotel room window (where I was dramatically backlit), spun around and declared, "Once you have eliminated the impossible, whatever remains, however improbable, must be the truth!"

I yanked the mattress off the bed and heaved up the box spring. There, cowering in a hole in the fabric, was Sweetie. She meowed at me—a half-scolding, half-horrified meow that seemed to say, *"Where were you, Papa?! First you leave me in this tiny hotel room with no window perch, then you're gone all day. I'm very upset with you, Papa!"* I kissed her and put her in the carrier.

However my and Sweetie's relationship became indelible much earlier than that—within a month of bringing her home from the pet store.

It was Christmas Day, 2001. The family, including Alexas and me, my parents and younger sister, were spending the holiday at our vacation house in Maine. A couple days earlier, there had been a blizzard and the countryside was cloaked in a foot and a half of snow.

That afternoon, to give the fire a better draw, my father opened the door to the porch. After a few minutes, noticing the door was open, I looked around for the cat and asked, "Where's Sweetie?" Instantly my father's face matched the snow outside.

"Jeezis," he said, "she couldn't of gotten out! I only had it open a minute or two."

I went to the door and threw it open. Sure enough, a tottering trail of tiny footprints headed out the door, broke through the crust on the foot-deep snow, and disappeared off the porch. I glanced at the outdoor thermometer: 3°F—scary cold, and if you're a kitten, deathly cold. It was three o'clock, which in Down East Maine meant there were maybe two hours of daylight left. Desperate to find her, I ran outside in my socks and a sweater.

I knew that adult feral cats were capable of surviving outside in winter, but a 16-week-old kitten, alone? Trudging through the snow, I feared the worst, expecting any moment to find her frozen stiff. Or she might have fallen into a deep pocket of snow and suffocated. Her tracks were faint, and a wind was starting to come up, blowing away the loose powder atop the crust. If I didn't find her soon, I'd lose my one and only chance.

Before the wind erased her paw prints, I followed them across our backyard, towards a small gully between our property and the next-door neighbors'. I squatted down and noticed that the snow on the opposite bank was disturbed, like something had clawed its way up. Peering over the bank, I scanned the horizon from her perspective, inches off the ground, and asked myself, *"If I were a kitten—cold, disoriented and seeking warmth—where would I go?"* The only shelter nearby was a low porch attached to my neighbors' house.

My family had all gone to the front of the house and were calling the cat's name, a tactic whose value I questioned, since Sweetie still wasn't responding to her name 100% of the time. By now my feet were freezing, but there was no time to go back and get my boots. The sun was low in the sky, throwing deep blue shadows across the snow. I went to the porch, dropped to my stomach and crawled partway underneath, a task complicated by my being fifty pounds overweight at the time. I managed to squeeze in about 6' before my back ran out of clearance. A gray light filtered in from the one side where the snow hadn't banked against the porch.

"Sweetie? Sweetie, honey, where are you?"

I closed my eyes and listened. At first I heard only the wind, but as it subsided I made out the smallest meow. I called out again, and she replied again. It was coming from somewhere against the house foundation. I didn't have a flashlight. I would have to do this solely by ear and feel.

I kept calling to her in the dark and homing in on her cries, which, like a Geiger counter, grew stronger and faster the closer I approached. *"Papa, Papa, I'm here,"* she seemed to say. Claws were scratching on metal. She was leading me towards one of those metal culverts around a basement window. I groped around, praying I wasn't about to put my hand into a skunk's winter nest, reached into the bowl-like hollow, felt a tail, then a wet nose. I pulled her out, backed up and emerged in the half-light with her. She was shivering. I tucked her under my cashmere sweater against my T-shirt with her head sticking out of the neck hole. My father marched toward us clutching a snow shovel.

"You found her! Thank God!"

"Yeah, let's go in."

I spent the next hour with her by the fire, bundling her in towels warmed in the clothes dryer. Sweetie was completely still, unbothered by being confined. In fact, she purred and gazed lovingly at me until her eyes became heavy. *"You rescued me, Papa,"* her sleepy look said. *"Someday I'll rescue you."*

She was, by anyone's definition, a fraidy-cat, something for which I am probably as much to blame as her genetics. Even nine years later, several of my friends and relatives who cared for her when we were traveling had only ever seen her as a dark blur disappearing into a closet. Some doubted that we even had a cat.

The only two people Sweetie was consistently unafraid of were Alexas and me. Since then, I learned that in order for cats to be effectively socialized, they need to be around a variety of people and situations, two things that Sweetie did not get in her critical first months. The apartment was quiet, and, with the exception of the clacking of a typewriter or my swearing at a recent rejection, I too was quiet. This meant that whenever we had overnight guests, or if relatives, the building super or the UPS guy showed up, she went into panic mode, stopping short behind me and staring at the door saucer-eyed as it opened. Invariably whoever was there frightened her and she would squat to the floor, elongate herself like a ferret and scurry away (a behavior that struck me as a bit *off*, since plain-old running was far more efficient) to one of her many hidey-holes.

What was Sweetie's Alamo, you ask? A bookcase bottom shelf, in the hollow space behind some dusty reference books.

Like other cats, Sweetie had her idiosyncrasies, some adorable, some exasperatingly not. For five years after 9/11, I was an adjunct English lecturer at Baruch College in Manhattan. I routinely came home with piles of papers to grade, which I spread out next to me on the bed. Sweetie would join me, and I quickly discovered that she enjoyed rolling around on certain students' work more than others'. Studying the names on the papers she preferred, I quickly deduced the common thread: they were the one I'd believed to be stoners. When I returned their papers, for fun I called those students aside.

"Go easy on the ganja, folks," I said, to which they incredulously replied, "What? How…how did you know?"

I never revealed my secret weapon: Super Sweetie.

Some of Sweetie's other habits may not have been unique to her, but they were no less adorable or annoying. Contrary to the conventional wisdom that says you can't bathe a cat, from the time Sweetie was a kitten, Alexas and I used a three-bucket system she'd seen on Martha

Stewart to wash her. After we dried her in towels, Sweetie retreated to the Alamo for an hour to groom herself and pout, but when she emerged, her coat full and gleaming and redolent of baby shampoo, she strutted back and forth in front of us, basking in our praise: "Oh, Papa, look," Alexas would say, "look at the beautiful girl!"

Not so beautiful was her predilection for snacking on bugs; disgusting is what it was, but, Alexas assured me, "It's what cats do." Another habit of hers was annoyingly sneaky, yet in a strange way I respected her for it. Before I would acquiesce to give her some "cheeser" or a piece of shrimp, she had to be standing on the dining table rug, *not* on the kitchen floor. It was still begging, but this at least put her at a distance so I wouldn't trip over her. While she started out observing the rule, gradually she became a living slippery slope, worming her way out half an inch here, two inches there, until only the tip of her tail was on the rug.

"*Sweetie,*" I'd say.

She'd chirrup in reply, as if to say, *"Hey, I am on the rug. See my tail, Papa? See? Now how's about coming across with some of them shrimps?"*

By age three, she began to have a lot of problems keeping her food down. In other words, she puked—three or four times a day. So often that we had to buy paper towels in bulk. Eventually we had to remove all wet food from her diet. Nothing but Science Diet Sensitive Stomach, the salad and oatmeal of cat food. Vet appointments were useless, the trauma often provoking more puking while yielding *no* answers as to its cause. There were stomach medications, thyroid medications and more.

Shortly after she turned six, the Night Crazies started. From the time Sweetie was a kitten, Alexas and I had let her sleep with us, always without incident. I slept on my back, with my sock-covered feet sticking out from beneath the covers, but apparently, after years of coexisting with them, Sweetie suddenly found my feet an irresistible temptation. At three o'clock in the morning, she would pounce on them and bite them. I'm ashamed to admit that I never learned to react with saintly kindness and understanding; instead, I would yell death threats, grab the nearest magazine and chase her out of the room.

Why she did it, I have no idea. She might have been startled out of a deep sleep and seen my long, gaunt feet towering over her (a scary prospect, if you knew my feet), or perhaps like her Papa she was having violent nightmares, waking up and lashing out at the nearest threat. Or, maybe she was bored, and biting my feet was the most fun a cat could have at 3 a.m.

Whatever the reason, as she grew older this tendency became more pronounced, as did her waking up from naps disoriented and hissing. Eventually we had to ban her from the bedroom at night, which stopped the biting but didn't change her other night behavior: confused yowling, door scratching, and growling at things outside. Several times Alexas awoke to see what was the matter and to comfort her, but she never saw what, if anything, Sweetie was reacting to outside. She appeared to be seeing things. Or not seeing them, as in the case of her begging to have food put in her dish when it was already full.

Her increased vocalizations continued during the day, too, becoming so frequent and irritating that several times, in the middle of writing, I snapped at her to "Stop it!" or "What is it?"—as if she could tell me. She also became clingier, wanting to lie on me every chance she got, and at first I welcomed her attachment. My fondest memories of her are of my writing in bed and her crawling up to lie on my stomach while I wrote with the clipboard resting on her. She seemed not only *content* to share me with my clipboard and eraser-less pencil, but I think she took a little pride in her role as clipboard propper-upper, knowing that she was helping Papa.

Many, many times she saved me, too, hopping on the bed and walking tentatively over to lie on me. It saddens me to remember that there were a few times when I pushed her away. Sweetie could always sense when I was in a depression and would stay close to me for hours, days, weeks. Once, overwhelmed by rejections from multiple publishers and a Hollywood studio that had been considering *A Real Piece of Work* for a movie, I was lying on my back, staring at the ceiling, seriously contemplating the best way to commit suicide, when Sweetie crawled on my chest purring, sat down and licked my nose. A cynic would call it coincidence, but I know better. More than once, that little cat was an instrument for higher forces. More than once, Sweetie saved my life by giving me something tangible—herself—to love.

Which is why it broke my heart when the attacks started. One morning after Sweetie had been up in the night growling at imaginary threats outside, Alexas mimicked for me the sounds the cat had made, and Sweetie tore across the room at Alexas. I jumped in front of her, and the cat clawed my leg. Shouting at her, fending her off with a chair like a lion-tamer, I eventually got her to settle down. Later I learned that her behavior was known as "redirected aggression." She had become riled up by real or imaginary threats, but being unable to attack the irritating interloper, she took out her aggression on us instead.

I knew that my own mood swings, which are erratic and often unprovoked, had contributed to her perpetual nervousness and tension. More than one person in my life has said that being around me is tantamount to walking on eggshells, through a minefield. So I could almost understand why, after nine years, she finally snapped and attacked me. Maybe I deserved it. Deciding that it was an anomaly, I forgave her.

Our final morning together began peacefully, like the attack at Pearl Harbor. I awoke at my usual time of 5:00 or 5:30, made coffee, showered, dressed and started to write. At a few minutes before 7:00, I went into the kitchen to refill my coffee, and Sweetie hissed out at the patio. I had the sliding door open with the screen in place. Sweetie was up against the screen, staring and growling at the neighbor's beagle. She had never done this before. I let her drive the dog away, said, "Okay, Sweetie, you won," then closed the sliding door. Within seconds, she sprang at me, screeching, clawing, biting. She raked my arm, ripped my T-shirt down the chest. I threw her off, but she came at me again, this time leaping at my neck. I slapped her in midair, hitting her hard in the mouth (and puncturing my hand on her fangs), knocking her against the kitchen drawers. Momentarily stunned, she poised herself for another attack. I reached for the chair and swung it between us. I shouted at her, she backed away, and I went into the bathroom.

As I cleaned and dressed my wounds, I realized how much more ferocious this second attack had been, and in that instant I realized her behavior wasn't normal. She was sick. The years of vomiting, the aggression, the Night Crazies—it all made sense. I sensed that she had a brain problem of some kind, and with a shiver of agony I knew what had to be done. I would have to put her to sleep.

What were my other choices? Continue to live with the cat, but in constant fear of another, even worse, attack, and in fear that I would have to hit her even harder next time, when hitting her once had already made me sick? Send her to a "home" for troubled animals, if such a thing even exists? Consult an array of pet therapists? Put her through a long battery of tests, further traumatizing her with stays in hospital kennels, and all without any guarantee that she would be restored to her sweet self? Observing her behavior over time, it was clear to me that she was suffering from something, or a combination of things, that caused the puking, the nervousness, the hallucinating, the yowling, and the aggression. However, as is often the case in life, the most ethical and humane option was perforce the most difficult one.

Twenty years earlier, I had taken a course in Ethical Issues in Medicine. As an argument in support of euthanasia I posited the idea that in addition to preventing her own sustained suffering, a dying patient has the right to determine how others will remember her. In most cases the patient would not want her suffering to erode others' good memories of her. In the case of Sweetie, I felt that she had a right to be remembered by Alexas and me for her beautiful attributes, not for making us fearful in her final days.

I told Alexas of my decision, instructing her not to try and talk me out of it. The pain that clutched my stomach was bad enough to go through once; I wasn't going through it a second time.

I think Sweetie sensed my decision, but she wasn't fearful about it. Almost as if to console me for having to make it, she walked over to me and gave me a sustained tail-hug. I lay a hand on her side, and we sat there for some time. Inexplicably, I had the feeling that Sweetie had been trying for quite a while to communicate to me that she wasn't well and was relieved to have finally gotten through to me.

On the way to the vet with Sweetie in her carrier, I talked to Alexas about the various options, saying "the egg" instead of the cat's name because I didn't want to upset her. Alexas agreed that we had no choice.

The first appointment that we could get was at 10 o'clock. Still not certain about the decision, I had Alexas stop at a church on the way home. We went in and prayed. I felt like an executioner and wanted some sense that I was doing the right thing.

When I opened my eyes, I had the gut feeling, the knowing, that Sweetie was indeed suffering, that she in fact had a brain tumor. Then, at precisely that moment, the church bell tolled nine times.

Nine times. Nine lives. Nine years old.

I don't know what else I could have asked for in terms of confirmation.

The veterinarian spoke with us for half an hour, during which we described Sweetie's behavior of the past several months. He concurred that there was most likely a brain tumor at work. Feral cats like Sweetie were prone to lesions, he said. The kindest thing we could do for her was to painlessly end her suffering. We told him to make the preparations.

When we went into the examination room, Sweetie lay stretched out on a soft quilt that was tucked in around her back to keep her warm. The doctor had administered a heavy sedative; so while she couldn't move, she could still hear us. He and the nurse departed so we could say our goodbyes.

Before going in, I had made Alexas promise that we wouldn't break down in Sweetie's presence. Although the cat was sedated, I knew she would still be able to sense our fear or sadness, and I was determined to make her final moments peaceful. I placed a hand on Sweetie and talked softly to her.

"Papa loves you, Sweetie," I said. "Papa loves you."

I told her how much she had meant to me, and I thanked her for nine wonderful years of companionship, years during which I'd needed her more than I ever realized. Several times as I spoke, Sweetie's muscles twitched; Alexas said this was her way of communicating back to me, and I think she's right.

Then I sang a song to Sweetie, a lullaby I had made up and sung to her when she was a kitten:

> *Sweetie, O Sweetie, how'd you get so swee-eet?*
> *Sweetie, O Sweetie, how'd you get so sweet?*
> *Bought you in a pet store,*

Your friends were sound aslee-eep.
Then you jumped into my arms,
Now my life's complete.

I kissed her, then Alexas kissed her, and the veterinarian returned. He gently shaved her back leg near the ankle, found a vein and injected the strong barbiturate. Alexas and I stood at the side of the table, tightly holding hands and trembling, but not crying, while the vet checked for breathing and a pulse. There were neither.

We stayed with her for a few more minutes. What I most vividly remember about those final moments is how warm she still was. I pet her belly—something she almost never let me do—expecting, I think, she would suddenly come back to life.

She didn't.

I kissed her head for the last time and walked out, leaving instructions with the nurse to donate Sweetie's carrier to another family.

And then, outside in the warm and breezy summer morning, I did something unexpected, something I hadn't done since my grandfather died, much less in public.

I steadied myself on the walkway railing, stomped my foot at the gods, and sobbed.

10

The Prodigal Student Returns

I was in our Cambridge, Massachusetts hotel room staring down at a crew team rowing on the Charles River. The early morning water ahead of the lead scull was still, but as the scull whisked smoothly downriver, it sent ripples across the water to either bank. More sculls followed, and from the colors on the rowers' oars, I saw that my college was down there. So were Harvard and a couple of schools I didn't recognize.

Alexas was attending a work conference in Cambridge, right across the river from Boston, where the two of us had gone to college (different schools, four years apart). Having heard me wax sentimental about my former professors, she suggested I tag along on her trip and look them up. The notion of seeing them, 20 years after graduation, was both exciting and nerve-wracking.

You have to understand: when I was between the ages of 18 and 22, these guys were my heroes. Everything in the world worth knowing—the Ontological Argument, the correct usage of me and I, the Hamilton–Burr Duel—I had learned from them, in lovely, neatly packaged views of the world called "courses." As a student, I was fairly accomplished, graduating *summa cum laude*, Phi Beta Kappa, with a 3.9 GPA in philosophy.

Since graduation, I had only kept in touch with one of my professors—Prof. L. ("Rex")—but I didn't get to see him often because those visits were usually squeezed in during business trips. With the exception of a brisk walk through my campus in December 2001, during which I noted new buildings where parking lots used to be, the only contact I'd had with my alma mater was in the form of solicitation letters from the alumni association (which I immediately trashed) and the alumni magazine, which I glanced at less for news about the school, and more to keep tabs on my classmates. I had it in my bag and planned to browse it on my way over to the college that morning.

I was watching the last of the sculls disappear downriver when Alexas came up behind me and rubbed my back.

"Whatcha looking at?" she asked.

"The crew teams," I said. "Did I ever tell you—"

"—how your freshman year a couple guys on the team wanted you to join because you were so strong, but you told them you thought crew was boring and you couldn't row? Yes, you've told me this before."

My thoughts drifted away from the scene on the Charles to a foliage-resplendent Sunday afternoon in October 1986. The family Subaru had rolled into the pond, and I maladroitly rowed my father out to the car so he could tie a rope to the back bumper and attempt to pull the car to shore. Despite our best efforts, the car sank.

Outside the hotel window, the sun glared above the horizon and the entire river sparkled gold. Leaves rained down on the riverbanks. Alexas tapped my shoulder.

"Who are you having lunch with today?"

"No idea. I was going to wander over there and see who's around. Is it weird?"

"A little bit. Most of us don't keep in touch with our old professors."

"But I haven't kept in touch. That's the whole point. With the exception of Rex, I haven't seen some of these guys in twenty years."

She grabbed her makeup bag and walked into the bathroom. I followed and leaned on the doorjamb.

"I emailed them, but none of them replied. I hope it's not because they read the email and were like, 'Not that schmuck. Maybe if I ignore him, he'll go away.'"

"I'm sure none of them think that," Alexas said. "Some of them might not even use email."

"Maybe."

"So, what's your plan?" She sponged on foundation. "Just walk into their offices?"

"That or their classrooms, if they're teaching."

She smiled and shook her head.

"What?" I said.

"You. I think it's sweet. And I bet they're going to be thrilled to see you."

"We'll see."

I went back out to the bedroom, sat in the reading chair and imagined their reactions to seeing me again. The ideal scenario? I would walk into the philosophy department conference room, all of my former professors would be there, and they'd leap out of their chairs, crowd around me, and hang on my every word about what I've been doing since graduation.

"You were a newspaper reporter?" one blurts out. "That must have been exciting. Chris, I'm writing a paper about how philosophy helps people become better writers. Did you find this to be the case? Your insights would really help me to flesh this out. May I take you to dinner tonight? Do you like lobster?"

"Are you still reading any philosophy?" asks another. "I recently finished a marvelous little volume on Hume's atheism. Let me loan it to you!"

"Tell us what else you've been doing!" cries another, shaking my arm. "We have to know!"

"Gentlemen, gentlemen," I say soothingly, "please. You're philosophers for God's sake. Control yourselves. One at a time, please."

But I know it won't go like this, and I'm actually glad for it. I'm afraid that if they do remember me, they're going to be distinctly unimpressed with my achievements, such as they are. Besides, I'll feel less pressure if they're laid back or even ambivalent about my being there, as in, "Ah, hello, Orcutt. We were discussing Berkeley's '*esse est percipi*.' Care to join us?"

Alexas walked into the room and stood at attention. She slapped her hands against her sides.

"Reporting for inspection," she said.

"You look great. Pretty, yet businesslike." I grabbed my bag. "Let's go."

Outside, we boarded the hotel shuttle to Harvard Square. We were the only two people on the bus, and the driver set out immediately. There was a time when passing the hallowed brick buildings of Harvard University depressed me because they reminded me of my sophomore year, when I applied for transfer there. During an overnight campus visit, I'd bumped into a friend from high school, Eric Chen, who tried to dissuade me from transferring, telling tales of packed lecture halls, undergraduates treated like chattel, and cutthroat tactics employed by classmates; but his warnings were moot since I wasn't accepted anyway.

But now, as I kissed Alexas goodbye in Harvard Square, next to the newsstand where Bill Gates and Paul Allen had purchased the issue of *Popular Electronics* that inspired them to start Microsoft, I realized that if I'd gotten into Harvard, I might not have become a writer, and I almost certainly would not have met the love of my life, Alexas.

"What is it?" She smiled at me in the crisp October air. Her eyes were the pale blue of an iceberg.

" 'God gives each of us what is best for him,' " I said aloud.

"That's probably true," she said. "Have a good day, Toad."

"You too, Bunny."

I watched her cross Mass. Ave. and march through the iron gate into Harvard Yard. Then I took the escalator underground to the "T." Once I'd boarded the train to Boston, I pulled out the alumni magazine.

Two sections all alumni magazines have are "Class Notes" and "Deaths." Macabre bastard that I am, I opened straightaway to the Deaths section. I was simultaneously relieved and a little surprised not to find anyone I knew. Next I turned to the Class Notes section. Somebody in my class named Grover had gotten married, and a girl named Tanya had had a baby girl. I turned the page and read a note about someone I *had* known: one of my sophomore dorm suite-mates. He worked for the Internal Revenue Service and had just received a promotion with an impressive-sounding title: National Director, Corporate Revenue Enhancement.

At first I didn't think it was the same person; I couldn't reconcile the idea that a guy I knew in college, a guy who had been the ultimate ladies' man, now had a stultifying career in the least sexy government agency there is. True story: my sophomore year, this guy slept with so many coeds that, by April (after his own self-styled "March Madness"; he loved basketball), the springs on his dorm bed were shot. I can still remember the two facilities workers who came to replace the springs leaving his dorm room grinning and shaking their heads. Now this former ladies' man worked for the IRS. Ugh.

Well, I might not have worn out the springs on *my* bed in college, but at least I do something *cool* for a living today, and I'm not tied to a soul-sucking government office. I'm a novelist, Jack, and I answer to no one.

When the T reached Park Street in Boston, I put the magazine away, detrained and walked the rest of the way to campus. All of my professors' offices were still housed in an old factory building, so I went there and looked for them floor by floor. The philosophy department, I discovered, had been moved from its appropriate position on the first floor—philosophy being the foundation of all knowledge[22]—to a pathetic suite of offices on the third floor.

The reception area had the feel of a free clinic in an impoverished neighborhood. From this I deduced that the philosophy department no longer had quite the cachet with the college administration that it used to. When I was a philosophy major, the department secretary was a silver-haired woman, world-traveled and erudite, whose Luciano Pavarotti CDs resonated through the hallways on rainy afternoons. Today, the reception desk was occupied by a 19-year-old girl with resting bitch face texting on her phone.

I asked her if Professor Q. was around. Without looking up from her phone, she said he wasn't. I checked his posted hours on his office door; he had no hours scheduled today. I was on my way out when I spied another of my former professors.

Professor J., a teacher I'd had for courses on Moral Philosophy, Theory of Knowledge and Philosophical Problems in the Law—one of only two professors in the entire college to give me a grade of less than A-minus—was sitting in his office at his computer. His door was open. I knocked on the doorjamb.

"Professor J——?" I said.

"Yes?

---

[22] Physics, for example, used to be known as Natural Philosophy. Over the centuries, whenever philosophers started to learn something about a topic, other scholars would tear it out of Philosophy's purview and create a new discipline.

He swiveled in his chair to face me. I didn't expect him to remember me, so I spared him any potential embarrassment by telling him who I was.

"Anyway, professor, " I continued, "it's been twenty years, but I wanted to drop by and tell you how much your classes meant to me. You didn't give me an 'A' in any of them, but I'm actually glad about that. I realize now that you simply had really high standards."

"Well, Chris, that's nice of you to say, but I must admit that from time to time I wonder if my standards might be a bit too high."

"No, don't change a thing," I said.

I said this in part because I believed that Prof. J.'s higher standards were ultimately to a student's benefit, but also because, since he hadn't given me an "A," I didn't want other students to have that distinction.

"I suppose you're right," he said. "So, what have you been up to?"

I'd been rehearsing my answer to this question in my head for a week, so I was able to rattle off my work chronology in a couple minutes: newspaper reporter to teacher to entrepreneur to middle manager to adjunct lecturer to freelance speechwriter. While getting it out as quickly as possible, I could feel him studying me. Here it was, 20 years later, and the man still intimidated me. He stared at me with one eye shut and the other tightly squinted, a finger over his mouth and nodding slowly, like I was speaking gibberish and he was struggling to understand me.

Why the man intimidated me, I have no idea. He was still a diminutive 5'6" tall, maybe 150 pounds, but he had that *huge* head, huge in proportion to his narrow shoulders, and I knew what a big and powerful brain was in there. Alexander Hamilton had been another one of these small body-big brain guys; so had the best example in this situation: philosopher Immanuel Kant.

When I told him that I wrote speeches for corporate executives, maybe I was imagining it but I thought I saw a flash of disgust in his eyes, as if he wanted to say, "No, please don't tell me you're using your philosophy skills to help *those* people." Immediately I regretted telling him and wished I'd detailed my struggles to become a great writer instead. Until recently, my endeavors had been fraught with failure, but the professor probably would have respected me more.

I recalled to myself how Anton Chekhov once described his own life, and considered saying it to the professor: *"It is not much fun to be a great writer. To begin with, it's a dreary life. Work from morning till night, and very little to show for it. Money is as scarce as cats' tears."*[23]

I smiled; I loved that bit about "cats' tears."

Uncomfortable being the subject of attention anymore, I shifted the conversation back to Prof. J.

"So, professor," I said, "what have you been writing lately? Are you still as big a fan of John Stuart Mill as you used to be?"

His eyebrows sprang up so fast, I thought they'd fly off his forehead. "Wow, you remembered that?" he said.

"Sure," I said. "I still have my copy of *On Liberty*—bad highlights and all."

---

[23] Anton Chekhov in a letter to Mme. M.V. Kiselev, Moscow, Sept. 21, 1886.

He reached into a pile of papers on the couch where I was sitting and pulled out a pale blue volume. He held it lovingly. "This was an interesting project," he muttered. Once he was sure my hands were prepared to receive it, he passed it to me as one would a newborn.

"I was asked to edit Mill's *Principles of Political Economy*," he said. "The original text runs to over a thousand pages, so it was quite humbling having to sift through Mill's ideas and try to condense them down to their essence."

I flipped though the book. "I can only imagine."

At this point there was an awkward pause, during which I could tell he was expecting me to ask for a copy of the book. However, there was no way I was making any commitments (tacit or otherwise) to spend my leisure time reading a dense philosophy text. If I chose to spend my leisure time reading Kant or Kierkegaard, that was my business, but I didn't want to leave here with any kind of obligation to get in touch again in a month to discuss a book.

"You know, professor," I said, handing the book back to him, "I have to say, you don't look a bit different than I remember you twenty years ago. I mean, your hair is slightly grayer at the temples, but other than that it's as if I was still an undergraduate and I've come in for advice on my courses."

"That's very nice of you to say, Chris," Prof. J. said.

"I mean it. Seriously, it's amazing how little you've changed. Must be the philosophy. Maybe thinking great thoughts has a way of keeping you young."

"Maybe," he said.

I could tell that he was tiring of the conversation—fast. Clearly, my discourse wasn't as scintillating as the work of John Stuart Mill. The professor eyed his book dreamily, probably hoping that I'd clear out ASAP so he could crack it open to a favorite passage about unproductive labor.

"Well," I said, standing up, "it's been great seeing you, professor."

"Likewise." He shook my hand. "Good luck with your writing, and whatever else you're doing."

"Thanks. Maybe I'll drop by again in five or ten years."

"I'm not sure I'll be here, but if I am, it would be nice to see you then."

Perhaps I was imagining it, but he seemed to put undue emphasis on the word "then," as in, "See you *then*, but not before, please."

"And good luck to you, professor."

On my way out of his office, I glanced down the hall at Prof. Q.'s door. It was still closed. I went out to the industrial stairwell and clunked downstairs. I decided to go someplace for a snack and to kill time, then come back in an hour and skulk around some more.

This, I mused as I trod down the stairs, was probably as close to the experience of being a "fan" as I would ever get. Autograph hounds and paparazzi must do an awful lot of this skulking and aimless waiting in order to catch their quarry. For a moment I considered getting a sandwich and sitting on a bench across from the entrance to the faculty offices. But it felt too much like work. After all, I was on vacation. I decided to check out the revamped student center across campus.

My walk was during a class change, and while I didn't see any of my professors, I did have a chance to make some observations about the student body. According to the most recent *U.S. News & World Report* top colleges issue, my alma mater was now officially ranked among the top 50 colleges in the country, and its newfound prestige showed in the serious, studious faces I saw passing me by, students with high SAT scores who were sure of their career plans, who seemed to gaze into the future as if these four years were but an annoying layover on their journey to achievement. None of the kids had that bleary-eyed, dissipated and disheveled look that so many of us had exhibited when I went here.

The other sign the school had made a turn for the better was the overall attractiveness of the girls; there were far more objectively gorgeous girls here now than when I had attended. Most of them were walking briskly while typing frenetically on smart phones, oblivious to me and everyone else around them. It was an unseasonably warm morning, and many of them wore short skirts. For a moment, I was 20 years old again, but with the wisdom and confidence of middle age. I felt like I could march up to any of them, ask them out, and receive a grateful and stammering "y-ye-yes" in reply.

That is, until a statuesque young woman strutted purposefully toward me. Her hair was the same fiery orange as the sugar maples lining the walkway, and with a toss of that hair she threw me a slit-eyed smirk that said, *"I know you. You're one of those middle-aged men with a redhead fetish. Hmmph. Well, you're cute, but…about twenty years too late. Sucks for you!"*

Recalling beautiful Anne Bernay, I stopped, steadied myself on a bench, and watched this statuesque redhead fade into the throng. My chest ached. Where had the time gone? It didn't seem fair. Especially now that I was older and so much wiser.

Continuing my hike to the student center, I passed a string of places that conjured pleasant memories: the top-floor window of the old library, where I'd once tossed a copy of Anaïs Nin's erotica *Delta of Venus* out the window and later retrieved it down in the alley, rather than suffer the ignominy of checking it out from the librarians; the steps of the new library, where K.M., a pale and sullen brunette gal-pal, and I had huddled together in our ratty overcoats against the wind between Shakespeare classes, smoked Dunhill blue cigarettes, and conversed in extemporaneous iambic pentameter; the lecture hall where I took an Intro to Political Science course, and the professor (a tall German woman who bore an uncanny resemblance to the singer Annie Lennox) flirted with me after class, but I didn't realize what she'd been hinting at, the opportunity I'd missed, until a year later, after she'd returned to Munich; the dorm where I'd missed another opportunity, a Willy Wonka Golden Ticket opportunity, an opportunity that would haunt me forever, this one with a mind-blowing blonde from down the hall, a blonde with the body of a *Penthouse* centerfold and the face of a pastor's daughter, a blonde from Pawtucket, Rhode Island who danced nights at a strip club in the Combat Zone under the stage name "Goldilocks," who had, like, a *wicked* crush on me, but who allegedly was a raving nymphomaniac, which rumor turned me off because I didn't care to boldly go where lots of other men had gone before, then learning later on that the poor girl had dropped out of school and died of a drug overdose; the law school building, where I'd taken my first criminalistics course from the then-head of the Mass. State Crime Lab; the law school courtyard, where I'd been filmed for the college's national TV commercial; the faculty cafeteria, where, as the guest of Prof. G., I made a group of professors laugh to tears with my story about the Subaru rolling into the pond and my father and I trying to pull it out; the campus auditorium, where my friends Bill and Tom and I went stoned one evening to listen to a lecture by physicist Stephen Hawking; the theatre department building, where I performed the lead in my own dramatic adaptation of *The Great Gatsby*, with C., a strikingly Junoesque pre-law student, as Daisy. And finally, as I neared the student center, the registrar's office, where I once stood in the dim, empty hallway at 8:00 a.m., waiting for them to open, and a 30-something redhead in a short skirt and ribbed black stockings stomped to the office door, found it locked, swore, then turned to me and said, "That's the way of the world these days, honey: Nobody starts on time. But *you*"—she winked at me *con brio*, nearly causing me to ejaculate in my pants—"you're up *early*. Just keep being an early riser, honey, and you'll succeed at whatever you do. *Guaranteed.*"

The first indication that I was dealing with a wholly different student center was when I approached the entrance and the doors opened automatically. Once upon a time, when the doors had metal handles, I had watched a kid ahead of me try to open one at 7:00 a.m. in 10 below zero. His damp, ungloved fingers instantly stuck to the metal, forcing his buddy to run inside for a cup of water to peel them off. Today, however, I breezed through the automatic doors, winked at the perky work-study girl at the information desk, and used the bathroom.

Here was another area in which my college had improved over the last two decades. Whereas in my day the restrooms on campus resembled the ones you'd find in a second-tier city bus station, this one was bright, sparkling and palatial—nicer than the one at Tavern on the Green, for Pete's sake. Finishing my business, I watched a kid who could have been me 20 years ago. He primped his hair in a lighted mirror, washed his hands under an automatic faucet with foam soap and steaming hot water, and dabbed them dry on a linen-y-soft paper towel.

My jaw clenched. I wanted to block the doorway so I could lecture him about what the school's bathrooms were like in my day: flickering fluorescent bulbs if we were lucky, cold water with no soap, and certainly no hand towels. Instead we got those skin-chapping hand dryers popularized by McDonald's in the '70s, the ones with a monotone hum that sounded like a prop plane destined to crash deep in the Amazon.

"Nice bathroom you guys got," I said.

"Yeah, I guess," he said.

He'd given me an opening. Big mistake.

"You *guess*?" I said. "Let me tell you, when I went to school here, we didn't have anything like this."

"That's sad," the kid said, scooting around me. "Nice to meet you, but I gotta go."

"Hey...remember"—I stuck my head out the door as he left—"it wasn't always like this!"

Instead of feeling vindicated and empowered by my little speech, a hollowness and sense of desperation spread through me. *How pathetic can you get, Chris? That kid doesn't care about what the bathrooms were like in your day.* I had officially become one of those old, complaining curmudgeons, jealous of the new generation for having it so easy. This became even clearer to me when I exited the bathroom and spied the kiosks of shiny Apple computers for students to surf the web.

"Oh, come on!" I nearly shouted. "Where was all this cool stuff when I went here?!"

"Excuse me, sir?"

A young man in a tie was addressing me from a fold-up table with literature spread out on it. Next to him was a studious young woman, typing on a smart phone.

"Sir," the young man said, "did I hear you say you went to school here?"

"Yes."

Approaching their table, I saw bumper stickers, key chains, mugs and shot glasses with the college's logo on them.

"Sir, we're with the alumni association," he said. "May I ask, are you registered with us?"

"No, and—"

"Well, sir, we're offering a special promotion this week. If you give us your contact info, along with your class and major, you can take any of these things as a free gift."

The young woman, still boring her eyes into her cell phone screen, removed one hand from it long enough to wave at the merchandise. It was clearly rehearsed, but cute.

"Sorry, sonny," I said. "Not interested."

"Sonny?" the young man said. "What the hell, dude? How old are you?"

"Old enough to call you sonny.[24] Look, I have to go. Good luck with your proselytizing."

Nothing was preventing me from giving them a fake name and bogus class information so I could get the free trinket, but truth be told, I didn't want any reminders that I had gone to school here. The only aspects of the college that I truly enjoyed—its location in the heart of Boston, my professors, and the girls—had nothing to

---

24 This incident raises an important question: when *is* it appropriate to use the term "sonny"? Is use of this term dependent on the age gap between the person speaking and the person being "sonnyed"—an age gap of, say, at least 20 years—or is it really a term to which the right of use is restricted to the very old and crotchety?

For an answer, I referred to an incident at a nursing home when my father was visiting his mother. He rode his bike there, and as he was leaving, while trying to clip his biking shoes to the pedals, he tipped over into a flower bed. Seeing this, a whiskery old woman leaned forward on her patio chair and crowed (in a thick Down East Maine accent), *"Ride much, sonny?"*

Checking my dictionary (American Heritage, Fourth Edition), I was shocked to find "sonny" included. The definition reads as follows: "**sonny** (n') n., pl. **-nies** Used as a familiar form of address for a boy or young man. [Diminutive of SON.]"

Clearly my use of the word, which by now you have surely forgotten, was technically correct because it was closest to the denotative meaning of "sonny"; however, the old woman's use of the word made the most sense from a connotative perspective. Thus, in my little inquiry into the correct usage of "sonny," we arrive at an impasse: both are right.

do with the institution itself. And it wasn't as if being a graduate of the college had magically opened doors of opportunity for me.

He and the girl were shaking their heads at me as I walked away, but I didn't care. I was hungry.

The student center now had a full-service food court. *Spoiled bastards.* All of the usual fast-food outlets were here, along with a tiny place that sold nothing but soups, including clam chowder. I bought a large bowl of chowder and grabbed three bags of oyster crackers. The dining area was packed with students and their Sherpa-full knapsacks, so I went up the spiral staircase to the student lounge. There, I plopped down on the one thing on campus that hadn't changed in 20 years: the industrial-grade couches. So ass-numbingly hard, they discouraged sitting for more than five minutes.

The chowder was good, although not as good as the café's at the Copley Marriott (where Alexas worked when we first met). As I spooned it down, dumping in more crackers, I gazed up at the tiers of offices that contained the many student activities I'd been a part of. They also sparked memories of events I'd forgotten for 20 years.

For example, the election for Freshman Class President, and how the moment I was nominated and it became clear that I could win, I thought of all the *work* the job entailed and immediately withdrew, stating I would be a better guy "behind the scenes." I threw my support behind L.L., a very tall and confident guy I had met in Intro to Physics. L.L., who frequently wore bow ties, *looked* like a politician, and although he wasn't half the natural public speaker that I was, the other students literally looked up to him. Most importantly, he wanted the job; I didn't. I enjoyed getting people riled up, but I didn't want to *govern*. Boring.

All my life I've suffered from loving the thrill of the chase, but the second I get the thing that I *thought* I wanted, I don't want it anymore. (I know—"Boo-friggen-hoo." Cue Tchaikovsky's dirgeful *Marche Slave*.)

One of the offices on the second floor was in a glass fishbowl, and inside were several students working at computers. It was probably still the student magazine office. I had been a feature writer for the magazine with a humorous monthly "Man About Town" column. I recalled my most popular piece, "My Day at the MFA,"[25] as well as the time my friend Brian and I smoked a massive joint before an editorial meeting and sat through a scolding by the tight-assed editor as baked as macaroni and cheese.

Finished with my chowder, I threw out my trash and wandered around the lounge. There was some sort of career day going on, with a lot of big-name technology companies represented.

Not to mention, the Central Intelligence Agency.

These CIA recruiter clowns were here on campus when I was in school. Clearly, they were ensconced in here tighter than ticks. It wouldn't surprise me if they'd installed a secret office behind one of the stacks in the library. When I was a senior, a couple of friends and I had

---

[25] The "MFA" is the Museum of Fine Arts in Boston, Massachusetts. I still have a copy of this issue. Reading it over, I'm a little embarrassed to see how blatantly I mimicked Holden Caulfield's voice in *The Catcher in the Rye*. Still, the piece has some humorous moments.

completed the lengthy application process, only to hear *nothing* about our applications—not even a "thanks for applying" postcard with a picture of Langley on the front. Months later, we commiserated about it while drinking beer in paper bags on our dorm front stoop.

"You know what?" my friend Jesse pithily observed. "The CIA's a bunch of dicks."

Everyone nodded in agreement, clinked bag-bottles, and resolved never to apply to them again.

Well, here I had an opportunity to make a revenge fantasy come true. Not knowing when my professors would be in their offices, I decided to have some fun with these guys.

They were two young men, mid 20s, in dark suits and ties. One of them was Asian. He looked a lot like the Japanese kid in *Sixteen Candles*, so I decided to think of him as Long Duck Dong. The other one was blonde and had that husky, Iowa Farm Boy look, so thought of him as Farm Boy.

Since 9/11, the CIA had been aggressively recruiting people fluent in multiple languages, so I knew what one of their questions would be, and I was prepared for it.

"Hi," I said, "I'm interested in working for the CIA."

Long Duck Dong shook my hand first, then Farm Boy. They said their names, but I wasn't listening.

"Nice to meet you," Farm Boy said. "And you are…?"

"Not comfortable giving you my name yet," I said. "You can call me Dr. Jones for now."

Long Duck Dong nodded, smiling faintly. "Okay, Dr. Jones."

"Do you know any foreign languages, Dr. Jones?" Farm Boy asked. "And by 'know' I mean are you fluent in them?"

"Several," I said.

"Which ones?" asked Long Duck Dong.

"We'll get to that. Suffice it to say, gentlemen, that I am more than qualified to be a field operative for the Company."

"Okay." Farm Boy handed me a color slick describing positions in the Clandestine Service. "Why don't you take one of these and read it over when you have a chance."

"Sir," said Long Duck Dong, "why do you want to work for the CIA?"

"I love this country," I said. "My office was directly across the street from the World Trade Center on Nine-eleven. I actually completed an application a while back, but it must have gotten lost because I never heard from you guys."

"Where were you working during Nine-eleven?"

"American Express," I lied.

As lies go, this one was tame because American Express was only one building north of mine.

"And what did you do there, Dr. Jones?" Farm Boy asked.

"I was an international account manager," I said, spinning my yarn. "I traveled worldwide and worked with foreign offices to sell AMEX products and services to the local population. It's quite a bit like war propaganda, the history of which is something of a hobby of mine. You should see some of the techniques the Nazis used against Allied troops during World War II. Well, I'm ashamed to say that in some respects my job with AMEX was as a propagandist more than anything, but one has to make a living, right?"

The more I talked, the clearer it became that these two were new to the CIA because they seemed to be swallowing everything I said. Either I was a better liar than I thought or the Company hadn't trained them in recognizing visual cues. On my bookshelves at home were two books on the subject: *How to Read a Person Like a Book* and *Never Be Lied to Again*, so I knew what to look for. If they had known, they would have recognized that most of what I was saying was bullshit.

"You said 'was,' sir," Long Duck Dong said. "What do you do now?"

"I'm an adjunct professor at a college in New York City," I said.

"What languages do you speak again?" Farm Boy asked.

"I didn't say, did I? I speak fluent English, German, Italian, French, Spanish and Farsi."

"*Farsi*, really?" Farm Boy said.

"Really."

"Speak a little for us," said Long Duck Dong.

I snorted. "Why? You wouldn't understand what I was saying."

"What are your degrees in?" Farm Boy asked.

"International business and psychology. And I have a Ph.D. in linguistics."

"Where from?"

"Sorry," I said.

"Tell us more about the work you used to do for AMEX," Farm Boy said.

"No, I'd like *you* to tell me about the Clandestine Service."

"Well," drawled Farm Boy, "it's all in the brochure you have there. It's really about collecting intelligence, field work."

"Wait a minute." I clasped my hands behind my back and held the rolled-up brochure like a riding crop. "Are you telling me you guys don't have experience in the Clandestine Service yourselves?"

Long Duck Dong stared at the well-worn student lounge rug. Farm Boy took the opposite tactic: raising his chin and declaring defiantly, "No, we don't. We're Human Resource Officers."

I'd accomplished what I'd wanted, which was to have fun with these two, to get them all hot and bothered about my potential as a field operative, then disappear. Now I needed an exit strategy.

"Well, it's been nice chatting with you two," I said, "but I'm afraid before I go any further I'm going to need to speak with someone higher up in the food chain."

"Yes, yes, of course," said Long Duck Dong. He grabbed a clipboard and placed it on the table in front of me. "If you'll give us your name and phone number, we can have someone get in touch with you."

"Or your email if you'd prefer," added Farm Boy.

"I don't think so," I said. "Here's what we're going to do. I want somebody to write me a *letter*. Email or the phone is too easy. You see, gentlemen…there's a reason why most Zen monasteries are built on mountaintops.

They do it to discourage the dilettantes. If someone in a decision-making capacity writes me a *letter*, I'll know you guys are serious."

Farm Boy started to hand me a pen.

"Nice try," I said, "but I'll use my own. Nobody's running my prints until I get that letter."

"What?" Long Duck Dong said. "You've been watching too many movies, Dr. Jones."

"Sorry. Have somebody write me a letter at this address and I'll tell you everything."

Careful not to touch the clipboard or the table with my fingertips, I used my own pen to complete the info section, writing in ALL CAPS to throw off any Company graphologists in their handwriting analysis. For "Name," I wrote, "DR. JONES," and in the address field I entered a mailbox down the road from Tony's place in the Catskills. It was an address with an abandoned house that was well off the road, so the local post office didn't know it was vacant. Tony had used it a few times to receive items in the mail that he wasn't supposed to have, always using the surname "Jones" as the addressee. I completed the fields on the form and left it there without touching anything.

"Nice to meet you two. I hope to hear from somebody."

"You will, Dr. Jones. You will."

The table was full of CIA paraphernalia: mugs, mouse pads and lapel pins.

"May I take one of the pins?"

"Sure," said Farm Boy, "go ahead."

I did and put it on my sweater. We shook hands.

"Good luck in your careers, gentlemen."

"Nice to meet you, professor."

I walked away. When I reached the stairs, I glanced over my shoulder and saw Long Duck Dong snap open his cell phone. Not being trained in the reading of lips, I had no idea what he was saying, but from the eagerness in his face, I had to assume he was talking to a superior about this mysterious candidate he and his buddy had just met. Either that, or he was calling ahead to another agent somewhere on campus, someone who, based on Long Duck Dong's description of me, would tail me until he figured out who I really was.

To be on the safe side, to throw off any would-be tails, when I got to the ground floor I used my one advantage: intimate knowledge of the building's layout. I ducked into a stairwell and went up three flights to a bathroom, where I removed my leather jacket and bundled it inside my bag. Then I put on my black-framed Clark Kent glasses, the lenses of which darkened when I got outside. These two minor changes in my appearance would be more than enough to throw off any pursuers—certainly any CIA employees of such inferior caliber that their territory was a college campus.

"See," I said aloud to myself in the mirror, "you *would* make a good spy."

One of the cool things about my alma mater—and which I have to admit was one of the reasons why I went there—is that it has an elaborate network of tunnels connecting most of the buildings. This subterranean network comes in handy during blizzards or in situations like this: when you're a paranoid alumnus convinced the CIA is following you. I followed the tunnels to the building with the Provost and Bursar's offices, went upstairs and serpentined through the building to check for any tails. Disappointingly, there was nobody, and I descended to the tunnels again. Since my graduation, they had expanded the tunnels significantly, so I was able to follow them all the way to the other side of campus.

I emerged outside a classroom where I had once rallied my classmates to use Pavlov's findings against our smug psychology professor. The classroom was empty, so I went inside. It happened right…*there*: in retaliation for his subjecting us to a socialization experiment without our consent, I convinced my fellow students to act up and talk loudly the farther the professor strayed from the corner of the room. By the end of the semester, when we revealed to him how we'd used his own psychology tricks against him, he was teaching the entire hour from that corner, singeing his arm against an exposed steam pipe. Smiling, I took a deep breath of satisfaction at the memory, and exited the building.

Out on the street, 100 yards from the faculty offices building, I scanned the entire area. Unless the CIA had disguised operatives as Frisbee-throwers, no one was following me. I went to check for my professors again.

None of them were in their department offices, but on my way outside again, I spied Professor G. walking in. The moment I got outside on the entrance stairs, I regretted not having put some styling product in my hair that morning. Since I'd left the hotel that morning, the wind had picked up, and I could feel the hair on the sides of my head becoming "wingier" by the minute. In a lull between gusts, I did my best to smooth it out and smiled at the professor as he neared the stairs.

"Professor G——?"

He smiled and stared at me absently, like an Alzheimer's patient. For a moment I feared the worst.

"Yes?" he said. "Do I know you?"

"Professor, I'm Chris Orcutt. You were my American history professor twenty years ago."

His face snapped into recognition. "Of course! Chris!"

"I was in town and wanted to drop by and say hello," I said casually, as if this wasn't an all-out stalking operation. "Do you have a few minutes?" I held the door open for him.

"Actually, I'm going in this way," he said, pointing at the door to the elevator room.

"You're still on the second floor, aren't you?" I said.

"Yes, Chris, but when one gets to be my age, his bones begin to ache and he finds himself taking elevators."

"I think it's great. They're fun."

He chuckled. "Well, *this* elevator isn't much fun, but it works. Come along."

Considering the number of floors it spanned (one), that elevator ride was the slowest and most uncomfortable I'd ever had. It also took a full minute, during which I was packed in there with Professor G., Professor H. (whose daughter I had crushed on but who showed no interest in me), and six of the laziest 19-year-olds I'd ever seen. Prof. G. did his best to be gracious, like this was his parlor and we were simply waiting for tea to be served.

"So, Chris," he drawled, "are you still living in New York?"

"Yes, but we're back upstate now, my wife and—"

"Here we are!" Prof. G. said.

We squeezed out of the elevator.

"Now," he said, "did you wear glasses back then? I don't seem to recall your wearing glasses."

"Once in a while I did." I followed him down the hallway. "But I did it then as a fashion statement, and I'm afraid it became a self-fulfilling prophecy."

"Oh, dear…that's too bad." He switched on the conference room lights. "Sit down, Chris. I have to take care of something. I shall return momentarily!"

The conference room: the long, gleaming oak table encircled by black lacquer chairs with the college's seal on them, and a secondary set of chairs against the walls at the room's perimeter. This august space had always been reserved for faculty meetings and graduate student seminars.

Nothing had changed. The bookcase of graduate student theses was the same, the binders appearing not to have been moved in 20 years. This was very likely the same blue-gray indestructible rug, and the place even had the same smell, a contradictory smell I'd come to associate with history: mustiness and lemon furniture polish. Professor G. returned.

"So, Chris! How are you?" He chuckled. "The prodigal student returns!"

I had purposely left the chair at the head of the table free for him, and he sat in it.

"Very good," I said. "Were you returning from class?"

"I was!" he said. "My American Elites course!"

I smiled. He hadn't lost one of his most charming habits: forever projecting his voice to invisible students.

"American Elites—I loved that course," I said. "Well… everything except…are you still making the kids read that dreadful *Silas Lapham*?"

"Dreadful? That's a wonderful novel. Wonderful!"

"Professor, *you* were wonderful, but I hate to tell, you, that novel sucked."

He chuckled. "Now…you were writing for newspapers last I heard from you. Are you still a journalist?"

"Nope."

Having rehearsed my "What I'm Doing with My Life" monologue on Prof. J. earlier, this rendition went much faster. About a minute. I know because I timed it using the sweeping second hand on the ancient wall clock.

"*Speechwriting*?" Prof. G. said. "That sounds interesting. For political candidates as well?"

"No, only business executives for now. I applied to the Obama administration, but they've probably got more than their share of Harvard and Yale people, so I doubt they'll be calling."

"What's that pin on your sweater?"

"It's a CIA pin," I said.

He frowned. His neck shrunk, like a turtle retracting its head into its shell, bunching up his red bow tie around his Adam's apple.

"Don't tell me you're writing speeches for *them*!"

"No, I got it over at the student center," I said. "There were recruiters there."

"Did you apply to work there?" he asked.

His head began to shake. I couldn't tell if it was involuntary or not.

"No, it's a long story," I said. "Listen, I want to talk about you. You know, when I was teaching American history in Freeport, Maine, I used the notes I took in your courses as the foundation of my syllabus."

"Really?" he said.

"Yes. I still have those notes in fact," I said. "So are you teaching only the one course?"

He smiled mischievously and shook his head.

"Don't tell me you're still teaching a full course load," I said.

He nodded. Drumming his fully extended fingers on the edge of the table, he said, "I love it, and fortunately the faculty by-laws prevent them from getting rid of me."

"I think it's great, professor," I said. "Don't ever quit. It's got to be the reason why you look so good. Honestly, you haven't aged a day since I had you."

"Guess how old I am. Guess!"

I had an idea he was in his eighties, but over the years I've learned that when people ask you to estimate their ages, they want you to low-ball it. It's a little game we all play.

"I don't know. Seventy-one?"

He shook his head again. "I'm eighty-two."

"Wow, and teaching a full course load," I said. "That's really something, professor. I hope I can look like you when I'm your age."

"I swim a mile every day!" he boomed. "Let's go to lunch!" He slapped the end of the conference table with both hands and stood up suddenly. His spryness caught me off guard. "Have you seen the new student center?"

"No, well…I've seen it, but I haven't been inside."

"That settles it. Come, I'll buy you lunch."

I followed him across the hall to his office. He unlocked the door.

"Professor," I said, "you seem to be missing the point here. I'm taking *you* to lunch. I want to thank you for being such a great teacher. Students should be taking you out to lunch—hell, every meal—every day of your life. After sixty years of service, you shouldn't be paying for another thing, *ever*."

He chuckled. "Oh, Chris, I don't know about that."

I followed him into his office. He slipped on his coat. Twenty years ago, his office had looked like one of those Manhattan apartments you read about, where the occupant dies and when they finally cart the body out, they find towering heaps of newspapers that form a maze through the apartment. It didn't seem possible, but now it was even worse. Back then, I was *certain* he couldn't possibly cram one more folder, blue book, newspaper or textbook into the place, but somehow, in a blatant flouting of the laws of gravity, he had.

The piles towered higher than ever, several of them leaning precariously over his desk. I had always hoped that, when Prof. G. died, he went out like John Quincy Adams, the former President who died on the floor of the House of Representatives—Prof. G. just slumping over his lectern in the middle of a lecture on George Washington.

But the mountain of paper looming over his desk concerned me; I imagined it collapsing and burying him alive, like a skier caught in an avalanche.

"Professor," I said, "would it be okay if I left my bag here?"

"Of course!"

After taking out my umbrella, I placed my bag on top of a Royal KMM typewriter, which itself was balanced precariously atop a tower of magazines. I eyed the typewriter with a breathless, rapacious lust normally reserved for milky-skinned, 25-year-old redheads.

"Still have that old Royal, I see," I said. "By the way, if you ever decide to get rid of it, I like to write my first drafts on typewriters, so I'd be glad to buy it from you."

"Oh, that? The college owns it, Chris. I've simply been using it."

"*Using* it? For how long?"

"Since the day I started," he said. "In nineteen fifty-two."

"Surely they've forgotten about it by now," I said.

He didn't say anything. I dropped it.

We were walking down the hall when Professor O. bumped into us at the elevator. Twenty years ago, I'd branded him a pompous ass because he spoke with what sounded like a fake Boston Brahmin accent.[26]

"Professor O——," said Prof. G., "this is Chris Orcutt, one of our former students! He's here to take me to *lunch*!"

"Marvelous," said Prof. O.

---

26 According to one of his colleagues, Prof. O.'s accent was real. It was called "lace curtain Irish."

Prof. G. lowered his voice to the volume one would use to betray a secret.

"Guess what he does for a living. He writes speeches for all the big executives! Isn't that wonderful?"

"Mm," Prof. O. said. "So are you here writing a speech, Chris?"

"Actually, I'm on vacation."

"Pardon? You decided to come *here*? For your vacation?"

He looked at me askance, as though a person in his right mind wouldn't possibly want to visit his alma mater on vacation. I explained that I was accompanying my wife on a business trip, and while she was busy at her conference, I was exploring Boston and visiting my professors here at the college.

"Ah." He nodded, but continued to look at me circumspectly.

Out on the street, it occurred to me that I *had* seen the new student center. That was where I'd talked at length with the CIA boys. I didn't want to bump into them again.

"Professor," I said, "I *have* seen the new student center. I got it mixed up with the athletic center, which I haven't seen."

"You mean the fitness center?" he said.

"I guess so. Does it have a restaurant?"

"It does!" he said loudly. "They have soup! Soup and sandwiches!"

"Sounds great."

It was a revelatory lunch, because I saw an entirely different side of Professor G. than I'd ever seen before.

Initially he directed the conversation toward me, asking about my experiences teaching college English. I'd enjoyed the teaching part of it, I said, but the politics drove me out of it. I explained Alexas' theory on why the then-chair of the Baruch College English department pushed me out: when he'd expressed an interest in mentoring me while I got a Ph.D. in English, I unintentionally insulted him by replying I was a novelist and not interested in a doctorate.

Professor G. halted his spoon halfway to his mouth and clucked his tongue.

"English departments!" he said. "They're all like that—vicious little snipes!"

Eventually I steered the conversation back to him, and was soon uncomfortable as he shared details with me that contradicted the vision I'd always had of him as a history-teaching machine. As I listened to his confession that he was intimidated by the new technology the kids were using nowadays, my tomato-basil soup went cold.

"I'm absolutely lost, Chris," he whispered. "I don't know where I'd be without Professor H——."

He asked if I'd seen Rex lately, and I told him I'd be seeing him tomorrow, to take him to a doctor's appointment. Prof. G. closed his eyes and shook his head minutely, as though he couldn't believe what he was hearing.

"That won't be much fun for *you*, though, will it?" he said.

We commiserated about our mutual frustrations with Rex and how it seemed that anytime we called him, all he wanted to talk about were his medical issues—diagnoses, medications, internists, etc., always employing the royal "we," as in, "*We're* trying a new pill, Chris." I felt a little guilty about sharing a laugh with the professor at Rex's expense, but it was also a relief to know I wasn't the only person who felt this way.

All throughout lunch, I kept remarking to Prof. G. about how little he had changed, while inside I nursed doubts about whether I'd followed the right path in my own life. Had I done the right thing by not getting a Ph.D. and pursuing the academic life? For 60 years, Prof. G. had enjoyed job security, great health and satisfaction as a teacher. What the hell was I doing as a writer? What was I accomplishing—if anything?

We finished our lunch and headed back to the office. It had started to rain, but I opened my umbrella and held it mostly over Prof. G. as he talked. The professor's hero, George Washington, had allegedly died of a cold after being out in the rain,[27] and I was damned if I was going to let that happen to the professor.

"So," he said, "it looks like the College of Arts and Sciences is going to be splitting into three groups. It's a mistake! Sheer idiocy!"

A heartbeat later, I took his side, rapidly formulating and spouting off an argument against such a maneuver: that it would create walls between the fields of study, preventing interdisciplinary thinking.

"It's all about being able to think between disciplines," I said. "The problems that people face in the work world don't come pre-labeled with what subject you should use to solve them."

---

27 His doctors' bleeding him to treat the cold (a common 18th century medical practice) didn't help matters.

"Right!"

As we walked back to his office, I found myself getting into and enjoying the academic mindset again. Here, I thought to myself, is a world in which the pathetically insignificant is often elevated to cosmic importance. I'd missed the warm glow of certainty this world offered. Somewhat insulated from the mundane world, one was free to debate issues from the safe and rarified position of the ideal. It was fun, but I suddenly felt a twinge of pity for Prof. G.; I wondered if he had the breadth of life experience to see how petty this all was. Back at his office, I picked up my bag, and we shook hands.

"Chris," the professor said, "will you still be in town on Wednesday?"

"Yes."

"What are you doing at eight o'clock in the morning?"

"I'm not sure," I said. "What'd you have in mind?"

"I'd like for you to talk to my American survey class," he said.

"What about?"

"The importance of knowing history in the work world."

"I'd be honored, professor," I said.

"Excellent!" He gave me the building and room number, and shook my hand vigorously. "See you then, Chris!"

That night when Alexas got out of her conference, she found me down at the hotel bar, reading a book and drinking wine. It was a varietal I'd never had before—Pinot Noir. I was drinking it because it was mentioned several times in the depressingly inspired comic novel I was reading, *Sideways*. By the time Alexas got there, I'd had four glasses of the stuff. This was the most drunk I'd been in nearly a decade, when I'd gotten positively sloshed and behaved very badly.

"What's wrong?" she asked.

I shrugged. "Don't worry, I told the bartender to cut me off after this one."

"How many is that?"

"This? Number five."

She rubbed my back. "Bad day?"

"I don't know. It was going pretty well."

The trouble was, after the pleasant lunch with Prof. G., I'd made the mistake of walking around Boston and visiting old haunts that reminded me of the high hopes and big plans I'd for myself. Doing this only made me dwell on how far short I'd fallen in most areas. I told her that for the first time in my life I felt old, and I kept going on about how the professors I'd seen so far didn't seem to have aged a day. When I finished, Alexas took hold of my hands.

"First of all, you're not old," she said. "And you certainly don't look old, by any means."

"Really?"

"Come on, look at that hair!" she said, playing with it. "That's not the hair of an old man."

"It's just...seeing these guys and how successful they've been makes me wonder. I mean, I'm not where I thought I'd be at this age."

"Where did you think you'd be?"

After a long time of gazing around the hotel atrium, I chuckled to myself.

"What?" she said.

"Well, it's…I guess this is what a midlife crisis feels like, but as midlife crises go, this one's pretty lame. I feel like if I'm going to bother to have one, I might as well get some enjoyment out of it."

I raised my voice.

"Where's my seedy motel room?! Where's my bottle of Maker's Mark?! Where's my tall, sinuous, and most sinful redhead, whose gleaming hair when spilled over white pillows resembles molten lava?!

"Jesus, if I'm going to have a midlife crisis, it's gotta be worthwhile!"

The bartender walked over like someone approaching a bird on the Endangered Species List. Alexas smiled to let him know everything was okay.

"We'll take a check," she said.

"You got it," he said.

"Really, dude," she said to me when the bartender walked away, "get your priorities straight. If you're going to break down, break *down*."

"I don't know what's wrong with me," I said.

"You're way too hard on yourself, that's what's wrong." She signed the check to our room. "Come on, mama's taking you to dinner."

"I called Rex this afternoon," I said. "I'm going to drive him to the doctor and stuff tomorrow."

"That's good," she said. "You always feel better when you do something for someone less fortunate."

"Yeah. We'll see."

II

Early the next morning, I went back over to Boston, this time driving my car. I parked down the block from Rex's building on Arlington Street, across from the Public Garden.

Visiting Rex was always a pain in the ass. The trouble was, he was sick with a rare disease, he'd been ill with it for as long as I'd known him, and its chronic symptoms frequently interfered with whatever plans we'd made. It wasn't at all unusual for me to make plans to meet him in his lobby, only to get there, have the doorman call him up, and then be told by Rex to come back in an hour. This morning was no exception.

"It's too early," he said over the phone. "I haven't even had my *coffee* yet. Why don't you read the *Times* and you can brief me on it."

"But I loathe newspapers," I reminded him for the hundredth time, "you know that. I wrote for two of them, remember?"

"Well, take a walk or something. I need more time."

"Fine," I said. "I'll be back in an hour or so."

Ordinarily I'd read a book in Rex's plush lobby, but today I decided to stroll down to Copley Square and go inside Trinity Church. When I was in college, the place had had good spiritual juju for me. It was a place I could go when I needed answers, and I didn't have to be a regular parishioner to do it. I decided to give the place another try, see if it still had any of the old juice left.

When I got there, there was a line out the door for some reason. After standing in line for a minute, I finally figured out these people were waiting for tours of the church. I walked past them and went inside.

In the lobby, there used to be a simple donation box, but now there was a long counter and a sizable ticket booth, like a theater box office. No matter what, I was *not* paying to go inside a church. I stood near the counter and slowly removed my jacket.

"Excuse me," I said. "Miss?"

A college-aged woman clerk whisked to the end of the counter. A crucifix swayed from her neck.

"Yes sir?" she said.

"I was a parishioner here twenty years ago," I said. "I don't have to pay to go in and *pray*, do I?"

"No, sir, of course not." She smiled awkwardly, glanced around and lowered her voice to a whisper. "This is for people taking the tour. It also helps keep the homeless people out. We were having quite a bit of trouble with them a while back."

Now…I'm not a Holy Roller by any means, and in fact had only attended services here three times; but when I hear so-called Christians say something distinctly un-Christ-like, a switch inside me flips.

"You know, it's funny," I said, loudly enough that I caused the people waiting on line to look at me. "I seem to remember Jesus saying, 'He who cares for the least among you cares for Me also.' A lot of Jesus' disciples were homeless. Heck, so was Jesus himself."

"I'm sorry you feel this way, sir, but—"

"And another thing. When you guys set up your little shop here in the lobby, did anyone remember the part in the New Testament when Jesus turned over the tables of the moneychangers? You know…when they set up *in the temple*? I can't believe somebody didn't think of that."

"Sir, I'm really very busy," she said. "If you'd like to go in now…" She nodded at the doors.

"Yeah, yeah, okay."

I went inside and walked down to my lucky pew: #17. Every time I prayed here, I used this pew, and every time I got answers. Once, days before graduation, I came here and asked God what I was supposed to do with my life. Lying on my back, staring up at the ceiling, I posed the question over and over, until suddenly the answer boomed in my mind. It wasn't a voice as much as it was a feeling in my spirit, a feeling so strong that it seemed like it had been shouted at me: "WRITE!"

Now two decades later, I sat down in #17 to see if good old Trinity could deliver one more time. This time I wanted to know *what* I should write. You'll recall from the beginning of this book that a few years earlier the Alien Girls had expressed their opinion on what I should be writing. I'd taken their advice and begun to write about my own life, but I wanted confirmation from the Big Guy. Sorry, but I didn't entirely trust a pair of aliens in human hippie-girl form.

Before I asked my question, however, I began my prayer by expressing gratitude. Over the years I've learned that you tend to get more favorable results with your prayers if you thank the Almighty before launching into your shopping list. Once I'd done so, I asked gently, "God…what should I be writing?" Then I listened for the answer, which I knew would come. I had faith.

With my eyes tightly closed, I strained to hear something, anything. There was the faint murmur of street noise, a person coughing and then…the beep and click of a digital camera.

I opened my eyes. A male retiree I'd seen on line for the tour was snapping pictures of the ceiling and glass windows, and with every shot, his camera beeped and clicked. I stared at him. I couldn't believe this—in a church. Well, maybe I had to put up with people's nonsense like talking too loudly on cell phones in restaurants, but this was one place where I could rightfully expect silence. The second his camera beeped and clicked again, I turned around in the pew and spoke to him.

"Did you get your picture?"

"I'm sorry?" he said.

"Your picture. I hope it came out, because that's what this church exists for—for you to take pictures of it."

"What?"

It seemed that Bright Boy here had never been confronted with his inconsiderate behavior before. He looked back at me with his mouth slightly open.

"Your camera," I said. "Turn off the sound, please."

He shuffled away looking at the camera screen, and I didn't hear the beeping after that. Returning to my prayer, I smiled to myself, pleased that I had confronted someone on his rude behavior and won, and grateful that the miscreant had been a retired milquetoast and not an MMA cage fighter. I had the satisfaction of winning a showdown without getting my jaw broken.

And then my eyes sprang open again, as suddenly as they had that time in here 20 years ago, and the message was just as clear. It was the answer to the question of what I should be writing about.

This.

Situations like this one with the tourist. One man's battles with modern life, wherein he continually asks of himself and the universe, *"What is right? What should I do here? What is the lesson for me in this situation?"* In that moment, I realized that I didn't need to cast about for fictional story ideas because my own daily life was replete with drama, humor, tragedy and conflict, and there were more than enough interesting real people in my life to write about, so I didn't need to invent characters either. The Alien Girls had been right all along. Over the years, I'd worried that I didn't have anything to say as a writer, but considering it now, I almost had too much to say.

Then I remembered that I was in Boston, and it was time to meet Rex. I walked back to his building.

I was gazing across Arlington Street at the entrance to the Public Garden when Rex hobbled out onto the sidewalk with a cane. Rex had been complaining for years about having difficulty walking, so seeing him with the cane didn't come as a surprise. But now, as he tottered along the uneven sidewalk on the wobbling cane, I realized for the first time that not only was he truly ill, but, at 75 years old, he was officially elderly. All of this reminded me of the purpose of my visit today: to drive him to a doctor's appointment. I smiled to cover up the pity I felt for him.

"So," I said, "ready for a nice ride in the country?"

He pointed at my Honda Accord with his cane. "This is yours?"

"Sure is. What do you think?"

"It's terrific," he said. "You can't beat a Honda. Mine's around the corner. Twenty years old this year."

"That's something," I said. "Get in."

The moment we were both inside, I cranked the air conditioning because I knew that would be the first thing he asked for.

"Lead the way," I said. "You're the navigator."

"All right, then," he said, clearly pleased to be back in the position of lecturer. "We're taking Storrow Drive west, my boy, so drive down to Berkeley Street."

I'd forgotten what a joy driving around Boston was, especially with all the rotaries outside of the city. Instead of doing the hard work of civic planning and installing actual intersections with—oh, I don't know—*stop signals*, anytime road builders had reached the ends of a bunch of roads and they didn't know what to do next, they said, *"Screw it. Stick a rotary in there. The Sox are on tonight and I wanna get home."* Rex and I would get a couple of miles, and then he'd interrupt his conversation with a violent outburst about which rotary exit to take.

"Indubitably," Rex said, dissertating about Anton Chekhov, "there is no other short story writer whose work influenced so many writers who followed him. All of the modern masters owe a debt to the great medical doctor-cum-writer. Even Hemingway, who once notoriously quipped that Chekhov was, quote, 'an amateur writer who wrote only about six good stories'—even *he* was influenced by him. *Au contraire*, Mr. Hemingway, sir…*you* are the author of about six good stories! Chekhov, on the other hand…oh, goodness, Chris…author of

'The Lady with the Little Dog,' 'About Love,' and don't forget that little masterpiece, 'In the Cart'! His ability to *feel*, Chris…to empathize with his fellow man was nothing short of—*Turn! Turn! Now, Chris! Now!*"

I careened out of the rotary. Over the course of several more rotaries, Rex's discourse retrogressed from Chekhov to the "absolute necessity for a public option" in the healthcare reform legislation being debated, to the evils of the Medicare Part D Donut Hole (whatever the hell *that* was; I didn't know and hoped I died before I needed to know), to the medications "we" were taking right now.

Once upon a time, back when Rex was still teaching, I was able to deftly steer our conversations back to loftier topics, and didn't have to hear about his medical condition. But now, as I made the turn into the wooded hilltop office park where his doctor's office was, it became clear that since his retirement, the issues surrounding his health had, by necessity, absorbed all of his focus. Now, instead of directing his profound analytic skills at literary masterpieces, he was applying them to his ailments, his myriad medications, and his medical insurance deductibles.

I parked in a spot directly in front of the building and got out. Rex was having trouble standing up, but I had learned something from him and Ab: While little old ladies might like a helping hand from an attractive younger man, old men most certainly do *not*. So, I let him grunt and struggle.

"I don't want any help," he said stridently.

"Don't worry, I won't help you. In fact, if you fall, I'm leaving your crippled ass here."

He laughed and got to his feet. He stood for a moment on his cane, catching his breath. When he started to walk, I strolled alongside him but far enough away that he wouldn't think I was trying to assist him.

"You know," I said, "you get around pretty well on that thing."

He rapped on the side of his leg with the cane. The cane struck metal.

"It's the braces. I have them on both legs now. My knees are too weak."

"Braces," I said. "Like FDR."

"It's funny you should mention that," Rex said. "I've been thinking a lot about him lately. A lot."

"I can see how he'd be inspirational. I mean, look at all he accomplished in his condition. I know it's not a hell of a lot of consolation, but I guess it could be worse."

His jaw stiffened. He plodded ahead, but there was more determination, dare I say anger, in his movements.

"Boy, I hate it when people say that. 'It could be worse.' Of *course* it could be worse. But that doesn't negate the difficulty of the problems I'm dealing with right now."

"I know that," I said. "And my saying that wasn't meant to marginalize what you're living with. But…it seems to me that we can look at this one of two ways. We can dwell on everything you've lost, or we can focus on how many extra years you've gotten that you never thought you'd get. Think about Chekhov. He died of tuberculosis at forty-four, right? That's how old you were when you got your diagnosis. You've gotten thirty more years than he did. That must give you some consolation."

"I know all that," he said. "What I don't like is people presupposing they know what I'm going through. Because implicit in their saying 'it could be worse' is that they know the full extent of what I'm dealing with right now."

"Maybe," I said, opening the door as he climbed the steps, "but I think you're giving people too much credit of forethought. I think most people say 'it could be worse' because that's the only way they're equipped to express empathy."

When he reached the door, he stopped to take a breath.

"Let's drop it," he said.

"Okay."

The doctor's office was on the second floor. There wasn't an elevator, so we had to plod up 40 stairs together, one stair at a time, with me standing on the step behind him to catch him in case he tipped backward, but to the side so he couldn't accuse me of trying to help him. Ten minutes later, we reached the waiting room. Rex used the bathroom, and when he got out, the doctor, a portly man with one of the nicest ties I'd ever seen, greeted Rex.

"Professor L——. Great to see you."

"Doctor," Rex said, "this is a former student of mine, Chris Orcutt."

The doctor and I shook hands.

"Chris," Rex said, "I'll be out in fifty minutes."

"I'll be right here."

He followed the doctor down the hall. I sat in the waiting room next to an attractive black woman. She smiled at me, got up and handed the receptionist her clipboard. She said something, and although I couldn't make out what she was saying, her voice had a musical accent. Jamaican, I surmised. Habitually I reached down to pull a book out of my bag, but I hadn't brought my bag today, or a book. I frowned. I'd broken a cardinal rule for myself: *Never go anywhere without a book, because you never know when you'll have to wait.*

A mudslide of magazines covered the coffee table. The corners of the magazine covers, where the address labels went, were all torn off, and many of the magazines had foxed pages. I sifted through the pile until a copy of *Esquire* caught my eye. On the cover was Christina Hendricks, the voluptuous redhead on one of my favorite TV shows, *Mad Men*. Two of the headlines on the cover piqued my interest: "Eat Like a Man" and "NFL Preview from a Beautiful Woman." Flipping through the magazine, I spied a flash of red hair and alabaster cleavage. My breath faltered. I quickly closed the magazine and cleared my throat. I couldn't look at this in here, not with the Jamaican woman a foot away softly humming a tune, and the receptionist gazing down from her booth. Grabbing a *National Geographic*, which I laid atop the *Esquire* cover, I stood and went out to the car.

It was a beautiful day: deep blue almost indigo skies, sparkling sunshine, and lazily falling leaves. I opened the car windows and put on a classical music station while I browsed the magazine. I skimmed the NFL preview piece so I could tell myself that I'd read an article, then, with slightly trembling hands, turned to the Hendricks photo spread.

By posing her in an elegant little black dress in front of a dilapidated double-wide, the photographer was clearly trying to create counterpoint. And speaking of counterpoint, a sprightly Chopin piano etude, No. 21, came over the radio, sparking a pleasant memory of a girlfriend's mother—a beautiful classical pianist—who once played this very tune for me while wearing a baby blue halter top and Daisy Dukes. Tapping my thumb in time with the music, I turned the magazine page. In one photo, Hendricks dipped slightly forward at the waist. Her hair was up, but stray tresses dangled down her cheeks, and her protuberant womanhood formed a veritable knickknack shelf.[28] It was a lovely photo.

When I caught my breath, I laid the magazine on top of the steering wheel to admire the photo in the crystalline morning light. No sooner did I do that than I heard the clip-clop of a woman's heels approaching from behind the car. A shadow drifted past my window. There wasn't time to flip to another page, so I simply left the magazine where it was, with Ms. Hendricks spilling her milky-skinned goods in broad daylight. In my periphery I noticed that the approaching woman, middle-aged and overweight, wore a blue-checkered blouse. She muttered a sigh of disgust as she walked by, and went into the building.

I glanced at the other photos in the spread, but Ms. Hendricks' spell was broken. Besides, I saw now that her chest was so large as to be cartoonish; indeed, in a red sequin dress she would be the spitting image of Jessica Rabbit. I decided she was a bit too pneumatic for my taste, and when I read in the sidebar interview that she

---

[28] Credit for "knickknack shelf" goes to friend Tony Scotto, who once said it of a different woman, and I filed it away.

had recently gotten married, this new fact about her unavailability tipped the scales against her once and for all. I put down *Esquire* and read an article in *National Geographic* about whale sharks.

When forty-five minutes had passed, I went inside, bringing the magazines back with me. In the waiting room, Blue-checkered Blouse Lady looked up from her magazine and scowled at me. I pretended not to notice her and tossed my magazines on the table. The Jamaican woman gave me a big smile of the whitest teeth I'd ever seen. Flustered, I waved playfully with my fingertips in reply.

A lot of colds, not to mention the dreaded H1N1 virus, or "swine flu," were going around. Who knew what germs I'd picked up from the magazines, as well as the doors and handrails I'd touched. I went in the bathroom to wash my hands. Cranking the hot water full blast, mixing in just enough cold so I didn't melt my hands off, I wet my hands like a surgeon, squirted out eight or nine pumps of foam soap, lathered, rinsed and repeated. Finished, I dried my hands with a paper towel then started to shut off the faucets with the same paper towel. The valve for the cold water shut off, but the valve for hot kept spinning and spinning.

I'll never understand why, but objects have a habit of waiting for me to touch them before they break. As the water gushed in the sink, I experienced an adrenaline rush that sparked a memory. Late one summer morning when I was 17, my father brought home a brand-new Snapper lawnmower. He smiled as he pushed it down the hill to the pool, where I was tanning myself. I'd been looking forward to seeing my girlfriend that afternoon, but my father said I wasn't going anywhere until I did all the push mowing around my grandparents' property,[29] which would take hours. My father just stood there, expecting me to start mowing immediately. Now...I don't think what I did next was premeditated exactly; although I must admit that anticipating how my girlfriend and I would be spending the afternoon and evening together in her apartment off-campus from Vassar College was a strong motivator. Grabbing the starter cord handle, I peremptorily pulled it (well, "angrily yanked it" is more accurate) and ripped the handle off, causing the cord to zip into its hole like a snake and disappear. "*Jeezis*, what did you do?" my father asked, even though he had seen it and knew very well what I had done—nothing but pull the stupid cord. He trudged away, pushing the now-broken lawnmower back up the hill.

Well, at the moment, in Rex's doctor's office bathroom, I was faced with a similar crisis: the hot water was stuck, the mirror was fogged up, and steam filled the tiny room. Under the sink, I tried turning the emergency shutoff valve, but that wouldn't budge either, and I didn't want to force it, potentially snapping it off and creating a flood in the office. There was knocking at the door.

"Hello," Rex said. "Hello?"

"Be right out," I said.

"I have to use the bathroom," Rex said.

---

[29] When I say, "push-mowing," I'm referring to all of the "trim" mowing around the property—under trees, along fences, around buildings, on steep hillsides, etc. As for the 10 acres of *lawn*, my grandfather and the gardener mowed that with big golf course mowers.

"Okay."

I slipped out the door. Needless to say,[30] any designs I had of making a covert, speedy getaway with Rex before the broken faucet was discovered were now out of the question. Rex, the doctor, the receptionist, Blue-checkered Blouse Lady and the Jamaican woman were in the waiting room as I exited the bathroom and closed the door behind me. The lock shut with an ominous click, followed by utter silence and the sound of Niagara Falls emanating from behind the bathroom door. Most condemning of all, a billowing steam cloud had followed me into the waiting room.

"You forgot to shut the water off," the doctor said.

"Actually," I said, "it's broken. I tried shutting it off, but I couldn't."

"You broke the sink?" the secretary said.

Blue-checkered Blouse Lady muttered another sigh of disgust.

"No," I said, "the valve wouldn't shut off."

"Well," the doctor said, "you're not supposed to turn the faucet up all the way."

"It was an accident," I said. "Honest."

---

30 Suck it, Mrs. G. Yes, *you*, Mrs. G.—my 11th grade English teacher who gave me A's on all of my writing until one day when you returned a paper of mine with a "C+" on it. You have no idea how much that hurt me—to get a "C+" from the teacher of my favorite subject, and, adding insult to injury, from a woman with such beautiful, shimmering auburn-red hair! After I deciphered your red pen scrawl, I figured out what bothered you: my use of the phrase "needless to say." You had crossed it out and scribbled in the margin, *"IF IT'S NEEDLESS TO SAY, <u>WHY</u> SAY IT???!!!"* Well, Mrs. G., <u>*NEEDLESS TO SAY*</u>, I didn't accept your correction.

While I was defending myself, Rex had abandoned me, slipping into the bathroom. Behind the door, the water shut off.

"Got it!" Rex said.

The doctor nodded and walked away. The Jamaican woman winked at me. I don't know if she was flirting with me or if the wink was her way of saying, *"I know whatchu be doin' mon…you be brakin' duh sink."* She flashed those snowy white teeth of hers again. The office phone rang. The secretary whisked away.

"I wasn't trying to break it," I said to the Jamaican woman.

"Uh-huh," she said, grinning. She sat down and flipped through *People* magazine.

When Rex emerged from the bathroom, he grabbed my shoulder lustily.

"I'm hungry, my boy," he said. "How about you?"

"IHOP?" I said.

"Right."

We were halfway down the stairs when I brought up the sink.

"How'd you fix it, anyway?" I asked.

"I didn't. I just turned the shutoff valve underneath."

"I tried it, but it wouldn't turn."

"You were probably turning it the wrong way," he said.

"No, I wasn't. I know how to turn off a valve."

It made me feel mildly impotent to know that my semi-ambulatory former Russian literature professor was able to do something mechanical that I couldn't. Was it my imagination, or was he standing up straighter? I decided to give him his victory. Rex didn't get many chances to be a hero anymore, but I was young and, knock on wood, very healthy. There was always the possibility of my rescuing a child from a subway track, changing a flat tire for an old woman, or stabbing a would-be mugger with my Swiss Army knife (or, better yet, throwing my omnipresent cup of hot coffee in his face). Rex had none of these heroic acts to look forward to.

Without going into details, our brunch at IHOP was about what you'd expect: me, tortured by seeing Rex eat a Belgian waffle, a delicacy I hadn't had in a decade; and Rex, hobbling into the bathroom every five minutes and making incessant, fastidious requests of the waitress, as if he were at ritzy Locke–Ober asking for more brioche to go with our JFK lobster stew, and not at a chintzy pancake chain insisting on "five pieces of bacon, very crisp but not burned, instead of the potatoes." To Rex's credit, he had wanted to pay, but I snuck paying the check during one of his bathroom breaks.

Back in the car, the air conditioning roaring, I turned to him.

"Home?"

"No, I thought we were going to Target," he said. "I'm out of a lot of things in the apartment. Didn't I say—"

"Relax," I said. "Target it is. Tell me the way."

We'd only been together three hours, Rex and I, and fifty minutes of that time was spent apart, but already I was exhausted. Going shopping with the man was something I'd never done, even when he was fully mobile. The fun began as we searched for a parking spot.

"We should have brought my car," he said. "I have the handicapped sticker."

He was right. The lot was packed, and in aisle after aisle, only the handicapped spots were open, their bright blue wheelchair-guys gleaming from lack of use.

"Here's a spot!" I announced.

"All the way back *here*?" Rex said. "Chris, it will take me all afternoon to walk from here."

"Let me drop you at the door. I'll find a spot, and I'll meet you inside."

Rex considered my proposal with the same seriousness that I'd once seen him consider a question about Ivan Turgenev. He set his jaw and nodded once.

"Okay," he said. "I'll meet you at the pharmacy inside."

I dropped him at the front doors, idled at the curb until he made it inside, then parked in the remote parking space I'd spotted a moment ago. When I jogged inside, Rex was already at the pharmacy counter, speaking to the pharmacist. He was sitting on one of the store's complimentary scooters and fumbling with two prescription bottles.

Maybe it was the harsh lighting, or maybe it was because with Rex in the scooter the only way the pharmacist could speak to him was by leaning over the counter and literally looking down his nose (and over his half-glasses) at him, but the man did seem to be talking condescendingly to my old friend and mentor. The pharmacist glanced at me for sympathy, as if I would side with him against Rex.

Boy, did this clown have it wrong.

"What's going on here?" I said. "What's the problem?"

"It's all right, Chris," Rex said. "I've got this."

He started to say something else when he dropped the prescription bottles. They rolled in a neat arc, one chasing the other away from the counter, and turned down the dental care aisle.

"Chris!" Rex shouted. "We need those!"

"On it!"

By the time I made it down the aisle, a toddler had scooped them off the floor and was shaking them so the remaining pills rattled inside. The mother, who was examining children's toothbrushes with a level of care usually reserved for disabling time bombs, turned to me. I'm sure all she saw was a harried-looking middle-aged man staring at her young child.

"Can I help you?" she said.

"I'm sorry," I said, "but I need those bottles."

"Excuse me?"

"Those prescription bottles. The ones your kid is playing with. We dropped them."

The mother squatted in front of the child. "Honey, don't play with those. They came off the ground. The ground is dirty. This man needs them."

I wasn't keen on the syllogism this woman had created about me and the pills, especially not the proximity between the premises of the ground being dirty and "this man" (me) needing the bottles. Would the kid forever associate strangers with the dirty ground? Most annoying, however, was the fact that I needed the damn bottles and this mother was trying to reason with her 2-year-old.

"Come on, honey," the mom said. "Give them to the nice man."

The kid slobbered on the bottles. Now I wished I didn't need them. If I hadn't, I would have simply walked away. *Keep 'em, kid.* Along with your spit and snot.

"No, no, no," the mom said to the kid. "Now come on, honey, we—"

"*Lady*," I said sharply, "stop trying to reason with a two-year-old and give me the damn bottles!"

The child started to cry: another case of something breaking precisely when I interacted with it. The mother pried the bottles out of the kid's hands, which only increased the volume and ferocity of the crying.

"There," she said, slapping the saliva-ridden bottles into my hands. "I hope you're happy."

"Nice parenting skills," I said.

"Who the hell do you think you are?"

"Get lost, lady," I said and ran back to the pharmacy. The kid's crying had turned into a blood-curdling shriek.

"What happened?" Rex asked.

"A kid had them and wouldn't give them back." I put the bottles on the counter. The pharmacist sneered at the saliva on them. He looked at me and was about to say something.

"Don't say a word," I said.

He wiped them off with a Kleenex. Spotting travel packages of hand wipes at the end of the counter, I broke open a pack and wiped my hands down thoroughly.

"Rex, how about I take care of this while you do your other shopping?"

He sighed. "Okay, just make sure I get the generics," he said and drove away.

As soon as Rex was out of sight, the pharmacist peered over his glasses at me.

"Listen," he said, "that's what I was trying to tell the guy. When his doctor prescribed these, he stipulated 'D-A-W.' That means 'dispense as written.' That means I can't give him the generics, understand?"

"Look." I put my elbows on the counter and leaned forward. My leather jacket creaked. "First of all, he's not 'the guy.' He's one of the most highly regarded scholars in his field, and a winner of the National Book Award. He deserves respect. Second, don't give me that crap about 'I can't give him the generics,' because we both know you guys make mistakes. It's happened to me. If you 'made a mistake' and gave him the generics, no one would know about it. It's not like you'd be making any grand breach of ethics here. Give him the generics. Please."

He sucked his cheeks, like he was trying to extricate a raspberry seed from his teeth.

"All right," he said. "*This* time. But tell him he needs an updated prescription from his doctor, okay?"

"Okay, whatever," I said.

"It'll be forty minutes," he said.

"Forty?"

"Hey, I've got a lot of other prescriptions to get to. Your friend's isn't the only one, you know."

"I never said it was. Fine...I'll be back."

I walked along the aisles near the pharmacy, peering down each one, and when I finally caught up to Rex, he was intently reading the label of a personal care item. He didn't notice me behind him—and I didn't want to embarrass him by jumping into the aisle and saying, *"Hey, whatcha gettin'?"*—so I walked away. I found a few things I needed and caught up with Rex in the dental care aisle. Fortunately, the mother and screaming child were gone. I dropped my items in the basket on his scooter.

"Chris," he said, holding up two toothbrushes, "both of these say 'soft' but I want the softest one. Do you happen to know which one is softer?"

"How would I know that?"

"I thought maybe you'd used them and knew which was softer. What brand toothbrush do you use?"

I shrugged. "Alexas takes care of that stuff. I tell her when my current one is worn out and a new one magically appears the next morning."

He frowned, as if I was somehow cheating by having Alexas. He turned the toothbrush packages over and over in his hands, examining them from every angle.

"I wish there were an objective standard for these things," he said. "Like decibels for noise. I always get them home, try them once, and they're always too hard."

"That *is* annoying. Hmm."

I pulled out my notebook and jotted down a revenge fantasy: abduct all of the designers and engineers of toothbrushes, strap them to chairs, and brush their teeth every hour, on the hour, with the hardest damn toothbrushes available, until all the enamel is taken off their teeth.

As I put my notebook away, I said, "Look, Rex…I don't know what to tell you. Just get…" Rex was gone. As I set out to find him, I passed the pharmacy again. The pharmacist frowned at me from his elevated perch.

"They're *not* ready yet," he said.

"Relax, I'm looking for my friend," I said. "Did you happen to see him?"

"No."

Then, from somewhere in the other direction, I heard the beeping sound that scooters make when backing up. I jogged down the main traffic thoroughfare and found Rex in an aisle, driving back and forth, scanning painkillers. He'd go forward about five feet, see some other product that caught his eye, and back up.

"My God, Chris, will you look at this?" He held up a plastic jar of store-brand, extra-strength acetaminophen the size of a half-gallon of milk. He shook it. "A thousand tablets?! For this price? Terrific!"

Ordinarily I would have asked him if 1) he took that much Tylenol every day to justify such a comically large cache, and 2) if he had room in his apartment to store them, but I knew that the answer to both questions was yes. I also didn't want to say or do anything that would further delay us from getting the hell out of here. As it was, the endless aisles and the endless stuff and the crowds and the crying kids were closing in around me, and although I knew we'd been in the store for less than an hour, it felt like three.

I had grown to hate shopping. Especially with the elderly. In my early 20s, I would happily take my grandmother grocery shopping twice a week, but since her death I had been out of practice patiently accompanying an older person. I'd forgotten that for people like Nan and Rex it was less a matter of buying stuff, and more a matter of getting out of the house, having a daily goal and a purpose.

Glancing at my watch, I was shocked and dispirited to discover it was already 2:30 p.m.; we'd been together for nearly six hours. I was rapidly reaching my saturation point with Rex. It was time to get him back on task.

"Okay, Rex," I said, "what's next?"

"I don't know. Don't rush me, Chris. I have to *see* things, and they remind me of what I need."

"Don't you have a list?" I asked.

I hoped desperately that he did, because then I could tear through the aisles ahead of him, reconnoitering and reporting back on prices and availability like troop strengths and movements. Whenever Alexas went jeans shopping, for example, I accompanied her, gathering a dozen pairs in a range of brands, styles and sizes, and bringing them to her at the changing room door.

"No, I don't have a list," Rex said. "What time do you need to be back at the hotel?"

"Four o'clock," I lied. "I'm meeting Alexas for dinner, and I really don't want to get stuck in rush-hour traffic."

"Okay, we'll mind the time," he said.

From Healthcare and Personal Hygiene, I trailed behind Rex and his scooter to Home Entertainment, where he whirred down an aisle of music CDs. He stopped in front of the easy listening section, heaved himself up with the cane, and flipped through the S's. A young, red-shirted salesman appeared out of nowhere, as though from a trap door in the floor.

"Sir, can I help you find something?" he asked.

"I'm looking for the new Barbra Streisand album," Rex said.

"Sorry, we're sold out."

"*Already?*" Rex said.

"Yup. Sold out in like the first hour."

"Do you have any more in the back?" I asked.

"No, sir," the salesman said.

"How is it?" Rex asked.

The kid's eyes opened wide, and he leaned back on his heels.

"Rex," I said, "he doesn't listen to Streisand."

"How should I know?" Rex said. "I don't know what they listen to."

He got back on the scooter, saw that the end of the aisle was blocked by boxes, and put the scooter into reverse.

Beep…beep…beep…beep…beep…beep…beep!

When he reached the mouth of the aisle, he made a hard left, then a quick right and banged into a CD display for the Beatles. All of their albums has been recently re-mastered and re-released.

"Oh, this is interesting," he said. "You know, Chris, I've never been able to get into their music, even though everybody raves about it. I can't understand the lyrics. Which of these is the best?"

"Best how? You mean like emblematic? The best representation of their work?"

"Yes."

"*Abbey Road*, I guess."

He grabbed a copy and read the cover. "Can you understand the lyrics?"

"*I* can."

He put it back shaking his head. But when he hit the forward button on his scooter, he rammed into the

Beatles display. He tried backing up and only got a few inches before he rammed into the CD bin behind him. Somehow he had wedged the scooter between the two barriers like Austin Powers does his golf cart in the first Austin Powers movie.

He turned left.
Forward…forward…forward…BANG!
He turned right.
Beep…beep…beep…BANG!
He turned left.
Forward…forward…forward…BANG!
He turned right.
Beep…beep…beep…BANG!

The salesman ran over to him. "Sir! Sir, let me help!"

Putting his shoulder to the Beatles display, he shoved it to the side, making room for Rex to escape. Meanwhile, I had to walk away. I ended up in Sporting Goods, where a boxing heavy bag hung from a stand. I punched a few combinations, then stood still, breathing deeply, calming myself. Talk about exhausting. If this outing with Rex didn't end soon, I was afraid I'd say something hurtful to him, and I didn't want to do that. Slowly, I walked back to Home Entertainment and was standing in the main thoroughfare when he rolled up alongside me.

"I decided against *Abbey Road*," he said.

"Okay. Ready to go?"

"Just about. Come take a look at the TVs with me."

Before I could object, he accelerated down the aisle and stopped in front of a row of 50-inchers. They were all playing the same movie: *Out of Africa* on Blu-Ray disc. Admittedly, they couldn't have picked a better film to show off the high-res picture. The opening credits were playing. The picture was so clear, it was as if you were actually on a mountaintop watching a train vanish into a vast green valley below.

"So," Rex said, "do you and Alexas have a big-screen TV? A flat screen, I mean."

"No and no," I said. "We have a CRT. An elephantine one. Why?"

"I want to buy one for you."

"Excuse me?"

"Aren't you two movie buffs?" he said.

"Very much so."

"Well then…you need a nice big TV. I have one, a plasma, and I love it."

He inched the scooter along until he reached a 52" model. He started spouting off facts about the differences between LCD and plasma screens: which were the best brands, how much they'd come down in price, etc. Every now and then, Rex, already a very generous man, liked expressing his generosity with a Grand Gesture.

"Rex," I said, "I really appreciate the offer, but I can't accept. For one thing, how the hell would I get it home? I'm staying in Cambridge. I can't keep the car parked with an HDTV in the back. I don't even know if it would fit."

"But I want to give you two something to remember me by."

"You're giving us that painting, right? The Rockport, Maine seascape?"

"Let me do this for you," he said.

"But a *TV?*"

As I write this, I know that some of you (the greedy bastards anyway) are going to shout at the book, *"Do it! Take the TV! What kind of moron are you? A FREE HD TV? ARRRRGHHHHH!"* But in my defense, while I could see a future with one of these large, lovely, limpid screens on my living room wall, in order to make that happen with *this* TV, I would have to endure a minimum of another hour in this store with Rex.

I was feeling claustrophobic, and fed up with being superhumanly patient. All I wanted to do was go back to the hotel, take a long hot shower, and watch HBO. I glanced at my watch, holding it out for Rex to read.

"It's almost four o'clock, Rex," I said. "We really have to go."

He nodded grimly. "All right then. Another time. I have to get some socks."

"You get those while I pick up your prescriptions, and I'll meet you at the registers."

"Fine."

When we reached the main aisle, I watched him head toward men's clothing, then I ran back to the pharmacy. No one was there, but on the counter was a bell with a tented notecard that read "Ring 4 Service!" So I did: I smacked it—thrice. The pharmacist wandered out of the back office eating a sandwich.

"You didn't have to ring that," he said. "You could have simply called out. I was right in back."

I shook my head. "And forgo the chance to ring one of these old-timey page bells? Not a chance."

He flipped through the prescription bin, pulled two bags and tossed them on the counter in front of me.

"Tell me something," the pharmacist said as I paid, "is he really a distinguished scholar like you were saying?"

"Yes, absolutely."

"Who are you then? His healthcare worker?"

"No," I said, "his biographer. Good day, sir."

"Wait," he said as I was walking away. "Will this be in his biography?"

"Yes," I said.

He smiled. "Then *I'll* be in the book?"

"Yes. As the villain."

I looked over my shoulder one more time and saw him frowning, a tinge of regret etched into his forehead. Maybe he should have been nicer. Maybe if he had, he might have gotten better treatment in the biography of Rex I would never write.

Back in Boston, I double-parked for a moment and carried Rex's bags inside to the elevator. His face was ashen. It got like this when he overextended himself.

"Would you like to come up for a glass of wine?" he asked.

"Sorry, can't. I've got the car double-parked, and I'm meeting Alexas."

"How long are you in town for?"

"A couple more days," I said.

"Call me," he said, stepping on the elevator. "I'd like to take you two out to dinner."

"All right."

I made it back to the hotel in record-time and was able to swim, sit in the sauna, check my email, and take a long, hot shower all before Alexas returned from her conference. Once she'd joined me on the bed with HBO playing, I told her about my day.

"Hey," I said, "guess what Rex offered to buy us."

"What?"

"A flat-screen TV. Fifty-two inches."

"You're *kidding*," she said.

"Nope."

"I'm glad you didn't take him up on it."

"Really? Because I'm starting to think I should have. You know how long I've wanted one."

"Mmm," she said. "Hey...remember when Uncle Walt sent us that giant Thomas Kinkade and—"

"—we thought it was a TV? Yeah. Thanks for reminding me."

III

I was in Prof. G.'s 8:00 a.m. U.S. History to 1877 course, sitting conspicuously in a chair at the front as the professor introduced me.

"Mr. Orcutt has had quite a variety of careers. He's been gracious enough to come this morning and share some of his experiences, particularly on the many occasions when his knowledge of history came in handy. Please give him your undivided attention. Mr. Orcutt...?"

I stood. "Thank you, professor."

I had agreed to give this little lecture when the professor explained that, of all the classes he'd taught over his 60-year career, this particular class was the most obstinate and least interested in history, and that he was having profound trouble getting through to them.

However, the truth was, aside from the two years that I'd taught high school U.S. history, I couldn't point to many occasions when my knowledge of history had "saved the day." Regardless, during the T ride from Cambridge that morning, I'd made a list. Most of the examples were utter fiction, but the students wouldn't know that. It was really important to me that Prof. G. not look like a schmuck in front of his students.

"Hi, guys," I said, stepping up to the lectern. "It's great to be here. I had Professor G—— for this very course back in nineteen eighty-eight, and everything he taught has stuck with me all these years."

A girl in the second row stretched, yawned and lay on her desk.

"Well," I continued, "for my first example of how history helped me in the workplace, there's the time I was working for Merrill Lynch, I was up for a promotion, and I got it. Later I learned, the reason I got the job was because the boss had discussed U.S. history with me many times before, and he wanted someone around to talk about biographies with."

"Really?" said a wide-eyed kid sitting in the front.

"Absolutely," I said. "No matter what your career is in the future, when you get out in the work world, you'll see how important relationships with people are."

A girl with spiky blonde hair spoke up from the back: "Could you give us another example?"

Out of practice for this sort of thing, I had to glance down at my list on the lectern.

"All right," I said. "Once, I was in a bar on Wall Street after work, and they had these really obscure trivia questions. If you gave the right answer, you got five beers on the house. I had the right answer."

"What was the question?" asked the kid in the front row.

" 'What was the name of the other major speaker at the dedication of the National Cemetery at Gettysburg?' Anybody know?"

Prof. G. smiled. "Edward Everett."

"Correct."

"So you won the beers," the professor said.

"And a bowl of wings," I said.

The blonde in back rolled her eyes. "No offense, but who cares? I think you're grasping at straws, *Mr.* Orcutt."

"You know what, young lady? You're right." I tore up my index card, threw it in the trash and sat down on the table beside the lectern. "The thing is, it's tough to point to a few events or situations where knowledge of history has made the difference.

"Look...here's the deal," I continued. "When you graduate from college, there are going to be very few situations where right and wrong answers are so clear. Should the company lay off programmers? Hard to say. Should you and your spouse have children? Again, it's a tough call. But history is one of those definite things, where if you know a fact, you *know* it—it's usually not debatable. As you get older, it's nice to have something in your life where you can say, 'Don't believe me? Look it up.' It gives you a feeling of pride. The other value of history is that when you know it, it keeps paying you back by enriching other experiences. I once went to Dallas on a business trip, and while I was there I went to Dealy Plaza. Who can tell me what happened there?"

"Didn't somebody get shot or something?" said a boy in the corner, glancing up from his smart phone.

"Yes," I said. "President Kennedy. And the thing is, when I went and stood there, and saw what the place actually looked like, I was able to fill in the rest of the picture from what I knew about the assassination. It's knowing the stories behind a lot of these places and events. Like the Brooklyn Bridge, for example. Some of you might end up working in New York City. If you know what the bridge builders went through, when you walk across it you'll have a much deeper experience."

I glanced at Prof. G, who was nodding at me from his seat at the end of the front row.

"All right," I said, "I only have one more thing to say—the most important reason why you need to know history. And it has nothing to do with the work world. The philosopher and historian Santayana—he was at Harvard, I think—he once said, 'Those who do not know history are doomed to repeat it.' To me that means, if you know the events that have taken place over hundreds or thousands of years, you'll learn the patterns those events tend to follow.

"For example, if you know about the rise of dictators—dictators like Hitler, Stalin, Napoleon, Robespierre, and Genghis Khan—you'll see that these people rising to power follows a similar pattern. So then, when the *next* Hitler shows up in the world, maybe even runs for President of the United States someday, you'll have a better chance of recognizing that person for what he is. I say *he* because there haven't been many female despots in history. Anyway, that's my spiel. Thanks for listening."

It was disappointing to have them stare back at me with blank faces. Secretly, I'd hoped for my monologue to rouse them, like the English teacher's does in the movie *Dead Poets Society*, but what I got instead was crickets. The vibration of somebody's phone on a desk finally broke the dreadful silence.

"Okay," I said. "Any questions?"

"Yeah," said a kid wearing a Red Sox cap "gangsta" style. "How much do you make a year?"

Professor G. lunged to his feet and stepped behind the lectern.

"He's not answering that," he said, "and frankly, Mr. Heffernan, that's a rude question to ask! Mr. Orcutt writes speeches for all the major executives!"

I grinned, partly because that wasn't entirely true, but also because I was amused by the ludicrous *non sequitur* implicit in Prof. G.'s statement: The kid's question was rude *because* I wrote speeches for all the major executives.

"Thank you, Mr. Orcutt," the professor said.

I sat down among the students and listened to Prof. G.'s lecture about Aaron Burr and what a scoundrel he was, and about all of the great things Alexander Hamilton, whom Burr shot in a duel, did at the outset of our country. I enjoyed the lecture but had the eerie sense that I'd heard it all before, and exactly like this, right down to Prof. G.'s classic gestures at the lectern, including my favorite: stretching out both arms toward us students and wiggling his fingers, like he was casting a spell over us. I was suddenly 18 again, mesmerized by his presentation. After class, while the students filed quickly out, I waited for Prof. G. to pack up.

"Very good lecture today, professor," I said. "*Burr*. What a schmuck."

He chuckled. "Thank you, Chris. I appreciate your trying to get through to that bunch. But I'm afraid if it's not on one of those little screens, they don't have much use for it. Let's go, shall we?"

I followed him out. Ahead on the brick path were the two CIA guys from the other day.

"Hello, Dr. Jones," said Long Duck Dong, passing me.

"Gentlemen," I said.

When they'd passed, Prof. G. gave me a quizzical look.

"He called you 'Dr. Jones,' " he said. "What's going on?"

"These guys." I pulled my coat open and pointed at the CIA pin. "When I talked to them the other day, I didn't want them knowing who I really am, so I gave them a pseudonym."

He smiled. "Why doesn't that surprise me?"

"Do me a favor, professor?" I said. "If they, or anybody else, ask who I am, say, 'Dr. Jones.' Don't tell them my real identity."

"Okay. So long as nothing illegal is going on."

"Don't worry, there's—"

"I'm joking." He stopped in front of his building. "I'll have to say goodbye now, Chris. I have to meet with a graduate student in a few minutes. But the next time you're going to be in the Boston area—"

"I'll contact you ahead of time—"

"—and *I* will take *you* to lunch!"

"It's a deal," I said.

We shook hands. I waited for him to go inside, then followed a minute later and went upstairs to the philosophy office. The student-receptionist sighed when I came in the door.

"Not here, huh?" I said.

"Listen," she said, "if you want, give me your cell and I'll text you when he comes in."

"I don't have a cell phone," I said.

She looked at me as though I'd asked her to do a logarithm.

"Well…did you go to his class?"

"Whose class?" I said.

"Prof. Q.'s. He's teaching Philosophical Ideas in Film. Right now. It's in the Arts building, Room 409."

"I'll check it out. Thanks."

I was nervous about seeing Prof. Q. I'd given his last name to a suspect (who gets killed off) in one of my PI novels, and I was worried he'd somehow found out about it and was offended. I'd only done it because I was blocked at the time and couldn't come up with a decent-sounding character name, so I used his.

You're being irrational, I told myself, and hurried over to the Arts building.

When I reached the classroom, a flotilla of hipsters was drifting in. A coed smiled and held the door open for me. At first thought I thought she was flirting with me, but when I smiled back at her, I noticed that her eyes were glassy and she reeked of pot.

The smell immediately rekindled a memory of my first college fling and lust object, the tall, lithe and perpetually baked Deirdre.[31] I had fallen for her in my first philosophy class, which, coincidentally, was taught by Prof. Q.

"Coming in?" the coed chirped.

I nodded, and as she climbed the stairs to the top of the auditorium, I basked in her musky wake and took a seat behind her.

Prof. Q. glanced at me from the amphitheater floor, but I don't think he recognized me. He was sitting in front of the class exactly as he used to when I had him: atop a table, waggling his dangling legs like a child on a too-big chair. He asked the students about the differences between the novel *The Grapes of Wrath* and the film. He listened to their answers with his eyes closed, like he used to in my classes, and smiled and laughed when elaborating on a point, as if amused by a joke only he could hear.

---

31 Deirdre introduced me to the wonders of marijuana, taking a conspicuously "throw him in the deep end" approach. One Friday afternoon, she proposed we get stoned together and fool around. Never having tried pot, I assumed she meant a tiny joint or, at the most, something amusingly cigar-sized like in the Cheech & Chong movies. Instead, wearing nothing but her underwear, she sashayed across her living room—her impossibly long, saliva-inducing gams on full display—and snapped a bed sheet off a six-foot gravity bong. Climbing atop a rickety chair, she lit the pipe and demonstrated the proper technique.

The trouble was, Deirdre's hit seemed to have had no effect on her whatsoever; therefore, when my turn came, I seriously overdid it. Suddenly, all commands from my brain to my appendages stopped getting through. I was lucky I could still breathe, with the ultimate tragic effect being that, once we started fooling around, my equipment was as stoned as I was. Deirdre spent the better part of the evening trying in vain to get me erect, yanking on my thing like it was a broken lamp pull-chain.

In the seats around me, several boys surfed the web on laptops while a pair of girls conducted a texting conversation seated directly next to each other. Prof. Q. continued with his presentation, occasionally glancing at a typewritten sheet before going on to the next point. Maybe I was partially stoned from the miasma of pot surrounding the coed, or maybe sitting all the way in the back as I was gave me more perspective, but a mounting sense of déjà vu enveloped me. Like Prof. G., Prof. Q. hadn't changed physically in 20 years, and his teaching didn't seem to have changed either.

I told myself to shut up. They were both excellent teachers, and why fix something that isn't broken? The professor spoke a while longer, then nodded to his grad assistant, who played a 15-minute clip that showed the farmers being kicked off their farms. The lights came back on.

"So," Prof. Q. said, "if we were to construct a statement to articulate the theme in this part of the story, what might it be?"

He waited. Chewing gum popped. Someone coughed. The texting girls giggled softly.

"Come on, now, folks," the professor said. "It's very clear."

Unable to see one of my favorite professors suffer this indignity anymore, I finally raised my hand.

"Yes, you, in the back," Prof. Q. said. "Are you registered for this course?"

"Former student," I said. "Chris Orcutt."

"Ah-hah!" the professor said. "Yes...*Orcutt*. Go ahead, please."

"I'd say that a major theme in this scene, and throughout the entire story, is the idea of the indignity of capitalism, of private ownership of property. When the farmers have their land and homes taken from them, their humanity gets taken from them as well."

"Yes! Did everyone hear that? Maybe you could say it again, Chris?"

I did. Afterwards, the professor strove valiantly to get the students interested in Tom Joad as an antihero, but they had already mentally checked out. With ten minutes left, when it became too difficult for him to speak above the whines of knapsack zippers, he dismissed the class. He remained seated on the table as I walked down the aisle and shook his hand.

"Kyle," he said to the grad assistant, "this is one of my star students from the past." He gazed at me. "How long ago?"

"Twenty years," I said.

"Ah," Prof. Q. said, "well, the caliber of students that attend the college now is really something. You wouldn't *believe* their SAT scores."

"That's because they stand on the shoulders of giants," I said, smiling.

Prof. Q. chuckled.

"Nice to meet you, Chris," Kyle said. "Professor, I have to—"

Prof. Q. waved a hand; Kyle whisked out the door.

"Yes, I remember," he said. "Your class had several unusually capable people in it, and most of you seem to be doing quite well now. Do you remember Trask?"

I did, vaguely. His skill, as I recalled, consisted less of parsing and articulating philosophical ideas than it did of affecting introspective poses with his chin on his fist.

"Sure," I said.

"Well...it turns out he's insanely wealthy now. It seems that the family business was something healthcare technology-related and that for years he resisted his father's attempts to get him to take over. He finally did, and he has a great talent for it."

"If he has a lot of money," I said, "why doesn't he give it away, like Wittgenstein did?"

The professor laughed. "Yes, that would be something, wouldn't it. He's generous, Chris, but I don't anticipate that ever happening."

"So, professor, what are you up to right now?"

"Heading home. But you may join me back in my office for a while if you like."

Walking back to his office, I said I was astounded at how little he had changed.

"Really," I said, "it makes me wonder where the time went."

"Ah, well," he said, "it's something of a good thing that you dropped by this year, because I'm retiring after this one."

"Doing the emeritus thing, huh?" I said.

"Yes, I'll teach one course a year and get something like eighty percent of my salary for the first three years after I retire."

"Not bad."

"I'm going to be writing a book on the ideas in Kurt Vonnegut's work. He once remarked that he planted ideas in his writing 'like Easter eggs,' and I"—he tented his fingers and grinned like Descartes' Evil Deceiver—"*I know where most of the Easter eggs are.*"

"Sounds like a fun project."

"Oh, it is. So, what have *you* been up to?"

By the time he asked this, we were in his office and I was sitting on his customarily messy sofa. Having practiced my "what I've been up to" monologue twice already, I was able to recite it in under a minute this time.

"And that's it. Wait!" I snapped my fingers. "Before I forget, when I was teaching writing at CUNY, I used your Three C's model. I know the first two—Clarity and Concision—but I always taught the third one as 'Content.' But that's not it, is it?"

" 'Completeness,' " he said.

"Shoot. 'Completeness.' "

He leaned back in his chair, looked over his shoulder, and scraped at a paint chip with his fingernail.

"So, what did you think of today's class? It felt slow to me, like they're just not engaged."

When he asked me this, a question of my own formed in my head: *Is not telling the brutal truth, or telling a less brutal version of it, the same as lying?* This question was on my mind because a few nights earlier I had reread Kant's essay "On a Supposed Right to Lie because of Philanthropic Reasons." In it, Kant argues that it's never okay to lie. Even if a murderer is pursuing a man you have hidden in your house, if the murderer asks whether you're harboring the man, you *must* tell the murderer the truth, because if you lie and any harm subsequently befalls the man, *you* will be responsible. This argument, it seemed to me, included white lies intended to cheer up former professors, so I decided to give him a truthful response to a different question.

"I think it's still early in the semester," I said, "and that most of them haven't woken up to the fact that they're in college. You watch…they'll go away for the long weekend and come back much more serious students. At least some of them will. Some might not come back at all."

He was cupping his chin in his palm, staring at the rug.

"Yes, yes…I can see that. Okay. Listen, I have a confession to make."

I sat up. "What?"

I imagined all sorts of possibilities: that he had divorced his wife of umpteen years for a sassy redheaded former student, that he had never liked me, or that he *did* know about my using his last name in one of my mystery novels and wasn't happy about it.

"A few years ago," he said, "I was looking in the mirror one morning and I didn't like what I saw there. I saw an alien."

"Okay."

"By alien I mean that I looked deformed. I wasn't *losing* hair or *going bald* anymore; I *was* bald." He made an imploring gesture with his hands. "I thought of Aristotle's comment that there is something 'deformed' about a bald head, and it got me thinking. Well…I was at a faculty party one night, and the husband of a friend—he does hair restoration—he offered to give me a break on it. And I have to tell you, I thought about it for quite a long time, and finally went ahead and had it done."

The professor ran a finger across his forehead. "He said that for only a bit more he could give me a full head of hair, but I told him that all I wanted was a hairline again. And *that's* the reason why I probably don't look as if I've aged." He grimaced, turned to me. "What are your thoughts on this?"

"As in what," I said. "The ethics of it?"

"Your gut impression."

"Well...my gut impression is that most people don't go into this decision with the level of self-reflection that you clearly applied to it," I said. "It would have been one thing if you did it out of vanity, or for less than noble motives—like to bed a younger woman—but it sounds as though you decided to do it because your physical visage didn't jibe with your self-image. An analogous situation might be a woman who gets breast implants after a double mastectomy because her physical appearance is at odds with her feelings of femininity."

He nodded, over and over. "Hmm...I think that's sound, Orcutt. Very sound."

I glanced at my watch. It was four o'clock, and I was supposed to meet Alexas at Trinity Church to take her out for a birthday dinner.

"Are you heading home now?" I asked.

"I am."

"Could you give me a ride to Trinity?"

He winced. "I would, but that's actually in the exact opposite direction."

"Come on...I just gave you that sweet argument!"

"Yes, you did," he said. "Alrighty then."

His car was parked in the garage across the street. Ten minutes later, he dropped me in front of Trinity Church.

"If you have a retirement party," I said, "let me know."

"Will do."

I got out and watched him drive away, then went inside the church.

Compared to earlier in the week, today the church was empty and quiet, and the spiritual juju was strong, like it had been back in 1992 when I'd asked what I was supposed to do with my life. I went down to pew #17.

Without even asking the question I would have eventually asked, the answer came to me: By not pursuing an academic career, I *had* made the right choice. I'd followed the correct path for my life.

Sure, my professors had enjoyed satisfaction and security in their careers, but they had only experienced one world, whereas I had experienced many worlds.

They would never know the thrill of writing a newspaper article on a deadline, or selling a piece of software they helped design to a major corporation, or writing stories, plays and novels and having awestruck readers approach them in the grocery store to tell them how much they enjoyed their latest book.

My path was *my* path, and that's the way it was.

When I came out of my prayer and opened my eyes, Alexas was sitting next to me in the pew.

"Are you ready?" she asked.

"I am."

THE END

About the Author

Chris Orcutt has written professionally for over 25 years as a novelist, short story writer, speechwriter, journalist and playwright. *Perpetuating Trouble* is his tenth book.

Orcutt is the author of the critically acclaimed Dakota Stevens Mystery Series, including the Amazon bestseller *A Real Piece of Work*. Orcutt's short story collection, *The Man, The Myth, The Legend*, was voted by IndieReader as one of the best books of 2013. His modern pastoral novel *One Hundred Miles from Manhattan* (an IndieReader Best Book for 2014) prompted *Kirkus Reviews* to favorably compare Orcutt to Pulitzer Prize-winning author John Cheever. Early in 2017, Orcutt released *The Ronald And Other Plays*, which includes a full-length political satire and six short plays.

As a newspaper reporter Orcutt received a New York Press Association award, and while an adjunct lecturer in writing for the City University of New York, he received the Distinguished Teaching Award.

If you would like to contact Chris, you can email him at corcutt007@yahoo.com or tweet him @chrisorcutt. For more about Orcutt and his writing, or to follow his blog, visit his website: www.orcutt.net.

Excerpt from
One Hundred Miles from Manhattan

In this novel about a wealthy rural community—Wellington, NY—the hills and the seemingly quaint village conceal lives of love, lust, adultery, tragedy and small wars. Unlike other novels in the pastoral tradition, which often tell the story of a place through the eyes of a single character, this modern novel uses 10 narrators to shed light on this exclusive community. Following is the opening of the novel.

Until that early June evening in bed beside her much older husband, Caprice Highgate had never heard the screams of terrified cows. In fact, before moving upstate from Manhattan to Wellington she hadn't heard so much as a *moo* out of one. Even after three years, on nights like this she longed for the white noise of the city. The sustained silence of the country was deafening, and when there *was* noise, like now with the wailing cows and the howling coyotes, it more than startled her—it shredded her nerves. She waved a hand at the open windows.
"I wish you'd do something about that."

Hamilton was reading an armchair safari book: Robert Ruark's *Use Enough Gun*. He turned a page. Caprice glanced at the double-barreled shotgun hanging over the bedroom door.

"Maybe try *using* a gun instead of reading about them," she said. "Did you hear me?"

"What?"

"Your cows. There are coyotes out there, Hamilton. Hear them?"

"Coyotes?"

"Well, they're not wolves."

"Stephen's on top of it, I'm sure," he said. "Take a pill."

"That's your answer—take a pill."

"Caprice, don't be melodramatic."

She put on her robe and went downstairs.

She poured herself a glass of wine, padded into the great room, opened the French doors and sat in an armchair facing outside. For a minute it was pin-quiet, but then another burst of the melee shattered the silence: the calves' bleats for help, followed by the coyotes' eerie whistles. She sipped some wine and gazed out into the darkness. Half a mile away, Celia's bedroom lights glared across the long, narrow pond (a moat, really) in front of the mansion. Caprice wondered how the first Mrs. Highgate was faring and whether the carnage was keeping her awake, too. She hoped so. She hoped the bitch died from sleep deprivation so she and Hamilton could move into the mansion. This place had always felt like a child's playhouse by comparison.

In the morning after coffee, Caprice dressed in riding clothes and Wellies, got in her Range Rover and drove to the stables. One of the hands must have seen her coming because when Caprice got inside, Giorgio was already out of his stall with the saddle pad on his back. The air was thick with hay dust. She sneezed.

"Bless you," the stable hand said.

"Thanks. Stephen around?"

"Office, Miss Caprice."

She changed into her riding boots, grabbed her crop and helmet, and marched into the office. Stephen was on the phone. He raised a finger to her.

Caprice stood at the window and pretended to watch Giorgio being walked out to the yard. Instead, in the reflection she watched Stephen trace the curve of her backside. Caprice knew her ass was good, but the breeches helped.

"Miss Caprice," Stephen said, hanging up the phone. "What can I do you for?"

She fastened her helmet strap. "Have you *heard* the cows at night, Stephen?"

"Heard what?"

"You're as bad as Hamilton. Don't tell me you haven't noticed. The cows, the coyotes."

"Coyotes? *No*…they're not big enough to go after cattle."

She stared at him. "So you think I'm hearing things."

"No, it's just—"

"Saddle up, Stephen. We're going riding."

"Where?"

"Wherever the cows are."

He leaned back in his chair. "That won't be so easy, Miss Caprice."

Stephen launched into a monologue about Hamilton's 200 head of cattle being spread across all 2,500 acres of the estate. Since the animals wandered freely spring through fall, the noises Caprice heard—*if* she'd heard them—could have come from anywhere. As the estate manager, he knew about these things.

"Humor me then," she said.

"You're the boss." Stephen grabbed a rifle from behind his chair.

"What's that for?"

"In case you're right."

They rode all morning, scouring patchworks of fields separated by dense hedgerows. The weather was clear, affording a beautiful view of the Village of Wellington and the endlessly undulating, tree-dappled hills. They also saw a lot of Hamilton's cattle—Black Angus, Stephen informed her—as they searched for signs of the violence that had kept her awake last night.

As the noon fire horn carried faintly from the village, Stephen pulled up beneath the ancient oak that sheltered the Highgate family cemetery. The earliest stone dated back to 1711. Tiger lilies grew wild along the picket fence. Caprice loathed coming to this spot on the estate; headstones awaited Hamilton and Celia, but there was no space earmarked for her…

www.ingramcontent.com/pod-product-compliance
Lightning Source LLC
Chambersburg PA
CBHW070137100426
42743CB00013B/2729